Martin Buber on Psychology and Psychotherapy

The Martin Buber Library

Martin Buber on
Psychology and Psychotherapy

Essays, Letters, and Dialogue

Edited by Judith Buber Agassi
With an Introduction by Paul Roazen

Syracuse University Press

First Edition 1999
99 00 01 02 03 04   6 5 4 3 2 1

The paper used in this publication meets the minimum requirements of
American National Standard for Information Sciences — Permanence of
Paper for Printed Library Materials, ANSI Z39.48–1984. ☻⁻

Library of Congress Cataloging-in-Publication Data
Buber, Martin, 1878–1965.
[Selections. English. 1999]
Martin Buber on psychology and psychotherapy : essays, letters,
and dialogue / edited by Judith Buber Agassi ; with an introduction by
Paul Roazen.
p.   cm.
Includes bibliographical references and index.
ISBN 0-8156-0582-X (hardcover : alk. paper) /
ISBN 0-8156-0596-X (pbk : alk. paper)
1. Psychology. 2. Psychotherapy. 3. Buber, Martin, 1878-1965 —
Views on psychology. 4. Buber, Martin, 1878-1965 — Views on
psychotherapy. I. Buber Agassi, Judith II. Title. III. Series:
Buber, Martin, 1878-1965. Martin Buber library.
BF121.B837 1999
150 — dc21   98-37835

Manufactured in the United States of America

Contents

Preface

It was Paul Roazen who first suggested collecting and publishing in one volume Martin Buber's influential writings on psychology and psychotherapy, and he then agreed to write the introduction. Why was this not done before, even though many important therapists have declared that he had influenced them greatly? Perhaps it is because they were influenced less by those writings of Buber that address issues pertaining directly to psychology or to psychotherapy and more by his most well-known philosophical work, *I and Thou* (1923), as well as by works of wisdom such as *The Way of Man According to the Hasidic Teaching* (1948).

Buber's lifelong interest in psychology, psychopathology, and psychotherapy was tied to his philosophical concerns, religious, ethical, and anthropological. He was neither a psychotherapist nor a psychologist. As a young student he had studied three semesters of clinical psychiatry in Leipzig and Berlin and with Bleuler in Zürich, yet he never seriously considered a professional career in psychiatry. He also decided against a university career; he became a university lecturer only in 1923, when he was forty-five. His interests were broad. He showed active interest in a large variety of subjects and topics that are usually classified as belonging to the humanities or to the human or the social sciences, to exclude the natural sciences. In other fields he read, corresponded, wrote, and sometimes lectured and organized social action.

In his young days his self-image was that of a writer, a poet, and a *Nachdichter*, that is, a poetic translator, of myths. He earned his living as editor (*Lektor*) at the publishing house of Rütten

vii

und Loening — editing in the course of six years (1906–12) a
series of forty monographs bearing the title Die Gesellschaft:
Sammlung sozialpsychologischer Monographien (Society: A Col-
lection of Sociopsychological Monographs) on social phenomena,
institutions, movements, professions, occupations, and fashions.
Among the authors writing there were several of the then most
original thinkers in the German language, including Georg Simmel,
Werner Sombart, Gustav Landauer, Fritz Mauthner, Ferdinand
Tönnies, Eduard Bernstein, Ellen Key, and Lou Andreas-Salomé.
The name of the series testifies to the fluidity of the border between the sociological and psychological.

In 1908 Buber approached Freud, apparently with a request
to contribute to the series, and offered to visit to discuss this
request with him. In a brief, polite letter Freud left open the
door to a visit by Buber for further clarification, but hinted at
circumstances that regrettably might prevent his writing for the
series. Lou Andreas-Salomé, who became a member of Freud's
circle in 1911, had by 1910 completed her contribution to Buber's series and was engaged in discussion with him about a fitting title, in the course of which they became great friends. She
visited the Bubers apparently in 1916 in their new home in Heppenheim. By that time, he was challenged by Freudian psychoanalysis and intended to publish a critical study on it. Apparently
she dissuaded him then from executing his plan to publish on the
ground that the movement still needed time to mature. (In his
old age he told this to Grete Schaeder, who later authored the
excellent biographic introduction to his correspondence.)

I heard from Margot Cohn (first his secretary and since his
death the director of the Martin Buber Archive in the National
and University Library, Jerusalem) that Buber was convinced
that he had once written a critical essay on Freud. He was then
preparing the most valuable of his still-unpublished manuscripts
for the volume *Nachlese* (1965); as he wished to include this essay
there, he asked her to conduct a search and was disappointed
that it proved unsuccessful.

Yet in his correspondence he continued to criticize Freud, especially his view of religion, as expressed in *The Future of an Illusion*, and he repeated his expression of his intention to write about this (letter to Hermann Gerson of 30 Aug. 1928). Later on he also criticized Freud's central concept of guilt feelings (letter to Gerson of 23 Apr. 1937). A group of young Jewish immigrants from Germany to Palestine formed the collective settlement Hazorea and joined a Kibbutz federation that at the time dogmatically endorsed a philosophy that embraced both Marxist and Freudian views. One of the leaders of Hazorea was Gerson, who earlier had been greatly influenced by Buber. Buber argued with him not against psychoanalysis as such but against the extreme dogmatism of this philosophical school that was only seemingly progressive and critical (letter to Gerson 23 Apr. 1937). These letters are included in the second part of this volume.

On the first page of the preface to his *Moses* (1945), Buber dismissed Freud's book on Moses (*Der Mann Moses und die monotheistische Religion*, 1939). He said, "that a scholar of so much importance in his own field as Freud could permit himself to issue so unscientific a work, based on groundless hypotheses as his 'Moses and Monotheism' (1939), is regrettable." But not until 1957, with "Guilt and Guilt Feelings," did he publish his criticism of Freud's basic tenets.

With Carl Gustav Jung his relationship was different. Jung may have been present at Buber's lecture to the Psychology Club of Zürich in 1923 (see letter to Hans Trüb of 18 Oct. 1923). Trüb, then a disciple of Jung and a practicing Jungian psychiatrist, had invited Buber to lecture there shortly after the publication of *I and Thou*. Although the lecture's title was "On the Psychologizing of the World," its subject was not psychology but a rather demanding criticism of different forms of "psychologism." It exists only in notes; these were first published in 1965 in the already mentioned *Nachlese*. They include two short paragraphs of interest to the subject of this volume. One, on the analytic method, supports the assumption that Buber at this point in time considered Jung's method as not without merit and apparently even preferable to Freud's:

It expresses itself in the analytical method, more exactly 'analyti-cism', which applies this method as universally valid, which no longer knows, therefore, that it is a method and only usable and must always be ready to be given up. When the analysis longs for synthesis, it is not thus. When the man knows, now I must do this, I must, for example, seek a motive although I know that no motive exists, I must, for example, dissect the life of the soul, although it is a unity, that is not analyticism. In this wise restric-tion, I would gladly emphasize, I have often encountered the ana-lytical method precisely in the representatives of the direction prevailing here [Buber apparently meant Zürich and the Jungian school] as true scientific method.

The following short paragraph from the "Notes" contains Bu-ber's first tentative formulation of the significance of his dialogi-cal philosophy for psychotherapy:

Here another word about the problematic of the province of psy-chotherapy. The sicknesses of the soul are sicknesses of relation-ship. They can only be treated completely if I translate the realm of the patient and add to it the world as well. If the doctor pos-sessed super-human power, he would have to try to heal the rela-tionship itself, to heal in the 'between'. The doctor must know that really he ought to do that and only his boundedness limits him to the one side.

The lives and work of the two men appear to have intersected at various points, but nothing is known about any real conversation or correspondence between them. In August 1924, Buber was invited to lecture at the Jungian Eranos Conference in Ascona. Emma Jung, Carl Gustav Jung's wife, attended Buber's Am-ersfoort lecture series in the summer of 1925 as testified by her postcard of 25 December 1925; it reads: "With best wishes for the New Year and in grateful remembrance of Amersfoort, greets you, Emma Jung."

Jung was present at the conference on education in Heidel-

berg in summer 1925 where Buber delivered the keynote address, his "Über das Erzieherische" (On education). Apparently
he greeted "the Jungs" (husband and wife), but the prevailing
"conference atmosphere" discouraged conversation (see letter to
Trüb of 14 Aug. 1925).

According to Maurice Friedman (1991, 355) Buber wrote to
Hans Trüb as late as 14 August 1932 that in the past few years
he had read a few essays of Jung, which had made a positive
impression on him (he used the word "nearer"). (Unfortunately,
this letter is no longer in the Martin Buber Archive.) As Friedman mentions, Buber intended to meet with Jung in spring
1933, as he indicates in his letter of 22 March 1933 to Trüb.

Buber and Jung may have attended the same Eranos conferences in Ascona in 1934, but after 1924 Buber was never invited
to lecture there. Much later, when he and his wife vacationed in
Ascona, late in summer 1947, after Buber's first postwar European lecture tour, Jung was in town, yet they did not approach
each other. Nothing is known about any significant conversation
or correspondence between them.

Some of their references to each other appear in the correspondence included in this volume. Critical attention to Jung's
views occupied an important place in Buber's ongoing, lifelong
special interest in psychopathology and psychotherapy that started
around 1923. The development of his thoughts and arguments is
possible to trace in his long correspondence with Trüb, who became a close friend and with whom Buber had frequent personal
contact. (The association lasted from 1923 until Trüb's death in
1951.)

Nine of Buber's essays form the first part of this volume. The
first essay was published in 1950, and the last in 1960. They
appear chronologically according to the dates of their first publication. These nine essays are included because they deal directly with Buber's critique of central teachings of Jung and of
Freud, or else with the significance of the philosophy of dialogue

for psychotherapy; some of the essays present Buber's philosophical-anthropological basis for his position on these matters.

The overall title of Buber's four lectures — or three lectures
and one seminar — held at the Washington School of Psychiatry
early in 1957, was "What Can Philosophical Anthropology Contribute to Psychiatry?" He included the essays "Distance and
Relation" and "Elements of the Interhuman" as parts of this
philosophical-anthropological basis. The essay "What Is Common to All" and parts of "Images of Good and Evil" constitute
the philosophical-anthropological preparation for "Guilt and Guilt
Feelings" — Buber's major critique of Freud — and for his approach to the unconscious and to dreams.

Buber advised his correspondent Robert C. Smith to read the
essay "The Word That Is Spoken," which concerns language as
such, in order to better understand his critique of Jung. It is the
last of the essays included here.

Eight of these essays appear here in their entirety as first published. "Healing Through Meeting" was first published as the
introduction (*Geleitwort*) to a posthumous book of Trüb's that
bears the same name, but it was soon published separately. Of
"Images of Good and Evil," only part 3 is included here, the part
relevant to psychology and psychotherapy. "Religion and Modern Thinking" is chapter 5 of the book *The Eclipse of God*; Jung's
reply and Buber's rejoinder to that reply are also included in that
chapter.

Although *The Way of Man* includes a short critical comparison
of the psychoanalytic approach with the Hasidic way of dealing
with the human problem of domestic conflict, it would be incorrect to classify this work as Buber's dealing with Sigmund Freud,
and so that text is not included in this volume.

———————

The second part of this volume begins with eighteen letters
exchanged between Buber and Hans Trüb that concern psychotherapy and Buber's reactions to Trüb's practical therapeutic experiences and efforts to formulate an alternative to Jung's ideas.

Buber's friendship with Trüb led him to regular contacts and correspondence with several other theoreticians and practitioners. Some relevant passages from letters to Rudolf Pannwitz, Ludwig Binswanger, and Ernst Michel are included here. The correspondence with Binswanger is particularly interesting as in it Buber explains at some length his dissent from the existentialists. He exchanged publications with all of them and shared with them not only criticism of Jung, but also concern with the proper place of faith in the theory and practice of psychotherapy. Buber's correspondence with Hermann Menachem Gerson concerning Freud and Freudian psychoanalysis has already been mentioned above.

In 1936 he received a letter from a Scottish clergyman, Ronald Gregor Smith, inquiring about the influence and relevance of Buber's writings, especially for Protestant theology. The part of Buber's reply to Smith (28 Dec. 1936), where the writings of Trüb are listed as examples of applications of his dialogical philosophy to psychological problems, is here included.

After the publication of several of his writings in the United States and his several lecture tours there, he received in March 1956 an invitation to come and teach for some time in 1957 at the School of Psychiatry in Washington D.C. The letter section includes some correspondence with Leslie Farber, the director of the school, and with Maurice Friedman, who was then very active in the arrangement of this event, which took place in March and April 1957, as well as of the dialogue with Carl Rogers in Ann Arbor on 18 April 1957 that is included in the third part of this volume. These letters illustrate the views and expectations of Buber's American hosts as well as his thoughts and choices in the face of the challenge as he was asked for the first time — for a presentation and a discussion of his teachings specifically for a group of American psychologists and psychiatrists.

The last letters included here are different. As late as 1960 Robert C. Smith, then a young American Protestant minister and a doctoral student at Temple University, sent to Buber as well to Jung — both then in their eighties — letters with the same long list of questions, for the purpose of gathering information for his planned dissertation on "Religious Knowledge and Experience in

the Writings of Carl Jung and Martin Buber," which eventually
became *A Critical Analysis of Religious and Philosophic Issues Between
Buber and Jung.* A lively correspondence ensued. This exchange
provided an opportunity for Buber to amplify his position vis-
à-vis Jung. Smith also sent Buber copies of his own letters to
Jung and Jung's three replies, and Buber then also responded to
Jung's position as expressed in these letters. Buber subsequently
also read and commented on Smith's dissertation and gave permission to quote from this correspondence and reproduce it. Yet
as Jung expressly refused to give any such permission, Buber
had to exclude his reactions to Jung's letters from his permission. Jung died in 1961, Buber in 1965. Smith published ex-
cerpts of his letters to Buber and Buber's replies to him in the
Review of Existential Psychology and Psychiatry. Originals and copies
of the entire correspondence remain in the Martin Buber Archive. Later, the first and the third replies of Jung to Smith were
published in Jung's *Collected Letters.* The publishers kindly granted
permission to include them here. Thus all relevant parts of this
curious correspondence, two-pronged but not fully triangular,
are published here in chronological order for the first time.

There are fifty-seven letters in this volume. Twenty-four of
them were written in English in the original; five others had already been translated from the German for the American volume
The Letters of Martin Buber; twenty-eight were translated from the
German for the first time for this volume by the editor with
the help of Adi Schilling. Most of these were first published in
the second or the third volume of the *Martin Buber: Briefwechsel
aus sieben Jahrzehnten.*

Most letters — from and to Buber — do not appear here in their
entirety, as they are only partly relevant to the subject matter of
this volume.

The third part of this volume consists of two special texts —
dialogues. The first text comprises notes taken by Maurice Friedman of the three-session seminar on *The Unconscious,* presented
by Buber at the School of Psychiatry, Washington D.C., in

March and April 1957. Although it was mainly Buber who spoke, there were about thirty interjections from the participants, who were a group of American psychotherapists. These interjections stimulated, broadened, and sharpened Buber's discourse.

As far as I know, this is the only time that Buber attempted to present to a professional audience his own view of psychology. He presented his ideas about the unconscious, especially to its being both physiological and psychological, and about the mind, the self, dreams, repression, free association, hypnosis, transference, and so on. He did not suggest a psychotherapeutic method to compete with existing ones but centered on two theses. First, the unconscious is not what Freud, Jung, and Adler assumed it to be. Second, the preconceived categories and habits of interpretation employed in professional psychotherapy put in jeopardy the immediacy of the meeting between patient and healer. He observed that Freud had not followed up any of his criticisms of his early hypotheses, and that his followers clung to these hypotheses dogmatically.

After Buber's return to Israel in 1958, he was asked by Friedman to develop these notes into a monograph, and he intended to do so. When during his last illness it became clear that he could not complete the work, he gave permission to publish the notes as they stood (in English and in German).

The second text is a transcript of a taped dialogue between Martin Buber and Carl Rogers held before an audience in Ann Arbor Michigan on 18 April 1957. It is a more accurate transcription of the original tape than the one previously published by Friedman, who was the initiator of the encounter. It was made by Kenneth N. Cissna and Rob Anderson, both professors of communication, at the University of South Florida, Tampa, and at Saint Louis University, St. Louis, Missouri, respectively. The transcription has recently been published in book form.

Considering the fact that Buber was reluctant to have a dialogue before an audience, and about its being taped, we are fortunate that Friedman succeeded in convincing him to do it anyway, as it resulted in a very easygoing yet very detailed and careful exposition of Buber's ideas and reservations concerning

the use of the dialogical method in psychotherapy. This is particularly remarkable, as the interlocutor in this dialogue is the
famous founder of the method of client-centered therapy. Surprisingly, Buber appears to have been more practical-minded and
more humble in his claims for the dialogical method than was the
leading practitioner.

Bibliographical information about the texts, the letters, and
the dialogues, is given in the list of sources. It is followed by a
selected reading list on Buber's contribution to psychotherapy,
his critique of Jung, and his impact on the nonanalytic schools of
psychotherapy.

Herzlia, Israel   Judith Buber Agassi
August 1998

Acknowledgments

My thanks to Professor Paul Roazen for his initiative in suggesting the compilation of this volume and for writing its introduction.

My thanks also to the publishers of the *Collected Works* and the *Letters* of C. G. Jung for granting permission to reprint here Jung's "Reply to Martin Buber" of 1952, as well as two of Jung's letters of reply to Robert C. Smith, who in 1960 had sent a list of identical questions to Jung and to Buber. I also thank Professor Smith for granting permission to publish here for the first time his entire correspondence with Buber and Jung.

My thanks to Professors Kenneth N. Cissna and Rob Anderson for their kind offer to include in this volume their new transcription of the original tape of the dialogue between Martin Buber and Carl Rogers of 1957. My special thanks to the kind and unstinting help given by Mrs. Margot Cohn and the Martin Buber Archive at the National and University Library in Jerusalem; also to Mr. Richard Balkin, agent of the Martin Buber Estate, for his patience and continued efforts in bringing this project to realization.

I especially acknowledge here the considerable contributions to this project of Mrs. Adi Schilling for her devoted cooperation in the work of translating the letters, and of Ms. Harriet Unruh for her efficient assistance in the editing work.

Finally I thank Joseph Agassi for compiling the indexes.

Introduction

Paul Roazen

When one looks back over the intellectual history of the twentieth century, there can be little doubt that Sigmund Freud stands out as the most prominent single psychologist. The stature of the creator of psychoanalysis partly comes from his extraordinary abilities in founding a school that carried on his work well after his death. But a central part of Freud's power came also from his literary talents; he was such a great writer that people started saving his letters even while he was a young man, and when all his correspondences finally appear in print they will over-shadow in size the works that Freud actually published.

Acknowledging Freud's preeminence does not mean that it is necessary to ignore where he went wrong, and often badly so. He proposed sweeping theories and also had concrete practical recommendations; a central sources of Freud's commanding presence has been the extent to which his concepts not only formed a consistent body of ideas, but led directly to clinical consequences. In practice we now know that Freud could set aside his theories, and violate some of his most famous therapeutic principles. For example, he was in reality by no means as uninvolved in the lives of his patients as he usually liked to pretend. Freud captured his personal adherents by a variety of means, and these disciples, beneficiaries of Freud's flexibility, often disguised his idiosyncratic actual practices from the outside world. The impact of psychoanalysis became so great because

Freud had constructed a system of thinking that was integrated enough to be a self-sustaining inspiration.

Freud's success in the history of ideas has been such that it can take a special effort to recall that right from the outset of his work he had critics of his who respectfully disputed his central contentions. These pioneering skeptics have rarely been given an adequate hearing. Sometimes those who rejected psychoanalysis had no personal familiarity with it, but opposed Freud on a variety of theoretical grounds. Although Freud had great success with organizing a personal following, he also ran into pupils who disagreed enough with him that they were deemed "deviators" who had to be expelled from the psychoanalytic "movement." All these ideological squabbles were in themselves a tip-off to many that in spite of Freud's position within medicine he had in fact created a secular religion. Psychoanalysis became a "cause" that demanded intense loyalty as well as the scapegoating of occasional "dissenters."

Recently in the English-speaking world, the pendulum has swung so far that seemingly unremitting Freud-bashing has achieved novel heights, and it has become fashionable to think of psychoanalysis solely as involving either unprovable hypotheses or else notions that have long since been falsified. Within medicine, Freud's reputation is about as low now as it has ever been; analysts are once again, as at the beginning of the century, outsiders at odds with the conventional status quo of the professional universe.

As a philosopher, however, Freud's reputation is more substantial than ever, so the confrontation between Martin Buber and Freudian thinking becomes a special and largely unknown aspect of the history of ideas. Both Freud and Buber were Austrian and Jews; it would be impossible to understand either of them apart from their cultural and religious backgrounds. Out of the remarkably cosmopolitan maelstrom of old world civilization they went in startlingly opposite directions. Although Buber never undertook the full-scale reconsideration of Freud that he is reported to have contemplated, there is plenty of evidence about the divergent ways of their respective thinking and how they bear on one another. We know that in the spring of 1908 Buber had visited Freud and asked, unsuccessfully, that he write a book for a series Buber was editing.[1] At a time shortly thereafter, when Buber thought of writing a critical book about psychoanalysis, he allowed himself to be dissuaded by Lou Andreas-Salomé, Nietzsche's old friend who came to Freud's circle before World War I; apparently Lou argued that psychoanalysis was still a young doctrine in need of getting established, and this seems to have convinced Buber.[2]

Although intellectual historians today would not challenge Freud's stature, his specific therapeutic recommendations are not likely to be highly recommended now. Even a disciple like Lou Andreas-Salomé took a different tack from Freud himself, and he allowed her a great deal of latitude if only because of her special talents as well as the historical tradition she had come to represent. Despite all the controversies associated with Freud, Buber ranks as one of the most prescient skeptics who expressed the enduring suspicion that Freud's real intentions went far beyond modest-sounding psychology itself.

At times Freud claimed to be merely a ploddingly neutral scientific investigator. Although Buber rarely specifically took Freud on, Freud's old "crown prince" Carl G. Jung, who became a psychoanalytic renegade, replied to Buber's criticisms of what Jung called his "analytical psychology." Jung, despite all his other differences with Freud, alleged that he was just a dispassionate scientific investigator, and Jung protested that Buber was ignoring Jung's so-called findings. Despite all the deep cleavages between Freud and Jung, they continued to have much in common: they had a similar outlook on the methodology

1. Ernest Falzeder and Eva Brabant, with the collaboration of Patrizia Giampieri-Deutsch, eds., *The Correspondence of Sigmund Freud and Sandor Ferenczi*, vol. 2 (Cambridge: Harvard Univ. Press, 1996), 179.

2. Maurice Friedman, *Martin Buber's Life and Work: The Early Years, 1878–1923* (Detroit: Wayne State Univ. Press, 1988), 172.

of science, and neither Freud nor Jung was readily able to acknowledge the extent to which their respective psychologies
were enmeshed in implicit world views.

It may seem ironic that Buber should have tangled with Jung,
and not Freud, in that Freud had been the one to have been
especially savage about religious belief. Part of the falling-out
between Freud and Jung came over the question of religion, and
how to approach it psychologically. Jung, a pastor's son, was
from Freud's point of view far too tolerant of what could be
learned from comparative religious beliefs, and Christianity itself
seemed to Freud a great rival. Buber was remarkably open to
Christian teachings, but he suspected something in Jung's reasoning that was at odds with the promotion of genuine faith.
Jung and Buber argued partly because they were on something
of the same wave-length, whereas Freud steered as clear of Buber as Buber did Freud. The outlooks that Freud and Buber
represented were so at odds with one another that they could
not share enough common ground to make a genuine dispute
feasible.

Freud's prophetic pronouncements, against religion for example, prove that he had not succeeded in detaching psychology
from philosophy. By now it should be clear that everything he
wrote has to be understood in the light of certain central values
and beliefs that Freud was trying to promote. Buber intuitively
knew that Freud was a moral theorist, and one with whom Buber felt he had too little in common to make possible a genuine
dialogue.

Oddly enough, it is the most abstract side to Freud's thought,
linking him to Nietzsche and all other previous writers who have
sought to inquire about how the good life ought to be lived, that
has helped keep his work alive and relevant. For despite what
has happened within American medicine, where psychoanalysis
now plays a minor role, psychoanalysis is more central today
throughout European and Latin American intellectual circles
than at any previous time. Freud's theories, and those of his followers, have become part of university higher education, where
this subject is being studied as part of normal academic life

and not by people who only want to go on to be therapists themselves.

Although Freud might have writhed at his current preeminence as a philosopher, he also would have especially disdained Buber's sort of critique. Freud might not have been surprised at the quarrel between Buber and Jung, even though to Freud they both appeared to be too close to mysticism. Jung was at least ready to acknowledge his own genuine links to philosophizing, and in particular to theology, while Freud was trying to withdraw with quiet contempt from precisely those issues that would turn out in the long run to have been paradoxically responsible for ensuring the contemporary vitality of psychoanalysis's contribution.

Each of the papers in this volume are an aspect of the larger issue of how to relate Freud and Buber. It will be necessary to tease out from the individual slivers offered by a great system-builder like Buber the exact relevance now for what he had to say, not just about the practice of psychotherapy but about the moral direction in which he was proposing that humanity move.

Freud could have agreed, for instance, with the conceptual contrast Buber drew between guilt and guilt "feelings." Freud steered clear of any romantic-sounding association with theories of self-enhancement, unlike Jung's own interest in what he called "individuation." Freud himself took a rather dim view of such theories of self-enhancement and stood on the side of therapy that entailed a stoical compromise between known evils.

As hard-working a clinical practitioner as Freud was, he did not pitch his teachings on his success as a therapeutic helper. Nor did he think of himself as in any way on the same moral level as those he treated. Psychoanalytic patients might learn to become superior, and Freud thought that out of the treatment setting a new set of moral standards might arise; but both inequality and hierarchy were both taken for granted by Freud as he proceeded to work with neurotic clients.

Buber's whole orientation, implying that the therapist has as much to learn as the patient, would have made no sense at all to Freud. Psychoanalysis was not designed to be a kind of level playing field. But then the scope of Buber's interests sought out the existential problems of people far more disturbed than the garden-variety neurotics Freud wanted to specialize in. Buber, oddly enough, probably had more formal psychiatric experience, as a young student just starting out in his studies, than had Freud, who was trained as a neurologist but had little familiarity with psychiatry.

Buber came to play a role in the development of so-called third force psychology, and Buber's contact with Carl Rogers was an aspect of Buber's significance for psychotherapeutic matters. In the exchange between Buber and Rogers one can see how far they both were from the world of Freud, which presumes an omniscient analyst dealing with curiously foolish neurotics. Freud's aloofness might have been self-deceptive, but he never advocated anything like the mutual give-and-take that Buber and Rogers had in mind. Even Jung, unknown, evidently, to Buber, was critical of the power implications built into the orthodox Freudian analytic situation.

Buber did become aware of some of the humanistic strands within psychoanalysis, and in particular the proposals of Harry Stack Sullivan, who had worked with psychotics and made self-esteem a central part of what the therapist must concentrate on maintaining. Others within psychotherapy challenged the kinds of goals Freud had in mind. Freud said he had limited objectives, to enable the patient to make autonomous choices. Ideals like authenticity and health were not ones with which Freud felt comfortable, yet since his death most analysts have more or less conceded the necessity of coming to terms with areas Freud had wanted to bypass with silence.

Although the idealism behind a contrast between a "true" as opposed to a "false" self would have seemed alien to Freud, it has not prevented his school being centrally concerned with exactly that distinction. The whole notion of selfhood became one of prime importance within modern psychotherapy. As one reads these essays by Buber, and comes across a concept like that of "confirmation," it is hard not to think that he succeeded in having more of an impact on the profession of psychotherapy than most have been willing to acknowledge. Key concepts like anxiety, transference, and the unconscious itself need to be reexamined in the light of Buber's teachings. Much has recently been written about the necessary reciprocity in the relationship between therapist and patient, although once again Freud himself never made any such concession from the point of view of orthodox theorizing. But his former apostle Otto Rank would use Buber-like language: in 1928, Rank maintained that "in contrast to I-psychology . . . one might designate ethics as Thou-psychology."[3] R. D. Laing also acknowledged Buber.[4]

Within Freud's thinking he missed out on the significance of the social and human context in which people exist. He even frowned on talking about national characteristics, as if cultural differences were superficial and not of true scientific interest. Freud reacted to his own Jewish background by an insistent yearning to universalize each of his insights, and he struggled to get beyond the confines of his own social beginnings. Acquiring Jung as a student had meant for Freud a breakthrough into the world of the Gentiles, and, in allying with a Christian, Freud could imagine that he was now securely able to challenge Christian teachings. Jung shared some of Freud's discontent with inherited religious doctrine, and although in the end religion was one of the fatal sources of their falling out, it had at the outset helped to bring them together.

Buber's mind was in another world from that of early psychoanalysis, and the passage of time has shown how relevant his thinking can be to how we approach the healing professions. Freud liked to think of himself as undermining some of the highest ideals of the West; each time he quotes Goethe's Mephistopheles we should remember with whom he took pride in allying himself. Humanitarianism, however, need not be the enemy of modern psychotherapy, and because of Buber's attempts

3. Otto Rank, *A Psychology of Difference: The American Lectures*, ed. Robert Kramer (Princeton: Princeton Univ. Press, 1996), 231.
4. Bob Mullan, *Mad to Be Normal: Conversations with R. D. Laing* (London: Free Association Books, 1995), 112, 115, 136.

to keep the Judeo-Christian tradition alive, his thoughts on psychology remain keenly pertinent.

Freud never made any public reference to Buber's writings, but he certainly knew what kind of standing he had attained. (Both failed to win Nobel prizes.) It turns out that in his consulting room Freud could compare himself with a Hasidic rabbi, and recount Hasidic tales in the course of clinical practice.[5] Freud once specifically mentioned Buber in a letter concerned with the possible reactions to the appearance of Freud's *Moses and Monotheism*. In the last year of his life while in exile in England, he wrote to a loyal disciple who lived in Palestine: "Martin Buber's pious phrases won't do much harm to *The Interpretation of Dreams*. The Moses is more vulnerable, and I am prepared for an onslaught by the Jews on it."[6] The whole inter-relation between Buber, Jung, Freud, and modern psychology in general makes a fascinating addition to our understanding of twentieth-century thought.

5. Paul Roazen, *Freud and His Followers* (New York: Knopf, 1975; New York: Da Capo, 1992), 408.

6. Quoted in Yosef H. Yerushalmi, *Freud's Moses* (New Haven: Yale Univ. Press, 1991), 115.

Essays

Distance and Relation

1

The question I wish to raise is that of the principle of human life, that is, its beginning.

This cannot be thought of here as a beginning in time. It is not sensible to try to discover when and how a certain species of life, instead of being content like the rest with the perception of things and conditions, began to perceive its own perceiving as well. The only way is to consider, in all its paradox and actuality, the category of being characterized by the name of man, in order to experience its ground and its beginning.

It would be quite wrong to make the reality of the spirit the starting point of the question. The one way to expose the principle of a being is first to contrast its reality with that of other known beings. But the reality of the spirit is not given to us apart from man: all the spiritual life which is given to us has its reality in him. Nature alone presents itself to us for this act of contrasting — nature which certainly includes man but which, as soon as we penetrate to his essentiality, is compelled to loosen its grasp and even to relinquish for our separate consideration this child which from its standpoint is an aberration. This separate consideration takes place thereafter not within nature, but starts from nature.

Starting from nature, that is, in this case, starting from the association of 'living beings' to which man, so far as he is a part

Trans. by Ronald Gregor Smith.

3

of nature, must be reckoned as belonging — does not mean noting those characteristics which distinguish him from the others, but it means examining the ground of being of those characteristics as a whole. Only in this way shall we learn both the fact and the reason for the fact that those distinguishing characteristics as a whole constitute not only a special group of beings but a special way of being, and thus constitute a special category of being. The act of contrasting, carried out properly and adequately, leads to the grasp of the principle.

In this way we reach the insight that the principle of human life is not simple but twofold, being built up in a twofold movement which is of such kind that the one movement is the presupposition of the other. I propose to call the first movement 'the primal setting at a distance' and the second 'entering into relation'. That the first movement is the presupposition of the other is plain from the fact that one can enter into relation only with being which has been set at a distance, more precisely, has become an independent opposite. And it is only for man that an independent opposite exists.

The double principle cannot be demonstrated in the first instance in man's 'inner life', but in the great phenomena of his connection with an otherness which is constituted as otherness by the event of 'distancing'. When the principle has been demonstrated in this way its working out in the inner life of the human person will become clear.

Modern biology speaks of an animal's environment (*Umwelt*), by which is understood the total world of objects accessible to its senses, as conditioned by the circumstances of life which are peculiar to this animal. An animal — something of this kind is said — perceives only the things which concern it in the total situation available to it, and it is those things which make its world (*Umwelt*). But it seems questionable whether the concept of a world is rightly used here, whether we are justified in regarding the context described as an environment as a kind of world, and not simply as a kind of realm. For by 'world' we must mean that which is extended substantially beyond the realm of the observer who is *in* the world and as such is independent. Even a 'world of the senses' is a world through being composed not of sense data alone, but through what is perceived being completed by what can be perceived, and it is the unity of these two which constitutes the proper 'world' of the senses. An animal's organism gathers, continuously or continually, the elements which meet the necessities and wants of its life, in order to construct from them the circle of its existence. Wherever swallows or tunny wander, their bodily being (*Leiblichkeit*) carries out this selection from 'nature', which as such is completely unknown to them, and on which they in turn have an effect, again as on something which they neither know nor can know. An animal's 'image of the world', or rather, its image of a realm, is nothing more than the dynamic of the presences bound up with one another by bodily memory to the extent required by the functions of life which are to be carried out. This image depends on, it clings to, the animal's activities.

It is only man who replaces this unsteady conglomeration, whose constitution is suited to the lifetime of the individual organism, by a unity which can be imagined or thought by him as existing for itself. With soaring power he reaches out beyond what is given him, flies beyond the horizon and the familiar stars, and grasps a totality. With him, with his human life, a world exists. The meeting of natural being with the living creature produces those more or less changing masses of usable sense data which constitute the animal's realm of life. But only from the meeting of natural being with man does the new and enduring arise, that which comprehends and infinitely transcends the realm. An animal in the realm of its perceptions is like a fruit in its skin; man is, or can be, in the world as a dweller in an enormous building which is always being added to, and to whose limits he can never penetrate, but which he can nevertheless know as one does know a house in which one lives — for he is capable of grasping the wholeness of the building as such. Man is like this because he is the creature (*Wesen*) through whose being (*Sein*) 'what is' (*das Seiende*) becomes detached from him, and recognized for itself. It is only the realm which is removed, lifted out from sheer presence, withdrawn from the operation of needs and wants, set at a distance and thereby given over to itself, which is more and other than a realm. Only when a structure of being is independently over against a living being (*Seiende*), an independent opposite, does a world exist.

The view could be put forward that this giving of independence to a world is the result of agelong developments of mankind, and that it can therefore not be constitutive of man as such. But it cannot concern us when and how the category of man has been realized; our concern is its ground. When a world exists, and to the extent to which it exists, there exists the man who conditions it, and he is there not in the sense of a species of living creatures, but of a category which has moved into reality. No matter where you meet man on his way, he always holds over against himself to some degree, in some way, that which he does not know as well as that which he knows, bound up together in one world, however 'primitive'. This is of course true of his connection with time no less than of his connection with space. An animal's actions are concerned with its future and the future of its young, but only man imagines the future: the beaver's dam is extended in a time-realm, but the planted tree is rooted in the world of time, and he who plants the first tree is he who will expect the Messiah.

Now the second movement has been added to the first: Man turns to the withdrawn structure of being (*Seiende*) and enters into relation with it. 'First' and 'second' are not to be taken in the sense of a temporal succession; it is not possible to think of an existence over against a world which is not also an attitude to it as a world, and that means the outline of an attitude of relation. This is to say no more than that an animal does not know the state of relation because one cannot stand in a relation to something that is not perceived as contrasted and existing for itself. The rainmaker who deals with the cloud that is sailing up beyond the orbit of his sight acts within the same category as the physicist who has worked out the existence of the still-unseen planet, and communicates with it at his desk.

We may characterize the act and the work of entering into relation with the world as such — and, therefore, not with parts of it, and not with the sum of its parts, but with it as the world —

as synthesizing apperception, by which we establish that this pregnant use of the concept involves the function of unity: by synthesizing apperception I mean the apperception of a being as a whole and as a unity. Such a view is won, and won again and again, only by looking upon the world as a world. The conception of wholeness and unity is in its origin identical with the conception of the world to which man is turned. He who turns to the realm which he has removed from himself, and which has been completed and transformed into a world — he who turns to the world and looking upon it steps into relation with it, becomes aware of wholeness and unity in such a way that from then on he is able to grasp being as a wholeness and a unity; the single being has received the character of wholeness and the unity which are perceived in it from the wholeness and unity perceived in the world. But a man does not obtain this view simply from the 'setting at a distance' and 'making independent'. These would offer him the world only as an object, as which it is only an aggregate of qualities that can be added to at will, not a genuine wholeness and unity. Only the view of what is over against me in the world in its full presence, with which I have set myself, present in my whole person, in relation — only this view gives me the world truly as whole and one. For only in such an opposition are the realm of man and what completes it in spirit, finally one. So it has always been, and so it is in this hour.

What has been indicated here must not be misunderstood as meaning that I 'establish' the world, or the like. Man's act of setting at a distance is no more to be understood as primary than his act of relation which is bound up with it. Rather is this the peculiarity of human life, that here and here alone a being has arisen from the whole, endowed and entitled to detach the whole as a world from himself and to make it an opposite to himself, instead of cutting out with his senses the part he needs from it, as all other beings do, and being content with that. This endowment and this entitlement of man produce, out of the whole, the being of the world, and this being can only mean that it is there for man as something that is for itself, with which he is able to enter into relation.

We must now look afresh at the twofold nature of the principle. Though the two movements are bound together in it very closely and with many strands, yet they are not to be understood as just two aspects of the same event or process. There is no kind of parallelism here, nothing that would make the carrying out of the one movement bring about the carrying out of the other. Rather it must be firmly maintained that the first creates the presupposition for the second — not its source, but its presupposition. With the appearance of the first, therefore, nothing more than room for the second is given. It is only at this point that the real history of the spirit begins, and this history takes its eternal rise in the extent to which the second movement shares in the intimations of the first, to the extent of their mutual interaction, reaction, and co-operation. Man can set at a distance without coming into real relation with what has been set at a distance. He can fill the act of setting at a distance with the will to relation, relation having been made possible only by that act; he can accomplish the act of relation in the acknowledgment of the fundamental actuality of the distance. But the two movements can also contend with one another, each seeing in the other the obstacle to its own realization. And finally, in moments and forms of grace, unity can arise from the extreme tension of the contradiction as the overcoming of it, which is granted only now and in this way.

2

He who, with his eyes on the twofold principle of human life, attempts to trace the spirit's course in history, must note that the great phenomena on the side of acts of distance are preponderantly universal, and those on the side of acts of relation preponderantly personal, as indeed corresponds to their connection with one another. The facts of the movement of distance yield the essential answer to the question, How is man possible; the facts of the movement of relation yield the essential answer to the question, How is human life realized. The first question is strictly one about category; the second is one of category and history. Distance provides the human situation; relation provides man's becoming in that situation.

This difference can be seen in two spheres, within the connection with things and within the connection with one's fellow men.

An animal also makes use of things. In fact it is in animals that we can observe using in the exact sense, when they turn something, on which they happen, round and round until they reach the possibility of using it for the attainment of a definite purpose, whether preconceived or arising at that moment. Monkeys make use of a stick they have found in order to force an opening which they could not have made with the arm, they make use of a stone to crack nuts. But they do not set aside any of these things, which for the moment have become tools, in order to use them the next day in a similar fashion; clearly none of them persists in their consciousness as a thing in which the faculty of the lever or the hammer dwells. These things are to hand, as occasion arises, in their realm; they never receive their place in a world. Only man, as man, gives distance to things which he comes upon in his realm; he sets them in their independence as things which from now on continue to exist ready for a function and which he can make wait for him so that on each occasion he may master them again, and bring them into action. A suitable piece of metal which has once been used as an auger does not cease to be an auger: it persists in the quality which has now been made known, this very piece of metal, this specific It with its known capacity now persists there; it is at one's disposal. Every change made in the stuff of things which is intended to make them more suitable for fulfilling a purpose, every strengthening and refining, every differentiation and combination, every technique is built on this elementary basis — that a person sets aside something which he finds, and makes it into something for itself, in which state, however, having become a tool, it can always be found again, and always as this same tool ready to carry out this same work. A monkey can swing the branch of a tree as a weapon; but man alone is capable of providing the branch with a separate existence, in that it is thenceforth established as a 'weapon' and awaits man's pleasure to be used again. Whatever is done to it after that to shape it into a proper cudgel, there is no further essential change: technique only fulfills what has been given by the primary choice and assignment, by a primary nomos.

But now something new and essentially different can enter the situation.

Let us think of a tribe which is close to nature, and which already knows the axe, a simple but reliable stone-axe. Then it occurs to a lad to scratch a curved line on his axe with the aid of a sharper stone. This is a picture of something and of nothing: it may be a sign, but even its author does not know of what. What was in his mind? Magic — to give the tool a more powerful effect? Or simply a play with the possibility presented by the empty space on the shaft? The two things are not mutually exclusive, but they mingle — the magical intention concentrates the play in more solid forms, the free play loosens the form decided on by magic and changes it — but even together these do not suffice to explain the unheard-of fact that a work has been carried out without any model, reaching beyond the technical purpose. We have to turn to the principle of human life in its twofold character in order to establish what has happened. Man sets things which he uses at a distance, he gives them into an independence in which function gains duration, he reduces and empowers them to be the bearers of the function. In this way the first movement of the principle is satisfied, but the second is not. Man has a great desire to enter into personal relation with things and to imprint on them his relation to them. To use them, even to possess them, is not enough, they must become his in another way, by imparting to them in the picture-sign his relation to them.

But the picture-sign grows to be a picture; it ceases to be accessory to a tool and becomes an independent structure. The form indicated by even the clumsiest ornament is now fulfilled in an autonomous region as the sediment of man's relation to things. Art is neither the impression of natural objectivity nor the expression of spiritual subjectivity, but it is the work and witness of the relation between the *substantia humana* and the *substantia rerum*, it is the realm of 'the between' which has become a form. Consider great nude sculptures of the ages: None of them is to be understood properly either from the giveness of the human body or from the will to expression of an inner state, but solely from the relational event which takes place between two entities which have gone apart from one another, the withdrawn 'body' and the withdrawing 'soul'. In each of the arts there is something specifically corresponding to the relational character to be found in the picture. Music, for example, can be understood in terms of categories only when it is recognized that music is the ever-renewed discovering of tonal being in the movement of 'distancing' and the releasing of this tonal being in the movement of relation by bodying it forth.

3

The twofold principle of human life can be still more fully clarified in men's relation to one another.

In an insect state the system of division of labor excludes not merely every variation, but also every granting of a function in the precise sense of an individual award. In human society at all its levels persons confirm one another in a practical way to some extent or other in their personal qualities and capacities, and a society may be termed human in the measure to which its members confirm one another. Apart from the technique of the tool and from the weapon, what has enabled this creature, so badly equipped 'by nature', to assert himself and to achieve lordship of the earth is this dynamic, adaptable, pluralistic form of association, which has been made possible by the factor of mutual individual completion of function and the corresponding factor of mutual individual recognition of function. Within the most closely bound clan there still exist free societies of fishers, free orders of barter, free associations of many kinds, which are built upon acknowledged differences in capacity and inclination. In the most rigid epochs of ancient kingdoms the family preserved its separate structure, in which, despite its authoritative quality, individuals affirmed one another in their manifold nature. And everywhere the position of society is strengthened by this balance of firmness and looseness. Man has always stood opposed to natural powers as the creature equipped with the tool which awaits him in independence, who forms his associations of independent single lives. An animal never succeeds in unravelling its companions from the knot of their common life, just as it never succeeds in ascribing to the enemy an existence beyond his hostility, that is, beyond its own realm. Man, as man, sets man at a distance and makes him independent; he lets the life of men like himself go on round about him, and so he, and he alone, is able to enter into relation, in his own individual status, with those like himself. The basis of man's life with man is twofold, and it is one — the wish of every man to be confirmed as what he is, even as what he can become, by men; and the innate capacity in man to confirm his fellow men in this way. That this capacity lies so immeasurably fallow constitutes the real weakness and questionableness of the human race: actual humanity exists only where this capacity unfolds. On the other hand, of course, an empty claim for confirmation, without devotion for being and becoming, again and again mars the truth of the life between man and man.

The great characteristic of men's life with one another, speech, is doubly significant as a witness to the principle of human life. Men express themselves to men in a way that is different, not in kind or degree but essentially, from the way animals express themselves to their companions. Man and many animals have this is common, that they call out to others; to speak to others is something essentially human, and is based on the establishment and acknowledgment of the independent otherness of the other with whom one fosters relation, addressing and being addressed on this very basis.[1] The oldest form of word, along with — and perhaps even before — the 'holophrastic' characterization of situations by means of words in the form of sentences, which signified the situations for those who had to be informed, may have been the individual's name: when the name let the companion

---

1. Animals, especially domestic animals, are capable of regarding a man in a 'speaking' way; they turn to him as one to whom they wish to announce themselves, but not as a being existing for himself as well, outside this addressing of him. On this remarkable frontier area, cf. Buber, *I and Thou*, 96 ff., 125 f., and *Between Man and Man*, 22 f.

and helper at a distance know that his presence, his and none other, was needed in a given situation. Both the holophrase and the name are still signals, yet also words; for — and this is the second part of the witness of speech to the principle of human life — man sets also his calls at a distance and gives them independence, he stores them like a tool he has prepared, as objects which are ready for use, he makes them into words which exist by themselves. Here in speech the addressing of another as it were cancels out, it is neutralized — but in order to come again and again to life, not indeed in those popular discussions which misuse the reality of speech, but in genuine conversation. If we ever reach the stage of making ourselves understood only by means of the dictograph, that is, without contact with one another, the chance of human growth would be indefinitely lost.

Genuine conversation, and therefore every actual fulfillment of relation between men, means acceptance of otherness. When two men inform one another of their basically different views about an object, each aiming to convince the other of the rightness of his own way of looking at the matter, everything depends so far as human life is concerned, on whether each thinks of the other as the one he is, whether each, that is, with all his desire to influence the other, nevertheless unreservedly accepts and confirms him in his being this man and in his being made in this particular way. The strictness and depth of human individuation, the elemental otherness of the other, is then not merely noted as the necessary starting point, but is affirmed from the one being to the other. The desire to influence the other then does not mean the effort to change the other, to inject one's own 'rightness' into him; but it means the effort to let that which is recognized as right, as just, as true (and for that very reason must also be established there, in the substance of the other) through one's influence take seed and grow in the form suited to individuation. Opposed to this effort is the lust to make use of men by which the manipulator of 'propaganda' and 'suggestion' is possessed, in his relation to men remaining as in a relation to things, to things, moreover, with which he will never enter into relation, which he is indeed eager to rob of their distance and independence.

Human life and humanity come into being in genuine meetings. There man learns not merely that he is limited by man, cast upon his own finitude, partialness, need of completion, but his own relation to truth is heightened by the other's different relation to the same truth — different in accordance with his individuation, and destined to take seed and grow differently. Men need, and it is granted to them, to confirm one another in their individual being by means of genuine meetings. But beyond this they need, and it is granted to them, to see the truth, which the soul gains by its struggle, light up to the others, the brothers, in a different way, and even so be confirmed.

4

The realization of the principle in the sphere between men reaches its height in an event which may be called 'making present'. As a partial happening something of this is to be found wherever men come together, but in its essential formation I should say it appears only rarely. It rests on a capacity possessed to some extent by everyone, which may be described as 'imagining' the real: I mean the capacity to hold before one's soul a reality arising at this moment but not able to be directly experienced. Applied to intercourse between men, 'imagining' the real means that I imagine to myself what another man is at this very moment wishing, feeling, perceiving, thinking, and not as a detached content but in his very reality, that is, as a living process in this man. The full 'making present' surpasses this in one decisive way: something of the character of what is imagined is joined to the act of imagining, that is, something of the character of an act of the will is added to my imagining of the other's act of will, and so on. So-called fellow feeling may serve as a familiar illustration of this if we leave vague sympathy out of consideration and limit the concept to that event in which I experience, let us say, the specific pain of another in such a way that I feel what is specific in it, not, therefore, a general discomfort or state of suffering, but this particular pain as the pain of the other. This making present increases until it is a paradox in the soul when I

and the other are embraced by a common living situation, and
(let us say) the pain which I inflict upon him surges up in myself,
revealing the abyss of the contradictoriness of life between man
and man. At such a moment something can come into being
which cannot be built up in any other way.

The principle of human life which we have recognized sug-
gests how making present may be understood in its ontological
significance. Within the setting of the world at a distance and the
making it independent, yet also essentially reaching beyond this
and in the proper sense not able to be included in it, is the fact of
man's himself being set at a distance and made independent as
'the others'. Our fellow men, it is true, live round about us as
components of the independent world over against us, but in so
far as we grasp each one as a human being he ceases to be a
component and is there in his self-being as I am; his being at a
distance does not exist merely for me, but it cannot be separated
from the fact of my being at a distance for him. The first movement of human life puts men into mutual existence which is fundamental and even. But the second movement puts them into
mutual relation with me which happens from time to time and by
no means in an even way, but depends on our carrying it out.
Relation is fulfilled in a full making present when I think of the
other not merely as this very one, but experience, in the particular approximation of the given moment, the experience belonging
to him as this very one. Here and now for the first time does the
other become a self for me, and the making independent of his
being which was carried out in the first movement of distancing
is shown in a new highly pregnant sense as a presupposition — a
presupposition of this 'becoming a self for me', which is, however, to be understood not in a psychological but in a strictly
ontological sense, and should therefore rather be called 'becoming a self with me'. But it is ontologically complete only when the
other knows that he is made present by me in his self and when
this knowledge induces the process of his inmost self-becoming.
For the inmost growth of the self is not accomplished, as people
like to suppose today, in man's relation to himself, but in the
relation between the one and the other, between men, that is,

preeminently in the mutuality of the making present — in the making present of another self and in the knowledge that one is made present in his own self by the other — together with the mutuality of acceptance, of affirmation and confirmation.

Man wishes to be confirmed in his being by man, and wishes to have a presence in the being of the other. The human person needs confirmation because man as man needs it. An animal does not need to be confirmed, for it is what it is unquestionably. It is different with man: sent forth from the natural domain of species into the hazard of the solitary category, surrounded by the air of a chaos which came into being with him, secretly and bashfully he watches for a Yes which allows him to be and which can come to him only from one human person to another. It is from one man to another that the heavenly bread of self-being is passed.

Healing Through Meeting

A man who follows an intellectual profession must pause time after time in the midst of his activity as he becomes aware of the paradox he is pursuing. Each of these professions stands, indeed, on paradoxical ground. When he pauses, something important has already happened. But this happening only becomes significant if he does not content himself with taking such fleeting upheavals of a well-ordered world into the register of the memory. Again and again, not too long after the completion of the thus interrupted activity, he must occupy himself, in strenuous yet dispassionate reflection, with the actual problematic to which he has been referred. With the involvement of his living and suffering person, he must push forward to greater and still greater clarity of that paradox. Thus a spiritual destiny, with its peculiar fruitfulness, comes into being and grows — hesitating, groping, while groping wrestling, slowly overcoming, in overcoming succumbing, in succumbing illuminating. Such was the destiny of Hans Trüb.

But the particular profession that is in question here is the most paradoxical of all; indeed, it puts forth out of the sphere of the intellectual professions not less than do these ordered intellectual activities, taken together out of the totality of the professions. Certainly the lawyer, the teacher, the priest, no less the doctor of the body, each comes also to feel, as far as conscience genuinely infuses his vocation, what it means to be concerned with the needs and anxieties of men, and not merely, like the pursuer of a nonintellectual profession, with the satisfaction of their wants. But this man here, the psychotherapist, whose task

is to be the watcher and healer of sick souls, again and again
confronts the naked abyss of man, man's abysmal lability. This
troublesome appendage had been thrown into the bargain when
that process unknown to nature was acquired, which may be
characterized in the specific sense as the psychic.[1] The psychotherapist meets the situation, moreover, not like the priest, who is
armed with sacred possessions of divine grace and holy word,
but as a mere person equipped only with the tradition of his
science and the theory of his school. It is understandable enough
that he strives to objectivize the abyss that approaches him and
to convert the raging 'nothing-else-than-process' into a thing that
can, in some degree, be handled. Here the concept of the unconscious, manifoldly elaborated by the schools, affords him invaluable help. The sphere in which this renowned concept possesses
reality is located, according to my understanding, beneath the
level where human existence is split into physical and psychical
phenomena. But any of the contents of this sphere can in any
moment enter into the dimension of the introspective, and
thereby be explained and dealt with as belonging to the psychic
province.

On this paradoxical foundation, laid with great wisdom and
art, the psychotherapist now practices with skill and also with
success, generally, too, with the assistance of the patient, whom
the tranquilizing, orienting, and to some extent integrating procedure for the most part pleases. Until, in certain cases a therapist is terrified by what he is doing because he begins to suspect
that, at least in such cases, but finally, perhaps, in all, something
entirely other is demanded of him. Something incompatible with
the economics of his profession, dangerously threatening, indeed,
to his regulated practice of it. What is demanded of him is that
he draw the particular case out of the correct methodological
objectification and himself step forth out of the role of professional superiority, achieved and guaranteed by long training and
practice, into the elementary situation between one who calls and

1. By this nothing else is meant than the series of phenomena that opens
itself to the introspective activity.

one who is called. The abyss does not call to his confidently functioning security of action, but to the abyss, that is to the self of the doctor, that selfhood that is hidden under the structures erected through training and practice, that is itself encompassed by chaos, itself familiar with demons, but is graced with the humble power of wrestling and overcoming, and is thus ready to wrestle and overcome ever anew; Through his hearing of this call there erupts in the most exposed of the intellectual professions the crisis of its paradox. The psychotherapist, just when and because he is a doctor, will return from the crisis to his habitual method, but as a changed person in a changed situation. He returns to it as one to whom the necessity of genuine personal meetings in the abyss of human existence between the one in need of help and the helper has been revealed. He returns to a modified method in which, on the basis of the experiences gained in such meetings, the unexpected, which contradicts the prevailing theories and demands his ever-renewed personal involvement, also finds its place.

An example, sketched only in general outline, may serve here for clarification of what has been set forth and show something further concerning it.

A man saddles himself with guilt toward another and represses his knowledge of it. Guilt, this fundamental life occurrence, is only rarely discussed in the psychoanalytic literature, and then generally only in terms of its subjective side, and not within the circumference of the ontic reality between man and man; that is, only its psychological projection and its elimination through the act of repression appear to be relevant here. But if one recognizes the ontic, in fact, suprapersonal ontic character of guilt, if one recognizes, therefore, that guilt is not hidden away inside the human person, but that the human person stands, in the most real way, in the guilt that envelops him, then it also becomes clear that to understand the suppression of the knowledge of guilt as a merely psychological phenomenon will not suffice. It hinders the guilty man, in fact, from accomplishing the reconciliation whose ontic nature has, to be sure, been rather obscured by some discussions of moral philosophy and moral theology. It hinders him from thereby influencing the suprapersonal facts of the case through setting right the disturbance engendered in the human constellations — a setting right of which the "purification" of the soul is only the accompanying manifestation within the person. Reconciliation cannot take place merely in relation to the man toward whom one has become guilty (and who is perhaps dead), but in relation to all and each, according to the path of his individual life, according to his surroundings and his circumstances. What matters is only that, starting with the fact of guilt, life be lived as a reconciling, a making good.

Let us assume that the man who has repressed his knowledge of guilt falls into a neurosis. He now comes to the psychotherapist for healing. The therapist draws what is especially favored by him within the all-containing microcosmos of the patient — Oedipus complex or inferiority feeling or collective archetype — from the unconscious into the conscious, and then treats it according to the rules of his wisdom and art; guilt remains foreign to him or uninteresting. In one case of which I am thinking in particular, a woman took another woman's husband, later suffered the same loss herself, then "crept away into her soul," only to be visited and unsettled by vagrant pains. The analyst (a well-known disciple of Freud) succeeded so thoroughly in "healing" that the pain fully ceased, the patient "came forth out of the soul" and lived her life to the end amid an abundance of agreeable and, to her mind, friendly social relationships: that incessant and highly painful reminder of the unreconciled, the disturbed relation-to-being that must be set right, was eradicated. I call this successful cure the exchange of hearts. The artificial heart, functioning entirely satisfactorily, no longer feels pain; only one of flesh and blood can do that.

To the psychotherapist who has passed through this crisis of the paradox of his vocation, such "healing" is barred. In a decisive hour, together with the patient entrusted to and trusting in him, he has left the closed room of psychological treatment in which the analyst rules by means of his systematic and methodological superiority and has stepped forth with him into the air of the world where self is exposed to self. There, in the closed room where one probed and treated the isolated psyche according to the inclination of the self-encapsulated patient, the patient was referred to ever-deeper levels of his inwardness as to his proper world; here outside, in the immediacy of one human confronting another, the encapsulation must and can be broken through, and a transformed, healed relationship must and can be opened to the person who is sick in his relations to otherness — to the world of the other which he cannot remove into his soul. A soul is never sick alone, but there is always a between-ness also, a situation between it and another existing being. The psychotherapist who has passed through the crisis may now dare to touch on this.

This way of frightened pause, of unfrightened reflection, of personal involvement, of rejection of security, of unreserved stepping into relationship, of the bursting of psychologism, this way of vision and of risk is that which Hans Trüb trod. After repeated wrestlings with the word for the unfamiliar, he has set forth his findings ever more maturely, ever more adequately, until its maturest and most adequate expression in this work, which he was not able to finish. His foot can no longer push on, but the path is broken. Surely there will not be wanting men like him — awake and daring, hazarding the economics of the vocation, not sparing and not withholding themselves, risking themselves — men who will find his path and extend it further.

Images of Good and Evil

Our Point of Departure

It is usual to think of good and evil as two poles, two opposite directions, the two arms of a signpost pointing to right and left; they are understood as belonging to the same plane of being, as the same in nature, but the antithesis of one another. If we are to have in mind, not ethical abstractions, but existent states of human reality, we must begin by doing away with this convention and recognizing the fundamental dissimilarity between the two in nature, structure, and dynamics within human reality.

It is advisable to begin with evil, since, as will be shown, at the original stage, with which we shall deal first, the existent state of good in a certain matter presupposes that of evil. Now the latter, however, though concretely presented to extraspective vision also, in its actions and effects, its attitudes and behavior, is presented in its essential state to our introspection only; and only our self-knowledge — which of course, everywhere and always requires to be supplemented by our cognizance of the self-knowledge of others — is capable of stating what happens when we do evil (only we are wont to make far too little use of this self-knowledge when we look around in the circles of evil and are, at the same time, making some attempt to understand it). Since, on the other hand, such experience must have reached a high degree of objectivity to be capable of providing us with a knowledge of the subject, it is necessary to proceed from the viewpoint of a man looking back over his life, who has achieved the indispensable distance from even those amongst the remembered inner and outer occurrences which, for him, are bound up with the actuality of evil, but whose memory has not lost the no less requisite force and freshness. It follows from the foregoing that he must now be aware of the existent actuality of evil as evil, and that it is this which must be a specifically serious matter for him. Whoever has learnt to dispose of the matter to his own satisfaction within the more or less dubious sphere of so-called values, for whom guilt is merely the civilized term for *tabu*, to which corresponds no other reality than the control exercised by society and, attendant upon it, of the 'super-ego' over the play of the urges, is naturally unfit for the task in hand here.

At this point, however, it is necessary to draw an essential distinction in order to avert a misunderstanding which, nowadays, threatens every statement of this kind. What we are dealing with here is generically different from what is called self-analysis in modern psychology. The latter, as is the case in general with psychological analysis in our age, is concerned to penetrate behind that which is remembered, to 'reduce' it to the real elements assumed to have been 'repressed'. Other business is to call to mind an occurrence as reliably, concretely, and completely remembered as possible, which is entirely unreduced and undissected. Naturally, the memory must be liberated from all subsequent deletions and trimmings, beautifications and demonizations; but he can do this, to whom the confrontation with himself, in the essential compass of the past, has proved to be one of the effective forces in the process of 'becoming what one is'. Of leading significance to him in his work of great reflection will be the unforgotten series of those moments of electric spontaneity, when the lightning of the has-been flashed unexpectedly across the skies of the now.

If the questioner seeks to apprehend the common denominator between the self-knowledge thus acquired and the analogous self-knowledge of others which has become known to him, he will gain an image of the biographically decisive beginnings of evil and good which differs notably from the usual representations and provides an important confirmation of those Old Testament tales from the dawn of man.

Insight into the second stage, to which the Ancient Iranian
tales are to be related, must naturally be gained along a different
path.

The First Stage

Human life as a specific entity, which has stepped forth from
nature, begins with the experience of chaos as a condition perceived in the soul.

Only through this experience and as its materialization could
the concept of chaos, which is to be derived from no other empirical finding, arise and enter into the mythic cosmogonies.

In a period of evolution, which generally coincides with puberty without being tied to it, the human person inevitably becomes aware of the category of possibility, which of all living
creatures is represented just in man, manifestly the only one for
whom the real is continually fringed by the possible.

The evolving human person I am speaking of is bowled over
by possibility as an infinitude. The plenitude of possibility floods
over his small reality and overwhelms it. Fantasy, the imagery of
possibilities which, in the Old Testament, God pronounces evil
because it distracts from His divinely given reality and plays
with potentialities, imposes the form of its indefiniteness upon
the definiteness of the moment. The substantial threatens to be
submerged in the potential. Swirling chaos, 'confusion and deso-
lation' (Genesis 1:2) has forced its way in.

But as, in the stage I am speaking of, everything which appears or happens to man is transformed into motor-energy, into
the capacity and desire for action, so too the chaos of possibilities
of being, having forced an entry, becomes a chaos of possibilities
of action. It is not things which revolve in the vortex, but the
possible ways of joining and overcoming them.

This impelling universal passion is not to be confounded with
the so-called libido, without whose vital energy it naturally could
not endure, but to reduce it to which signifies a simplification
and animalization of human reality. Urges in the psychological
sense are abstractions; but we are speaking of a total concrete

occurrence at a given hour of a person's life. Moreover, these urges are, *per definitionem,* 'directed toward something'; but lack of direction is characteristic of the vortex revolving within itself.

The soul driven round in the dizzy whirl cannot remain fixed within it; it strives to escape. If the ebb that leads back to familiar normality does not make its appearance, there exist for it two issues. One is repeatedly offered it: it can clutch at any object, past which the vortex happens to carry it, and cast its passion upon it; or else, in response to a prompting that is still incomprehensible to itself, it can set about the audacious work of self-unification. In the former case, it exchanges an undirected possibility for an undirected reality, in which it does what it wills not to do, what is preposterous to it, the alien, the 'evil'; in the latter, if the work meets with success, the soul has given up undirected plenitude in favour of the one taut string, the one stretched beam of direction. If the work is not successful, which is no wonder with such an unfathomable undertaking the soul has nevertheless gained an inkling of what direction, or rather *the* direction is — for in the strict sense there is only one. To the extent to which the soul achieves unification it becomes aware of direction, becomes aware of itself as sent in quest of it. It comes into the service of good or into service for good.

Finality does not rule here. Again and again, with the surge of its enticements, universal temptation emerges and overcomes the power of the human soul; again and again innate grace arises from out of its depths and promises the utterly incredible: you can become whole and one. But always there are, not left and right, but the vortex of chaos and the spirit hovering above it. Of the two paths, one is a setting out upon no path, pseudo-decision which is indecision, flight into delusion and ultimately into mania; the other is the path, for there is only one.

The same basic structure of the occurrence, however, only become briefer and harder, we re-encounter in innumerable situations in our later lives. They are the situations in which we feel it incumbent upon us to make the decision which, from our person, and from our person as we feel it 'purposed' for us, answers the situation confronting us. Such a decision can only be taken by the whole soul that has become one; the whole soul, in whatever direction it was turned or inclined when the situation came upon us, must enter into it, otherwise we shall bring forth nothing but a stammer, a pseudo-answer, a substitute for an answer. The situations, whether more biographical or more historical in character, are always — even though often behind veils — cruelly harsh, because the unrecoverable passage of time and of our lives is so, and only with the harshness of unified decision can we prove ourselves equal to them. It is a cruelly hazardous enterprise, this becoming a whole, becoming a form, of crystallization of the soul. Everything in the nature of inclinations, of indolence, of habits, of fondness for possibilities which has been swashbuckling within us, must be overcome, and overcome, not by elimination, by suppression, for genuine wholeness can never be achieved like that, never a wholeness where downtrodden appetites lurk in the corners. Rather must all these mobile or static forces, seized by the soul's rapture, plunge of their own accord, as it were, into the mightiness of decision and dissolve within it. Until the soul as form has such great power over the soul as matter, until chaos is subdued and shaped into cosmos, what an immense resistance! It is thus understandable enough that the occurrence — which at times, as we know to be the case with dreams encompassing a whole drama, lasts no longer than a minute — so frequently terminates in a persistent state of indecision. The anthropological retrospective view of the person (which indeed is incorrectly termed 'view', for if our memory proves strong enough we experience such past occurrences with all our senses, with the excitation of our nerves and the tension or flaccidity of our muscles) announces to us as evil all these and all other indecisions, all the moments in which we did no more than leave undone that which we knew to be good. But is evil then not, by its nature, an action? Not at all: action is only the type of evil happening which makes evil manifest. But does not evil action stem precisely from a decision to evil? The ultimate meaning of our exposition is that it too stems primarily from indecision, providing that by decision we understand, not a partial, a pseudo decision, but that of the whole soul. For a partial decision, one which leaves the forces opposing it untouched, and certainly which the soul's highest forces, being the true constructional substance of the person purposed for me, watch, pressed back and powerless, but shining in the protest of the spirit, cannot be termed decision in our sense. Evil cannot be done with the whole soul; good can only be done with the whole soul. It is done when the soul's rapture, proceeding from its highest forces, seizes upon all the forces and plunges them into the purging and transmuting fire, as into the mightiness of decision. Evil is lack of direction and that which is done in it and out of it as the grasping, seizing, devouring compelling, seducing, exploiting, humiliating, torturing and destroying of what offers itself. Good is direction and what is done in it; that which is done in it is done with the whole soul, so that in fact all the vigor and passion with which evil might have been done is included in it. In this connection is to be recalled that Talmudic interpretation of the Biblical pronouncement of God concerning imagination or the 'evil urge', whose whole vigor must be drawn into the love of God in order truly to serve Him.

The foregoing is intended and able to give no more than an anthropological definition of good and evil as, in the last instance, it is revealed to the human person's retrospection, his cognizance of himself in the course of the life he has lived. We learn to comprehend this anthropological definition as similar in nature to the biblical tales of good and evil, whose narrator must have experienced Adam as well as Cain in the abyss of his own heart. But it is neither intended nor able to provide any criterion over and above that, either for the use of theoretical meditation concerning the entities 'good' and 'evil' nor, certainly, for the use of the questioning man, who is not spared enquiry and investigation into what, in the sense of design, is good and what evil, groping and feeling his way in the obscurity of the problematics, and even doubt as to the validity of the concepts themselves. The former and the latter will have to find their criterion, or their criteria elsewhere, will have to achieve it otherwise: the meditant seeks to learn something else than what happens, the designant cannot make his choice according to whether it will lead to his soul becoming whole. Between their requirements and our anthropological insight there is only one link, which is, of course, an important one. It is the presentiment implanted in each of us, but unduly neglected in each, the presentiment of what is meant and purposed for him and for him alone — no matter whether by creation, or by 'individuation' — and to fulfill which, to become which is demanded of and entrusted to him, and the resulting possibility of comparison time and again. Here too there is a criterion, and it is an anthropological one; of course, by its nature, it can never extend beyond the sphere of the individual. It can assume as many shapes as there are individuals — and nonetheless is never relativized.

The Second Stage

It is far more difficult to ascertain the human reality corresponding to the myths of Ahriman's choice and Lucifer's downfall. It is in the nature of the matter that here the assistance of retrospection is only very rarely open to us; those who have once surrendered themselves to evil with their innermost being will hardly ever, not even after a complete conversion, be capable of that deliberate, reliably recollecting and interpreting retrospection which can alone advance our insight. In the literature of those able to recount their fate we shall almost never encounter such a report; everything confronting us in this domain is, apparently of necessity, highly colored or sentimentalized, and so thoroughly that we are unable to distill out of it the occurrences themselves, inner and outer likewise. What psychological research on phenomena of a similar nature has brought to light are naturally purely neurotic borderline cases and, with very few exceptions, not capable of illuminating our problem. Here our own observations, whose methods are adapted to that which is essential to our purpose, must set in. To supplement them, by far the richest contribution is offered by historical and, in particular, biographical literature. It is a question of concentrating our attention on those personal crises whose specific effect on the person's psychic dynamic is to render it obdurate and secretive. We then find that these crises are of two clearly distinguishable kinds: negative experiences with our environment, which denies us the confirmation of our being that we desire, underlie the one; negative experiences with oneself, in that the human person cannot say Yes to himself, underlie the other — the only one that concerns us here; we will leave aside mixed forms.

We have seen how man repeatedly experiences the dimension of evil as indecision. The occurrences in which he experiences it, however, do not remain in his self-knowledge a series of isolated moments of nondecision, of becoming possessed by the play of the fantasy with potentialities, of plunging in this possession upon that which offers itself: in self-knowledge, these moments merge into a course of indecision, as it were into a fixation in it. This negativation of self-knowledge is, of course, again and again 'repressed', as long as the will to simple self-preservation dominates that to being-able-to-affirm-oneself. To the extent, on the other hand, to which the latter asserts itself, the condition will change into one of acute auto-problematics: man calls himself in question, because his self-knowledge no longer enables him to affirm and confirm himself. This condition now either assumes a pathological form, that is, the relationship of the person to himself becomes fragile and intricate; or the person finds the way out where he hardly expected it, namely through an extreme effort of unification, which astonishes him himself in its power and effectiveness, a decisive act of decision, precisely that therefore, which in the amazingly apposite language of religion is called 'conversion'; or a third process takes place, something entitled to a special status amongst the singularities of man and to the consideration of which we must now turn.

Because man is the sole living creature known to us in whom the category of possibility is so to speak embodied, and whose reality is incessantly enveloped by possibilities, he alone amongst them all needs confirmation. Every animal is fixed in its thisbeing, its modifications are preordained, and when it changes into a caterpillar and into a chrysalis its very metamorphosis is a boundary; in everything together it remains exactly what it is, therefore it can need no confirmation; it would, indeed, be an absurdity for someone to say to it, or for it to say to itself: You may be what you are. Man as man is an audacity of life, undetermined and unfixed; he therefore requires confirmation, and he can naturally only receive this as individual man, in that others and he himself confirm him in his being-this-man. Again and again the Yes must be spoken to him, from the look of the confidant and from the stirrings of his own heart, to liberate him from the dread of abandonment, which is a foretaste of death. At a pinch, one can do without confirmation from others if one's own reaches such a pitch that it no longer needs to be supplemented by the confirmation of others. But not vice versa: the encouragement of his fellow men does not suffice if self-knowledge demands inner rejection, for self-knowledge is incontestably the more reliable. Then man, if he cannot readjust his self-knowledge by his own conversion, must withdraw from it the power over the Yes and No; he must render affirmation independent of all findings and base it, instead of on 'judgment-of-oneself,' on a sovereign willing-oneself; he must choose himself, and that not 'as he is intended' — this image must, rather, be totally extinguished — but just as he is, as he has himself resolved to intend himself. They are recognizable, those who dominate their own self-knowledge, by the spastic pressure of the lips, the spastic tension of the muscles of the hand and the spastic tread of the foot. This attitude corresponds to what I have called the third process, which leads out of auto-problematics 'into the open': one need no longer look for being, it is here, one is what one wants and one wants what one is. It is of this that the myth is speaking when it recounts that Yima proclaimed himself his own creator. Just this too Prudentius reports of Satan, and the great legendary motif of the pact with him is clearly derived from the view that he who has achieved self-creation will be ready to assist men to it.

From this point, the meaning of that paradoxical myth of the two spirits, one of whom chose evil, not without knowing it to be evil, but as evil, is also revealed to us. The 'wicked' spirit — in whom, therefore, evil is already present, if only *in statu nascendi* — has to choose between the two affirmations: affirmation of

himself and affirmation of the order, which has established and
eternally establishes good and evil, the first as the affirmed and
the second as the denied. If he affirms the order he must himself
become 'good', and that means he must deny and overcome his
present state of being. If he affirms himself he must deny and
reverse the order; to the yes-position, which 'good' had occupied,
he must bring the principle of his own self-affirmation, nothing
else must remain worthy of affirmation than just that which is
affirmed by him; his Yes to himself determines the reason and
right of affirmation. If he still concedes any significance to the
concept 'good', it is this: precisely that which I am. He has chosen himself, and nothing, no quality and no destiny, can any
longer be signed with a No if it is his.

This too explains altogether why Yima's defection is called a
lie. By glorifying and blessing himself as his own creator, he
commits the lie against being, yea, he wants to raise it, the lie, to
rule over being, for truth shall no longer be what he experiences
as such but what he ordains as such. The narrative of Yima's life
after his defection says with super clarity all that remains to be
said here.

Evil and Good

The images of good and evil which have been interpreted here
correspond, as I have shown, to certain anthropologically appre-
hensible occurrences in the life-path of the human person. They
include the images of evil belonging to two different stages on
this path, the Old Testament images to an earlier, the Iranian to a
later; whereas the images of good refer, in the main, to the same
momentum, which may occur at either the first or the second
stage.

To the Biblical images of evil corresponds, in the first stage of
living reality, the purpose of man to overcome the chaotic state
of his soul, the state of undirected surging passion, in appearance
only, instead of really overcoming it and breaking violently out of
it wherever a breach can be forced, instead of achieving direction
by unifying his energies — the only manner in which it can be

achieved. To the ancient Persian images corresponds, in the second stage of living reality, man's endeavour to render the contradictory state, which has arisen in consequence of his lack of direction and his pseudodecisions, bearable and even satisfying, by affirming this state, in the context of the total constitution of the personality, absolutely. In the first stage man does not choose, he merely acts; in the second he chooses himself, in the sense of his being-constituted-thus or having-become-thus. The first stage does not yet contain a 'radical evil'; whatever misdeeds are committed, their commission is not a doing of the deed but a sliding into it. In the second stage evil grows radical, because what man finds in himself is willed; whoever lends to that which, in the depths of self-awareness was time and again recognized by him as what should be negated, the mark of being affirmed, because it is his, gives it the substantial character which it did not previously possess. If we may compare the occurrence of the first stage to an eccentric whirling movement, the process of the freezing of flowing water may serve as a simile to illustrate the second.

Good, on the other hand, retains the character of direction at both stages. I have already indicated that for true human decision, that is, decision taken by the unified soul there is only One direction. This means that to whatever end the current decision is reached, in the reality of existence all the so diverse decisions are merely variations on a single one, which is continually made afresh in a single direction. This direction can be understood in two ways. Either it is understood as the direction toward the person purposed for me, which I only apprehend in such self-awareness that divides and decides, not thrusting any energy back, but transforming undirected energies into it by conferring direction upon them: I recognize ever more clearly that which is purposed for me, precisely because I confer the direction upon it and take the direction toward it—the experience of vital hours provides us with the key to this paradoxy, its actuality and its significance. Or else the single direction is understood as the direction toward God. This duality of comprehension, however, is no more than a duality of aspects, provided only that I do not apply the name 'God' to a projection of myself or anything of that kind, but to my creator, that is, the author of my uniqueness, which cannot be derived from within the world. My uniqueness, this unrepeatable form of being here, not analyzable into any elements and not compoundable out of any, I experience as a designed or preformed one, entrusted to me for execution, although everything that affects me participates in this execution. That a unique human being is created does not mean that it is put into being for a mere existence, but for the fulfillment of a being-intention, an intention of being which is personal, not however in the sense of a free unfolding of infinite singularities, but of a realization of the right in infinite personal shapes. For creation has a goal and the humanly right is service directed in the One direction, service of the goal of creation which we are given to surmise only to the extent necessary within this scope; the humanly right is ever the service of the single person who realizes the right uniqueness purposed for him in his creation. In decision, taking the direction thus means: taking the direction toward the point of being at which, executing for my part the design which I am, I encounter the divine mystery of my created uniqueness, the mystery waiting for me.

Good conceived thus cannot be located within any system of ethical co-ordination, for all those we know came into being on its account and existed or exist by virtue of it. Every ethos has its origin in a revelation, whether or not it is still aware of and obedient to it; and every revelation is revelation of human service to the goal of creation, in which service man authenticates himself. Without authentication, that is, without setting off upon and keeping to the One direction, as far as he is able, *quantum satis*, man certainly has what he calls life, even the life of the soul, even the life of the spirit, in all freedom and fruitfulness, all standing and status — existence there is none for him without it.

Buber and Jung

Religion and Modern Thinking

1

I shall speak of the relation of modern thought to religion. By this I do not mean the attempts to think from the standpoint of religious reality, or to create an understanding between it and philosophy based on mutual tolerance. My subject shall rather be modern thought only insofar as it undertakes to give a verdict as to whether or under what conditions or within what limits the character of a living human reality can be ascribed to religion. We find a judgment of this sort in the ontological sense, on the one hand, in the so-called existentialism of Sartre and Heidegger, and in the psychological sense, on the other, in Jung's theory of the collective unconscious. Basic to both positions is the assumption that the outcome of the crisis in which religion has entered depends essentially upon the judgments which are made by modern ontological or psychological thought. It is this assumption that we must examine.

In naming Heidegger and Sartre together, I by no means imply that they have the same attitude toward religion. On the contrary, in this respect as in so many others they are without doubt radically dissimilar, and accordingly the reply to the one must be entirely different from the reply to the other.

The essay "Religion and Modern Thinking" became chapter 5 of *Eclipse of God*.

34

Sartre proclaims his atheism; he says,[1] "The atheistic existentialism, which I represent. . . ." Among the representatives of this position he has, to be sure, included Heidegger; but Heidegger has refused to allow himself to be thus classified. We must therefore deal with Sartre by himself. He clearly wishes his atheism to be understood as a logical consequence of his existential philosophy. We undoubtedly have here before us an atheism which is basically different from any materialistic one. That it follows, however, from an existential conception of the world, that is, from one which proceeds from the reality of human existence, cannot be substantiated.

Sartre accepts Nietzsche's cry, or better shout, "God is dead!" as a valid statement of fact. Our generation appears to him as specifically the one which has outlived God. He says once[2] — although elsewhere[3] he most emphatically asserts, as one who knows, *"Dieu n'existe pas"* — that the fact that God is dead does not mean that he does not exist nor even that he no longer exists. In place of these interpretations he presents another which is singular enough. "He is dead," he says,[4] "he spoke to us and now is silent, all that we touch now is his corpse." I shall not deal here with the shockingly trivial concluding sentence. But let us turn to that which precedes it: "He spoke to us and now he is silent." Let us try to take it seriously, that is, let us ignore what Sartre really meant by it, namely, that man in earlier times believed that he heard God and now is no longer capable of so believing. Let us ask whether it may not be literally true that God formerly spoke to us and is now silent, and whether this is not to be understood as the Hebrew Bible understands it, namely, that the living God is not only a self-revealing but also a

---

1. *L'existentialisme est un humanisme* (1946), 21. All the quotations in this essay except one (see note 54) are translated directly and literally from the French or German original. For the context in translation cf. *Existentialism*, translated by Bernard Frechtman (1947), 18.

2. *Situations* I (1947), 153, Section *"Un nouveau mystique"* of 1943.

3. *L'existentialisme*, 33 f. Cf. *Existentialism*, 27 f.

4. *Situations* I, *loc. cit.*

self-concealing God.[5] Let us realize what it means to live in the age of such a concealment, such a divine silence, and we shall perhaps understand its implication for our existence as something entirely different from that which Sartre desires to teach us.

What Sartre desires to teach us, he says to us clearly enough.[6] "This silence of the transcendent, combined with the perseverance of the religious need in modern man, that is the great concern today as yesterday. It is the problem which torments Nietzsche, Heidegger, Jaspers." In other words, existentialism must take courage, it must give up once for all the search for God, it must "forget" God.[7] After a century-long crisis of faith as well as of knowledge, man must finally recover the creative freedom which he once falsely ascribed to God. He must recognize himself as the being through whose appearance the world exists. For, says Sartre,[8] "there is no universe other than a human universe, the universe of human subjectivity." The sentence that I have just quoted sounds like the thesis of a resurrected idealism.

The problem that "torments" the existentialist thinker of our age, insofar as he does not, like Sartre, dismiss it out of hand, lies deeper than Sartre thinks. It focuses finally in the question of whether the perseverance of the "religious need" does not indicate something inherent in human existence. Does existence really mean, as Sartre thinks, existing "for oneself" encapsuled in one's own subjectivity? Or does it not essentially mean standing *over against* the x — not an x for which a certain quantity could be substituted, but rather the *X* itself, the undefinable and unfathomable? "God," says Sartre,[9] "is the quintessence of the Other." But the Other for Sartre[10] is he who "looks at" me, who makes me into an object, as I make him. The idea of God, moreover, he also understands as that of an inescapable witness, and if

5. Isaiah 45:15.
6. *Situations* I, *loc. cit.*
7. *Ibid.*, 154.
8. *L'existentialisme*, 93. Cf. *Existentialism*, 60.
9. *Situations* I, 237, Section *"Aller et retour,"* probably of 1942.
10. *L'être et le néant* (1943), Section *"L'existence d'autrui."*

that is so, "What need have we of God? The Other is enough, no matter what other."[11] But what if God is not the quintessence of the Other, but rather its absoluteness? And what if it is not primarily the reciprocal relation of subject and object which exists between me and the other, but rather the reciprocal relation of I and Thou? Each empirical other does not, of course, remain my Thou; he becomes an It, an object for me as I for him. It is not so, however, with that absolute Other, the Absolute over against me, that undefinable and unfathomable X that I call "God." God can never become an object for me; I can attain no other relation to Him than that of the I to its eternal Thou, that of the Thou to its eternal I. But if man is no longer able to attain this relation, if God is silent toward him and he toward God, then something has taken place, not in human subjectivity but in Being itself. It would be worthier not to explain it to oneself in sensational and incompetent sayings, such as that of the "death" of God, but to endure it as it is and at the same time to move existentially toward a new happening, toward that event in which the word between heaven and earth will again be heard. Thus the perseverance of the "religious need," to which Sartre objects and which he thinks contradicts the silence of the transcendent, instead points directly to the situation in which man becomes aware of this silence as such.

Still more questionable is Sartre's demand,[12] reminiscent of Ludwig Feuerbach, that man should recover for himself the creative freedom which he ascribed to God and that he should affirm himself as the being through whom a world exists. That ordering of known phenomena which we call the world is, indeed, the composite work of a thousand human generations, but it has come into being through the fact that manifold being, which is not our work, meets us, who are, likewise, together with our subjectivity, not our work. Nor is this meeting, out of which arises the whole of the phenomena which we order into the "world," our work. All that being is *established*, we are estab-

11. *Situations* I, *loc. cit.*
12. *Situations* I, 334, Section *"La liberté cartésienne."*

lished, our meeting with it is established, and in this way the becoming of a world, which takes place through us, is established. This establishment of a universe, including ourselves and our works, is the fundamental reality of existence which is accessible to us as living beings. Contrasted with this reality, the demand that man recover his creative freedom appears as a demagogic phrase. That "creative freedom" which really belongs to us, our participation in creation, is established, as we ourselves. It is a question of using this freedom properly, that is, in a manner worthy of the fact that it is a freedom which is given to us, nothing less and nothing more. He who sets in the place of it the postulate of the "recovery of freedom" turns aside from true human existence, which means being sent and being commissioned.

Sartre has started from the "silence" of God without asking himself what part our not hearing and our not having heard has played in that silence. From the silence he has concluded[13] that God does not exist, at any rate not for us, for a god whose object I am without his being mine does not concern me. This conclusion is possible for Sartre because he holds the subject-object relation to be the primary and exclusive relation between two beings. He does not see the original and decisive relation between I and Thou, compared with which the subject-object relation is only a classifying elaboration. Now, however, Sartre goes further:[14] One "must draw the consequences." God is silent, that is, nothing is said to one that is unconditional or unconditionally binding. "There is no sign in the world."[15] Since, therefore, no universal morality can tell us what to do, since all possibility of discovering absolute values has disappeared with God, and since man, to whom henceforth "all is permitted,"[16] is at last free, is indeed freedom itself, it is for him to determine values. "If I have done away with God the father (*si j'ai supprimé Dieu le père*),"

13. *L'être et le néant*, 286 f., 341.
14. *L'existentialisme*, 33 ff. Cf. *Existentialism*, 25 ff.
15. *Ibid.*, 47. Cf. *Existentialism*, 33.
16. *Ibid.*, 36. Cf. *Existentialism*, 27.

Sartre says literally,[17] "someone is needed to invent values (*pour inventer les valeurs*). . . . Life has no meaning *a priori* . . . it is up to you to give it a meaning, and value is nothing else than this meaning which you choose." That is almost exactly what Nietzsche said, and it has not become any truer since then. One can believe in and accept a meaning or value, one can set it as a guiding light over one's life if one has discovered it, not if one has invented it. It can be for me an illuminating meaning, a direction-giving value only if it has been revealed to me in my meeting with Being, not if I have freely chosen it for myself from among the existing possibilities and perhaps have in addition decided with some fellow creatures: This shall be valid from now on. The thesis reminds me of that curious concept of Georges Sorel, the social myth, the classic example of which is the general strike. This avowedly unrealizable myth shall show the workers the direction in which they shall be active, but it can function naturally only so long as they do not read Sorel and learn that it is just a myth.

More important than these arguments of a remarkable psychological observer and highly gifted literary man, for whom genuine ontological considerations are always intermingled with entirely different matters, is that argument which Heidegger, who undoubtedly belongs to the historical rank of philosophers in the proper sense of the term, brings forward concerning the problem of religion in our time. These thoughts, it is true, are first explicitly expressed in the writings of his second period, from about 1943 on, but we already find indications of them earlier.

Like Sartre, Heidegger also starts from Nietzsche's saying "God is dead," which he has interpreted at length.[18] It is evident to him that Nietzsche wanted in this saying to dispense with not only God but also the absolute in all its forms, therefore, in truth, not only religion but also metaphysics. Heidegger believes that he can erect at the point of this extremest negation a new posi-

17. *Ibid.*, 89. Cf. *Existentialism*, 58.
18. *Holzwege* (1950), 193 ff., Section *"Nietzsches Wort 'Gott ist tot.'*

tion which will be a pure ontological thinking. It is the teaching
of being as attaining its illumination in or through man. In this
teaching the doctrine of Parmenides which posits being as the
original absolute which is prior to and above form is curiously
interwoven with the Hegelian theory of the original principle
which attains self-consciousness in the human spirit.

It has been possible for Heidegger to erect this new position
despite the "death of God" because being for him is bound to and
attains its illumination through the destiny and history of man,
without its becoming thereby a function of human subjectivity.
But by this it is already indicated that, to use an image that
Heidegger himself avoids, God can rise from the dead. This
means that the unfolding of the new ontological thought can prepare for a turning-point in which the divine, or as Heidegger, in
agreement with the poet Hölderlin, prefers to say, the holy, will
appear in new and still unanticipated forms. This thinking is consequently, as Heidegger repeatedly emphasizes, not atheism, for
it "decides neither positively nor negatively about the possibility
of God's existing."[19] Rather "through its adequate conception of
existence" it makes it possible for the first time legitimately to
ask "what is the ontological state of the relation of existence to
the divine."

Heidegger not only protests against our regarding this view as
atheism but also[20] against our regarding it as an indifferentism
which must deteriorate into nihilism. He by no means wants to
teach an indifference toward the religious question. The single
need of this hour is, to him, much more the thinking through of
the basic religious concepts, the cogitative clarification of the
meaning of words such as God or the Holy. "Must we not first
be able," he asks, "to understand and hear these words with the
greatest care if we, as men, that is as existing beings, are to
experience a relation of God to man?" But this in his opinion
would belong to a new thinking of being through man. Accord-

19. *Vom Wesen des Grundes* (1929), 28.
20. *Platons Lehre von der Wahrheit. Mit einem Brief über den Humanismus*
(1947), 102 f.

ing to Heidegger's conception,[21] to be sure, it is not for man to decide whether and how the divine will reappear. Such an appearance, he explains, will take place only through the fate of being itself. Since, however, he has stated[22] as the presupposition for this appearance that "beforehand and in long preparation being itself is clarified and is experienced in its truth," there can be no doubt as to what part is to be ascribed here to human thought about truth in the determination of "whether and how the day of the holy will dawn." It is indeed precisely in human thought about truth that being becomes illuminated. Heidegger usually conceives of this still uncertain surprise of the holy as the clear background before which "an appearance of God and the gods can begin anew."

Once[23] in interpreting Hölderlin, who had called our time an indigent one, he explains this as "the time of the gods who have fled *and* of the God who is coming." It is indigent because it stands in a double lack: "in the no longer of the departed gods and the not yet of the Coming One." As the denominating Word is wanting that could tell "who He Himself is who dwells in the holy,"[24] so is God Himself wanting. This is "the age in which God is absent";[25] the Word and God are absent together. The Word is not absent because God is absent, and God is not absent because the Word is absent. Both are absent together and appear together because of the nearness of man to being, which is at times, historically, illuminated in him. Thus, admonishes Heidegger, man living in this hour should not strive to make a God for himself, nor call any longer on an accustomed God.

Heidegger warns in this way against "religion" in general, but in particular against the prophetic principle in the Judaeo-Chris-

21. *Ibid.*, 75.

22. *Ibid.*, 85 f.

23. *Erläuterungen zu Hölderlins Dichtungen* (1944), 2nd ed. (1951), 44, Section *"Hölderlin und das Wesen der Dichtung"* of 1936. For an English translation of *"Hölderlin und das Wesen der Dichtung,"* cf. Martin Heidegger, *Existence and Being* (1949), *"Hölderlin and the Essence of Poetry."*

24. Ibid., 26.

25. Ibid., 27.

tian tradition. "The 'prophets' of these religions," he says,[26] "do
not begin by foretelling the word of the Holy. They announce
immediately the God upon whom the certainty of salvation in a
supernatural blessedness reckons." Incidentally, I have never in
our time encountered on a high philosophical plane such a far-
reaching misunderstanding of the prophets of Israel. The
prophets of Israel have never announced a God upon whom
their hearers' striving for security reckoned. They have always
aimed to shatter all security and to proclaim in the opened abyss
of the final insecurity the unwished-for God who demands that
His human creatures become real, they become human, and con-
founds all who imagine that they can take refuge in the certainty
that the temple of God is in their midst. This is the God of the
historical demand as the prophets of Israel beheld Him. The primal reality of these prophecies does not allow itself to be tossed
into the attic of "religions": it is as living and actual in this historical hour as ever.

This is not the place for a critical discussion of Heidegger's
theory of being. I shall only confess that for me a concept of
being that means anything other than the inherent fact of all
existing being, namely, that it exists, remains insurmountably
empty. That is, unless I have recourse to religion and see in it a
philosophical characterization of the Godhead similar to that of
some Christian scholastics and mystics who contemplate, or
think that they contemplate, the Godhead as it is in itself, thus as
prior to creation. It should also be noted, however, that one of
them, and the greatest of them all, Meister Eckhart, follows in
Plato's footsteps by placing above the *esse est Deus*, as the higher
truth, the sentence, "*Est enim (Deus) super esse et ens.*" Compare
this with Heidegger's statement:[27] "'Being'—that is not God and
it is not a ground of the world. Being is more than all that exists
and is, nonetheless, nearer than any existing thing, be it . . . an
angel or God. Being is the nearest thing." If by the last sentence,
however, something other is meant than that I myself am, and

26. Ibid., 108, Section *"Andenken"* of 1943.
27. *Platons Lehre,* 76.

not indeed as the subject of a *cogito,* but as my total person, then the concept of being loses for me the character of genuine conceivability that obviously it eminently possesses for Heidegger.

I shall, however, limit myself to his theses about the divine. These theses, out of the extremest consciousness of self-drawn boundaries, are only concerned with the "appearance" of the divine. They are concerned in particular with those presuppositions of future reappearances which pertain to human thought, human thought, that is, about being. The most surprising and questionable thing about these theses to me is the fact that they designate it or him, the possible reappearance of whom is their subject, as the divine or God. In all tongues since men first found names for the eternally nameless, those who have been named by this word have been transcendent beings. They have been beings who by their nature were not given to us as knowable objects, yet beings whom we nonetheless became aware of as entering into relation with us. They stepped into relation with us, form-changing, form-preserving, formless, and allowed us to enter into relation with them. Being turned toward us, descended to us, showed itself to us, spoke to us in the immanence. The Coming One came of his own will out of the mystery of his withdrawnness; we did not cause him to come.

That has always distinguished religion from magic; for he whom man imagined that he had conjured up could not, even if he yet figured as god, be believed in any longer as god. He had become for man a bundle of powers of which man's mysterious knowledge and might could dispose. He who conjured was no longer addressed nor was any answer any longer awakened in him, and even though he recited a prayer, he no longer prayed. And indeed, as Heidegger once said[28] in interpreting the words of Hölderlin, who understood poetry as the combined work of the inspiring gods and the men inspired by them, not only does man need god, but also "the heavenly need the mortal." God needs man independent — man has divined that from of old — as part-

---

28. *Erläuterungen,* 66, Section *"Wie wenn am Feiertage"* of 1941.

ner in dialogue, as comrade in work, as one who loves Him; God
needs His creature thus or wills to need him thus.

In no sphere or time in the history of the relations between the
divine and the human, however, has that proved true which
Heidegger further asserts, namely, that "neither men nor the
gods can ever of themselves bring about the direct relation to the
holy." Always, again and again, men are accosted by One who of
Himself disconcerts and enraptures them, and, although overcome, the worshipper prays of himself to Him. God does not let
Himself be conjured, but He also will not compel. He is of Himself, and He allows that which exists to be of itself. Both of these
facts distinguish divine from demonic powers. It may not be,
indeed, unimportant to God whether man gives himself or denies
himself to Him. Through this giving or denying, man, the whole
man with the decision of his whole being, may have an immea-
surable part in the actual revelation or hiddenness of the divine.
But there is no place between heaven and earth for an influence
of concept-clarifying thought. He whose appearance can be effected or co-effected through such a modern magical influence
clearly has only the name in common with Him whom we men,
basically in agreement despite all the differences in our religious
teachings, address as God. To talk of a reappearance of this conjured god of thought is inadmissable.

It is not that Heidegger is not somewhat aware of what is at
stake here. Once in 1936, again in a Hölderlin interpretation, he
came remarkably close to the essential reality to which I have
just pointed. Hölderlin says of us humans,

> Since we exist as talk
> And can hear from one another.

Heidegger explains this thus,[29] "The gods can only enter the
Word if they themselves address us and place their demand upon
us. The Word that names the gods is always an answer to this
demand." That is a testimony to that which I call the dialogical

29. *Erläuterungen*, 37.

principle, to the dialogical relation between a divine and a human spontaneity.

But since then we have not heard the like from Heidegger. In fact, if we set next to each other all of his later statements about the divine, it appears to us as if pregnant seeds have been destroyed by a force which has passed over them. Heidegger no longer shows himself as concerned with that which there is in common between the great God-impressions of mankind and the "Coming One." Rather he summons all of the power of his thoughts and words in order to distinguish him, the "Coming One," from all that has been. To one who observes the way in which Heidegger now speaks of the historical, there can be no doubt that it is current history which has pulled up those seeds and planted in their place a belief in the entirely new. How this has gradually come about can be clearly seen if one compares with one another the occasional utterances of different stages, e.g., the Rectoral address of May, 1933, with a manifesto to the students of 3 November of the same year. In the first,[30] Heidegger praises in general terms "the glory and the greatness" of the successful "insurrection" ("*Aufbruch*"). In the second,[31] the sinister leading personality of the then current history is proclaimed as "the present and future German reality and its law." Here history no longer stands, as in all believing times, under divine judgment, but it itself, the unappealable, assigns to the Coming One his way.

Heidegger, of course, understands by history something other than a list of dated events. "History," he said in 1939,[32] "is rare." And he explained: "History exists only when the essence of truth is originally decided." But it is just his hour which he believes to be history, the very same hour whose problematics in its most inhuman manifestation led him astray. He has allied his thought, the thought of being,[33] in which he takes part and to which he

---

30. *Die Selbstbehauptung der deutschen Universität*, 22.

31. *Freiburger Studentenzeitung* of 3 Nov. 1933.

32. *Erläuterungen*, 73.

33. It should be noticed that the term "thought" ("*das Denken*") in the late writings of Heidegger is used in essence to describe his own thought.

ascribes the power to make ready for the rise of the holy, to that hour which he has affirmed as history. He has bound his thought to his hour as no other philosopher has done. Can he, the existential thinker, despite all this, existentially wrestle, in opposition to the hour, for a freedom devoted to the eternal and gain it? Or must he succumb to the fate of the hour, and with it also to a "holy" to which no human holiness, no hallowed standing fast of man in the face of historical delusion, responsibly answers? The questions that I ask are not rhetorical; they are true questions.

Of the two who have taken up Nietzsche's expression of the death of God, one, Sartre, has brought it and himself *ad absurdum* through his postulate of the free invention of meaning and value. The other, Heidegger, creates a concept of a rebirth of God out of the thought of truth which falls into the enticing nets of historical time. The path of this existentialism seems to vanish.

2

In contrast to Heidegger and Sartre, Jung, the leading psychologist of our day, has made religion in its historical and biographical forms the subject of comprehensive observations. He is not to be blamed for including among these observations an abundance of phenomena which I must characterize as pseudo-religious. I characterize them so because they do not bear witness to an essential personal relation to One who is experienced or believed in as being absolutely over against one. Jung properly explains he does not wish to overstep the self-drawn boundaries of psychology. This psychology offers no criterion for a qualitative distinction between the two realms, the religious and the pseudo-religious, even as little as, say, sociology as Max Weber understood it enabled him to make a distinction in kind between the charisma of Moses and that of Hitler. What Jung is to be criticized for instead is that he oversteps with sovereign license the boundaries of psychology in its most essential point. For the most part, however, he does not note it and still less account for it.

There is certainly no lack in Jung of exact psychological statements concerning religious subjects. Many times these are even accompanied by explicit emphasis on the limited validity of the statement. An example is when[34] revelation, as "the disclosure of the depths of the human soul," is termed "to begin with a psychological mode . . . from which, of course, nothing, is to be concluded about what it may otherwise be." Occasionally, moreover, he declares[35] on principle that "any statement about the transcendent" shall "be avoided," for such a statement is "always only a ridiculous presumption of the human mind which is unconscious of its boundaries." If God is called a state of the soul, that is "only a statement about the knowable and not about the unknowable, about which [here the formula which has just been cited is repeated word for word] simply nothing is to be concluded." Such sentences express the legitimate position of psychology, which is authorized, like every science, to make objectively based assertions so long as in doing so it takes care not to overstep its boundaries.

They have already been overstepped if it is said[36] of religion that it is "a living relation to psychical events which do not depend upon consciousness but instead take place on the other side of it in the darkness of the psychical hinterland." This definition of religion is stated without qualification. Nor will it tolerate any. For if religion is a relation to psychic events, which cannot mean anything other than to events of one's own soul, then it is implied by this that it is not a relation to a Being or Reality which, no matter how fully it may from time to time descend to the human soul, always remains transcendent to it. More precisely, it is not the relation of an I to a Thou. This is, however, the way in which the unmistakably religious of all ages have understood their religion even if they longed most intensely to let their I be mystically absorbed into that Thou.

But religion is for all that only a matter of the human relation

34. *Psychologie und Religion* (1942), 133. This passage is not in the English edition.

35. Wilhelm-Jung, *Das Geheimnis der goldenen Blüte* (1929), 73. Cf. Wilhelm-Jung, *The Secret of the Golden Flower*, translated by Cary F. Baynes (1935), 135.

36. Jung-Kerényi, *Einführung in das Wesen der Mythologie* (1941), 109. Cf. C. G. Jung and K. Kerényi, *Essays on a Science of Mythology* (1949), 102.

to God, not of God Himself. Consequently, it is more important
for us to hear what Jung thinks of God Himself. He conceives of
Him in general[37] as an "autonomous psychic content." This
means he conceives of God not as a Being or Reality to which a
psychical content corresponds, but rather as this content itself. If
this is not so, he adds, "then God is indeed not real, for then He
nowhere impinges upon our lives." According to this all that
which is not an autonomous psychical content but instead produces or co-produces in us a psychical content is to be understood as not impinging upon our life and hence as also not real.

Despite this Jung also recognizes[38] a "reciprocal and indispensable relation between man and God." Jung immediately observes, to be sure, that God is "for our psychology . . . a function
of the unconscious." However, this thesis is by no means intended to be valid only inside the boundaries of psychology, for
it is opposed to the "orthodox conception" according to which
God "exists for Himself," which means psychologically "that one
is unaware of the fact that the action arises from one's own inner
self."

It is thus unequivocally declared here that what the believer
ascribes to God has its origin in his own soul. How this assertion
is to be reconciled with Jung's assurance[39] that he means by all
this "approximately the same thing Kant meant when he called
the thing in itself a 'purely negative, borderline concept'" is to
me incomprehensible. Kant has explained that the things in
themselves are not to be recognized through any categories because they are not phenomena, but are only to be conceived of as
an unknown something. However, that that phenomenon, for example, which I call the tree before my window originates not in
my meeting with an unknown something but in my own inner
self Kant simply did not mean.

37. *Die Beziehungen zwischen dem Ich und dem Unbewussten* (1928), 205. Cf. *Two
Essays on Analytical Psychology*, translated by H. G. and C. F. Baynes (1928),
"The Relation Between the Ego and the Unconscious," 267.

38. *Psychologische Typen* (1921), 340. Cf. *Psychological Types*, translated by H.
G. Baynes (1923), 300 f.

39. *Geheimnis*, 73. Cf. *The Secret of the Golden Flower*, 135.

In contradiction to his assertion that he wishes to avoid every statement about the transcendent, Jung identifies himself[40] with a view "according to which God does not exist 'absolutely,' that is, independent of the human subject and beyond all human conditions." This means, in effect, that the possibility is not left open that God — who, if the singular and exclusive word "God" is not to lose all meaning, cannot be limited to a single mode of existence as if it were only a question of one among many gods — exists independent of as well as related to the human subject. It is instead made clear that He does *not* exist apart from man. This is indeed a statement about the transcendent. It is a statement about what it is not and just through this about what it is. Jung's statements about the "relativity" of the divine are not psychological but metaphysical assertions, however vigorously he emphasizes "his contentment with the psychically experienceable and rejection of the metaphysical."[41]

Jung could cite in opposition to this a statement he once[42] made. "Metaphysical statements are expressions of the soul, and consequently they are psychological." However, all statements, if they are considered not according to the meaning and intention of their contents but according to the process of their psychic origin, could be described as "expressions of the soul." If, consequently, that sentence is to be taken seriously, the boundaries of psychology are forthwith abolished. These are the same boundaries that Jung says in still another place[43] that psychology must guard against "overstepping through metaphysical statements or other professions of faith." In the greatest possible contradiction to this, psychology becomes here the only admissable metaphysic. It is supposed to remain at the same time an empirical science. But it cannot be both at once.

Jung also supplies the idea of the soul which belongs to this

40. *Typen,* 340. Cf. *Psychological Types,* 300.

41. *Geheimnis,* 73. Cf. *The Secret of the Golden Flower,* 135.

42. Evans-Wentz, *Das tibetanische Totenbuch "Bardo Thödol"* (1936), 18; English trans., *The Tibetan Book of the Dead,* 3d ed. (1974).

43. *Psychologie und Alchemie (1944),* 28. *Psychology and Alchemy,* translated by R. F. C. Hull (1952).

conception. "It is the soul," he says,[44] "that produces the metaphysical expression out of inborn divine creative power; it 'sets'
the distinctions between metaphysical essences. It is not only the
condition for metaphysical reality, it is that reality itself." The
term "sets" is not chosen without reason; what is here set forth is
in fact a translation of post-Kantian idealism into psychology.[45]
But that which has its place within metaphysical thinking when
it is a product of philosophical reflection such as Fichte's I, can
demand no such place when it is applied to the concrete individual soul or, more precisely, to the psychic in an existing human
person. Nor can Jung indeed mean anything other than this.
According to his explanation,[46] even the collective unconscious,
the sphere of the archetypes, can enter ever again into experience only through the individual psyche, which has inherited
these "typical attitudinal figures."

The real soul has without question producing powers in which
primal energies of the human race have individually concentrated. "Inborn divine creative powers" seems to me, to be sure,
an all too lofty and all too imprecise designation for them. This
soul, however, can never legitimately make an assertion, even a
metaphysical one, out of its own creative power. It can make an
assertion only out of a binding real relationship to a truth which
it articulates. The insight into this truth cogitatively grows in this
soul out of what happens to it and what is given it to experience.
Anything other than this is no real assertion but merely literary
phraseology or questionable combination.

The real individual soul can never be regarded as "the metaphysically real." Its essential life, whether it admits it or not,
consists of real meetings with other realities, be they other real
souls or whatever else. Otherwise, one would be obliged to con-
ceive of souls as Leibnizian monads. The ideal consequences of
this conception, in particular God's eternal interference, Jung

44. *Totenbuch*, 19.
45. There is no expression similar to this to be found in the philosophers of
the preceding century who, like Fries and Beneke, wished to base metaphysics
on psychology.
46. Cf. *"Der Geist der Psychologie"* (*Eranos-Jahrbuch*, 1946), 460 ff.

would undoubtedly be most unwilling to draw. Or the empirical real realm of individual souls, that province given over to psychology, should indeed be overstepped and a collective being called 'soul' or 'the soul,' which only reveals itself in the individual soul and is thus transcendent, admitted. Such a metaphysical "setting" would then necessitate an adequate philosophical determining and foundation such as, to my knowledge, we nowhere find in Jung, even in the lecture on the spirit of psychology which specifically deals with the conception of the soul.

The decisive significance which this indistinct conception of the soul has for Jung's essential attitude toward religion becomes evident in the following two sentences[47] which have a common subject. "Modern consciousness, in contrast to the nineteenth century, turns with its most intimate and intense expectations to the soul." "Modern consciousness abhors faith and also as a result the religions that are founded on it." Despite his early protest that one can find in his teaching no "barbs . . . against faith or trust in higher powers,"[48] it is evident to any careful reader[49] that Jung identifies himself with the modern consciousness that "abhors" faith. According to Jung, this modern consciousness now turns itself with its "most intimate and intense expectations" to the soul. This cannot mean anything other than that it will have nothing more to do with the God believed in by religions, who is to be sure present to the soul, who reveals Himself to it, communicates with it, but remains transcendent to it in His being. Modern consciousness turns instead toward the soul as the only sphere which man can expect to harbor a divine. In short, although the new psychology protests[50] that it is "no world-view

47. *Seelenprobleme der Gegenwart* (1931), 417. Cf. *Modern Man in Search of a Soul*, translated by W. F. Dell and C. F. Baynes (1933), 239.

48. *Geheimnis*, 73. Cf. *The Secret of the Golden Flower*, 135.

49. Cf. especially the second part of the sentence cited above from "*Seelenprobleme*" 417: "Modern consciousness . . . wishes to *know*, i.e., to have primal experience" with the sentence contained in the same book (p. 83): "We moderns are directed to experience again the spirit, i.e. to make primal experience." Cf. *Modern Man*, 140.

50. Ibid., 327. Cf. *Modern Man*, 217 f.

but a science," it no longer contents itself with the role of an interpreter of religion. It proclaims the new religion, the only one which can still be true, the religion of pure psychic immanence.

Jung speaks once,[51] and with right, of Freud's inability to understand religious experience. He himself concludes his wanderings through the grounds and abysses of religious experience, in which he has accomplished astounding feats, far outstripping all previous psychology, with the discovery that that which experiences the religious, the soul, experiences simply itself. Mystics of all ages, upon whom in fact Jung also rests his position, have proclaimed something similar; yet there are two distinctions which must be kept in mind. First, they meant by the soul which has this experience only that soul which has detached itself from all earthly bustle, from the contradictoriness of creaturely existence, and is therefore capable of apprehending the divine which is above contradictions and of letting the divine work in it. Second, they understood the experience as the oneness and becoming one of the soul with the self-contained God who, in order to enter into the reality of the world, "is born" ever again in the soul.

In the place of that detachment of the whole man from the bustle of life, Jung sets the process of "individuation," determined by a detachment of the *consciousness*. In the place of that becoming one with the Self-contained, he sets the 'Self', which is also, as is well known, an originally mystical concept. In Jung, however, it is no longer a genuinely mystical concept but is transformed instead into a Gnostic one. Jung himself expresses this turning toward the Gnostic. The statement quoted above that modern consciousness turns itself to the soul is followed by the explication, "and this . . . in the Gnostic sense." We have here, if only in the form of a mere allusion, the mature expression of a tendency characteristic of Jung from the beginning of his intellectual life. In a very early writing, which was printed but was not sold to the public, it appears in direct religious language as the profession of an eminent Gnostic god, in whom

51. Ibid., 77. Cf. *Modern Man*, 135.

good and evil are bound together and, so to speak, balance each other. This union of opposites in an all-embracing total form runs since then throughout Jung's thought. It is also of essential significance for our consideration of his teaching of individuation and the self.

Jung has given a most precise expression to that which is in question here in one of his mandala-analyses. Mandalas, as Jung has found them, not only in different religious cultures, especially those of the Orient and of the early Christian Middle Ages, but also in the drawings of neurotics and the mentally disturbed, are circular symbolic images. He understands them as representations, arising in the collective unconscious, of a wholeness and completeness which is as such a unification of opposites. They are supposed to be "unifying symbols" which include the feminine as well as the masculine, evil as well as good in their self-contained unity. Their center, the seat of the Godhead according to Jung's interpretation, is in general, he says, especially accentuated.

There are supposed to exist, however, a few ancient mandalas and many modern ones in whose center "no trace of divinity is to be found."[52] The symbol which takes its place in the modern images is understood by the creators of these mandalas, according to Jung, as "a center within themselves." "The place of the deity," Jung explains, "appears to be taken by the wholeness of man." This central wholeness, which symbolizes the divine, Jung, in agreement with ancient Indian teaching, calls the self. This does not mean, says Jung, that the self takes the place of the Godhead in these images in which the unconscious of modern man expresses itself. One would grasp Jung's idea better if one said that from now on the Godhead no longer takes the place of the human self as it did in mankind up till now. Man now draws back the projection of his self on a God outside of him without thereby wishing to deify himself (as Jung here emphasizes, in contrast to another passage, in which, as we shall see, deification is clearly stated as a goal). Man does not deny a

52. *Religion*, 145 ff. Cf. *Psychology and Religion*, 97 ff.

transcendent God; he simply dispenses with Him. He no longer knows the Unrecognizable; he no longer needs to pretend to know Him. In His place he knows the soul or rather the self. It is indeed not a god that "modern consciousness" abhors, but faith. Whatever may be the case concerning God, the important thing for the man of modern consciousness is to stand in no further relation of faith to Him.

This man of "modern consciousness" is not, to be sure, to be identified with the human race that is living today. "Mankind," says Jung,[53] "is still in the main in a psychological state of infancy — a level which cannot be leaped over." This is illustrated by the Paulinian overcoming of the law which falls only to those persons who know to set the soul in the place of conscience. This is something very few are capable of doing.

What does this mean? By conscience one understands of old, whether one ascribes to it a divine or a social origin or simply regards it as belonging to man as man, that court within the soul which concerns itself with the distinction between the right and the wrong in that which has been done and is to be done and proceeds against that which has been determined as wrong. This is not, of course, simply a question of upholding a traditional law, whether of divine or social origin. Each one who knows himself, for example, as called to a work which he has not done, each one who has not fulfilled a task which he knows to be his own, each who did not remain faithful to his vocation which he had become certain of — each such person knows what it means to say that "his conscience smites him." And in Jung himself we find[54] an excellent explication of that which we call "vocation." "Who has vocation (*Bestimmung*) hears the voice (*Stimme*) of the inner man." By this Jung means,[55] it is true, a voice which brings near to us just that which appears to be evil and to which, in his opinion, it is necessary to succumb "in part." I think, however,

---

53. *Beziehungen*, 203 ff. Cf. *Two Essays on Analytical Psychology*, 267.

54. *The Integration of the Personality*, translated by S. M. Dell (1940), "The Development of Personality," 291 f. Cf. *Wirklichkeit der Seele* (1934), Lecture "*Vom Werden der Persönlichkeit*" of 1932, 197 f.

55. *Wirklichkeit der Seele*, 208 f. Cf. *The Integration of the Personality*, 302 f.

that he who has vocation hears at times an inner voice of an entirely different kind. This is just the voice of conscience, which compares that which he is with that which he was called to become. In clear distinction from Jung, moreover, I hold that each man in some measure has been called to something, which, to be sure, he in general successfully avoids.

But now, once again, what does it mean to set the soul in the place of the direction-giving and direction-preserving, the litigating and judging conscience? In the context of Jung's thought it cannot be understood in any other way than "in the Gnostic sense." The soul which is integrated in the Self as the unification in an all-encompassing wholeness of the opposites, especially of the opposites good and evil, dispenses with the conscience as the court which distinguishes and decides between the right and the wrong. It itself arbitrates an adjustment between the principles or effects the preservation of accord between them or their balancing out or whatever one may call it. This "way," which Jung certainly correctly qualifies[56] as "narrow as a knife-edge," has not been described and obviously is not suitable to description. The question about it leads to the question about the positive function of evil.

Jung speaks somewhat more clearly in another place[57] of the condition necessary for "the birth of the 'pneumatic man.'" It is "liberation from those desires, ambitions and passions, which imprison us in the visible world," through "intelligent fulfillment of instinctive demands"; for "he who lives his instincts can also separate himself from them." The Taoist book that Jung interprets in this way does not contain this teaching; it is well known to us from certain Gnostic circles.[58]

The "process of development proper to the psyche" which Jung calls individuation leads through the integration in the consciousness of the personal and above all the collective, or archetypal, contents of the unconscious to the realization of a "new

56. *Beziehungen*, 205. Cf. *Two Essays*, 267.
57. *Geheimnis*, 61. Cf. *The Secret*, 80.
58. Cf. *Religion*, 139 ff.; *Psychology and Religion*, 94 ff.

complete form" which, as has been said, he calls the self. Here a
pause for clarification is necessary. Jung wishes[59] to see the self
understood as "both that or those others and the I" and individuation as a process which "does not exclude, but rather includes
the world." It is necessary to grasp exactly in what sense this
holds good and in what it does not. In the personality structure
which arises out of the "relatively rare occurrence"[60] of the development discussed by Jung, "the others" are indeed included.
However, they are included only as contents of the individual
soul that shall, just as an individual soul, attain its perfection
through individuation.

The actual other who meets me meets me in such a way that
my soul comes in contact with his as with something that it is not
and that it cannot become. My soul does not and cannot include
the other, and yet can nonetheless approach the other in this
most real contact. This other, what is more, is and remains over
against the self, no matter what completeness the self may attain,
as the other. So the self, even if it has integrated all of its unconscious elements, remains this single self, confined within itself.
All beings existing over against me who become 'included' in my
self are possessed by it in this inclusion as an It. Only then when,
having become aware of the unincludable otherness of a being, I
renounce all claim to incorporating it in any way within me or
making it a part of my soul, does it truly become Thou for me.
This holds good for God as for man.

This is certainly not a way which leads to the goal which Jung
calls the self; but it is just as little a way to the removal of self. It
simply leads to a genuine contact with the existing being who
meets me, to full and direct reciprocity with him. It leads from
the soul which places reality in itself to the soul which enters
reality.

Jung thinks that his concept of the self is also found in Meister Eckhart. This is an error. Eckhart's teaching about the soul is
based on the certainty of his belief that the soul is, to be sure,

59. *"Der Geist der Psychologie,"* 477.
60. Ibid., 474.

like God in freedom, but that it is created while He is uncreated.[61] This essential distinction underlies all that Eckhart has to say of the relationship and nearness between God and the soul.

Jung conceives of the self which is the goal of the process of individuation as the "bridal unification of opposite halves"[62] in the soul. This means above all, as has been said, the "integration of evil,"[63] without which there can be no wholeness in the sense of this teaching. Individuation thereby realizes the complete archetype of the self, in contrast to which it is divided in the Christian symbolic into Christ and the Antichrist, representing its light and its dark aspects. In the self the two aspects are united. The self is thus a pure totality and as such "indistinguishable from a divine image"; self-realization is indeed to be described as "the incarnation of God." This god who unites good and evil in himself, whose opposites-nature also expresses itself in his male-femaleness,[64] is a Gnostic figure, which probably is to be traced back ultimately to the ancient Iranian divinity Zurvan (not mentioned, so far as I know, among Jung's numerous references to the history of religions) as that out of which the light god and his dark counterpart arose.

From the standpoint of this basic Gnostic view Jung recasts the Jewish and Christian conception of God. In the Old Testament the Satan, the "Hinderer," is only a serving element of God. God allows Himself to be represented by Satan, particularly for the purpose of "temptation," that is, in order to actualize man's uttermost power of decision through affliction and despair. Out of this God of the Old Testament Jung makes a demiurge who is himself half-Satanic. This god then for the sake of his "guilt," the miscarried creation of the world (I now quote literally from

61. "Since God alone is free and uncreated, he is like the soul in being free — but not in uncreatedness, for the soul is created." Sermon 13, Raymond Blakney, *Meister Eckhart, A Modern Translation* (1941), 159. For original cf. *Predigten*, ed. Quint, 13 f.

62. *"Über das Selbst"* (*Eranos-Jahrbuch*, 1948), 315. Cf. *Psychologie und Alchemie*, 61.

63. *Symbolik des Geistes* (1948), 385.

64. Ibid., 410.

Jung's speech of 1940,[65] the like of which is nowhere to be found
in the Gnostic literature to which he refers), "must be subject to
ritual killing." By this Jung means the crucifixion of Christ. The
Trinity, moreover, is enlarged to a Quaternity in which the autonomous devil is included as "the fourth."[66]

These, to be sure, are all, as Jung emphasizes,[67] "projections of
psychic events," "human spiritual products to which one may not
arrogate any metaphysical validity." The self seems to him the
prototype of all monotheistic systems, which are here unmasked
as hidden Gnosis. But, on the other hand, he sees it at the same
time as the *imago Dei in homine.* The soul must indeed, he says
once[68] in a formulation which so far as I know is without analogy
in his other statements, have within it something which corresponds to the being of God. In any case, the self, the bridal
unification of good and evil, is elevated by him to the throne of
the world as the new "Incarnation." "If we should like to know,"
he says, "what happens in the case in which the idea of God is no
longer projected as an autonomous essence, then this is the answer of the unconscious soul: the unconscious creates the idea of
deified or divine man."[69] This figure, which embraces Christ and
Satan within himself,[70] is the final form of that Gnostic god, descended to earth as the realization of the "identity of God and
man,"[71] which Jung once professed. He has remained faithful to
this god, repeatedly intimating its prospective appearance.[72]

Jung's psychology of religion is to be understood as the announcement of that god as the Coming One. To Nietzsche's saying, "All the gods are dead, now we desire that the superman
live!" Heidegger, in a note otherwise foreign to him, adds this

65. *"Das Wandlungssymbol in der Messe"* (*Eranos-Jahrbuch*, 1940-1941), 153 f.
66. *Symbolik*, 439. Cf. *Religion*, 108 ff.; *"Zur Psychologie der Trinitätsidee"*
(*Eranos-Jahrbuch*, 1940-41), 51 ff.; *Alchemie*, 212.
67. *Symbolik*, 417.
68. *Alchemie*, 22 f.
69. *Religion* 172 f. Cf. *Psychology and Religion*, 106.
70. *Symbolik*, 409. Cf. *"Selbst,"* 304.
71. *Religion*, 111. Cf. *Psychology and Religion*, 74.
72. Cf. especially *Religion*, 175 f. (*Psychology and Religion*, 107 ff.)

warning[73]: "Man can never set himself in the place of God because the essence of man does not reach to God's sphere of being. On the contrary, indeed, in proportion with this impossibility, something far more uncanny may happen, the nature of which we have still hardly begun to consider. The place which, metaphysically speaking, belongs to God is the place in which the production and preservation as created being of that which exists is effected. This place of God can remain empty. Instead of it another, that is, a metaphysically corresponding place can appear, which is neither identical with God's sphere of being nor with that of man, but which, on the other hand, man can, in an eminent relation, attain. The superman does not and never will step into the place of God; the place rather in which the will to the superman arrives is another sphere in another foundation of existing things in another being." The words compel one to listen with attention. One must judge whether that which is said or intimated in them does not hold true today and here.

Religion and Psychology:
C. G. Jung's Reply to Martin Buber[1]

Some while ago the readers of your magazine were given the opportunity to read a posthumous article by Count Keyserling,[2] in which I was characterized as "unspiritual." Now, in your last issue, I find an article by Martin Buber[3] which is likewise con-

73. *Holzwege*, 235. A comparison is to be recommended with Jung's expression "The interregnum is full of danger" in its context (*Psychologie und Religion*, 158), which means almost the opposite. (The passage is not in *Psychology and Religion*, which differs from the German edition.)

1. Written 22 Feb. 1952 as a letter to the editor, published as "Religion und Psychologie" in *Merkur* (Stuttgart) 6, no. 5 (May 1952), 467–73, and reprinted as "Antwort an Martin Buber" in *Gesam. Werke* 11, Anhang. The present translation was published in *Spring*, 1973.

2. Hermann Keyserling (1880–1946), "Begegnungen mit der Psychoanalyse," *Merkur* 4:11 (Nov. 1950), 1151–68.

3. "Religion und modernes Denken," *Merkur* 6, no. 2 (Feb. 1952). Trans., "Religion and Modern Thinking," together with Buber's reply to Jung (in the same issue with Jung's reply, *Merkur* 6, no. 5), in *Eclipse of God* (1953).

cerned with my classification. I am indebted to his pronouncements at least in so far as they raise me out of the condition of
unspirituality, in which Count Keyserling saw fit to present me
to the German public, into the sphere of spirituality, even though
it be the spirituality of early Christian Gnosticism, which has
always been looked at askance by theologians. Funnily enough
this opinion of Buber's coincides with another utterance from an
authoritative theological source accusing me of agnosticism — the
exact opposite of Gnosticism.

Now when opinions about the same subject differ so widely,
there is in my view ground for the suspicion that none of them is
correct, and that there has been a misunderstanding. Why is so
much attention devoted to the question of whether I am a Gnostic or an agnostic? Why is it not simply stated that I am a psychiatrist whose prime concern is to record and interpret his
empirical material? I try to investigate facts and make them more
generally comprehensible. My critics have no right to slur over
this in order to attack individual statements taken out of context.

To support his diagnosis Buber even resorts to a sin of my
youth, committed nearly forty years ago, which consists in my
once having perpetrated a poem.[4] In this poem I expressed a
number of psychological *aperçus* in "Gnostic" style, because I was
then studying the Gnostics with enthusiasm. My enthusiasm
arose from the discovery that they were apparently the first
thinkers to concern themselves (after their fashion) with the contents of the collective unconscious. I had the poem printed under
a pseudonym and gave a few copies to friends, little dreaming
that it would one day bear witness against me as a heretic.

I would like to point out to my critic that I have in my time
been regarded not only as a Gnostic and its opposite, but also as
a theist and an atheist, a mystic and a materialist. In this concert
of contending opinions I do not wish to lay too much stress on
what I consider myself to be, but will quote a judgment from a

---

4. *VII Sermones ad Mortuos*, by Basilides of Alexandria (n.d. [1916]), privately printed. English trans. by H. G. Baynes, privately printed 1925; reprinted in the 2nd ed. of *Memories, Dreams, Reflections*, appendix.

leading article in the *British Medical Journal* (9 February 1952), a source that would seem to be above suspicion. "Facts first and theories later is the keynote of Jung's work. He is an empiricist first and last." This view meets with my approval.

Anyone who does not know my work will certainly ask himself how it is that so many contrary opinions can be held about one and the same subject. The answer to this is that they are all thought up by "metaphysicians," that is, by people who for one reason or another think they know about unknowable things in the Beyond. I have never ventured to declare that such things do *not* exist; but neither have I ventured to suppose that any statement of mine could in any way touch them or even represent them correctly. I very much doubt whether our conception of a thing is identical with the nature of the thing itself, and this for very obvious scientific reasons.

But since views and opinions about metaphysical or religious subjects play a very great role in empirical psychology,[5] I am obliged for practical reasons to work with concepts corresponding to them. In so doing I am aware that I am dealing with anthropomorphic ideas and not with actual gods and angels, although thanks to their specific energy, such (archetypal) images behave so autonomously that one could describe them metaphorically as 'psychic daimonia'. The fact that they are autonomous should be taken very seriously; first, from the theoretical standpoint, because it explains the dissociability of the psyche as well as actual dissociation, and second, from the practical one, because it forms the basis for a dialectical discussion between the ego and the unconscious, which is one of the mainstays of the psychotherapeutic method. Anyone who has any knowledge of the structure of a neurosis will be aware that the pathogenic conflict arises from the counterposition of the unconscious relative to consciousness. The so-called "forces of the unconscious" are not intellectual concepts that can be arbitrarily manipulated, but dangerous antagonists which can, among other things, work frightful devastation in the economy of the personality. They are

5. Cf. G. Schmaltz, *Östliche Weisheit und westliche Psychotherapie* (1951).

everything one could wish for or fear in a psychic 'Thou'. The
layman naturally thinks he is the victim of some obscure organic
disease; but the theologian, who suspects it is the devil's work, is
appreciably nearer to the psychological truth.

I am afraid that Buber, having no psychiatric experience, fails
to understand what I mean by the "reality of the psyche" and by
the dialectical process of individuation. The fact is that the ego is
confronted with psychic powers which from ancient times have
borne sacred names, and because of these they have always been
identified with metaphysical beings. Analysis of the unconscious
has long since demonstrated the existence of these powers in the
form of archetypal images which, be it noted, *are not identical with
the corresponding intellectual concepts.* One can, of course, believe
that the concepts of the conscious mind are, through the inspiration of the Holy Ghost, direct and correct representations of
their metaphysical referent. But this conviction is possible only
for one who already possesses the gift of faith. Unfortunately I
cannot boast of this possession, for which reason I do not imagine that when I say something about an archangel I have thereby
confirmed that a metaphysical fact. I have merely expressed an
opinion about something that can be experienced, that is, about
one of the very palpable "powers of the unconscious." These
powers are numinous "types" — unconscious contents, processes,
and dynamisms — and such types are, if one may so express it,
immanent-transcendent. Since my sole means of cognition is experience I may not overstep its boundaries, and cannot therefore
pretend to myself that my description coincides with the portrait
of a real metaphysical archangel. What I have described is a
psychic factor only, but one which exerts a considerable influence on the conscious mind. Thanks to its autonomy, it forms the
counterposition to the subjective ego because it is a piece of the
objective psyche. It can therefore be designated as a 'Thou'. For me
its reality is amply attested by the truly diabolical deeds of our
time: the six million murdered Jews, the uncounted victims of
the slave labor camps in Russia, as well as the invention of the
atom bomb, to name but a few examples of the darker side. But I
have also seen the other side which can be expressed by the

words beauty, goodness, wisdom, grace. These experiences of the depths and heights of human nature justify the metaphorical use of the term 'daimon'.

It should not be overlooked that what I am concerned with are psychic phenomena which can be proved empirically to be the bases of metaphysical concepts, and that when, for example, I speak of 'God' I am unable to refer to anything beyond these demonstrable psychic models which, we have to admit, have shown themselves to be devastatingly real. To anyone who finds their reality incredible I would recommend a reflective tour through a lunatic asylum.

The "reality of the psyche" is my working hypothesis, and my principal activity consists in collecting factual material to describe and explain it. I have set up neither a system nor a general theory, but have merely formulated auxiliary concepts to serve me as tools, as is customary in every branch of science. If Buber misunderstands my empiricism as Gnosticism, it is up to him to prove that the facts I describe are nothing but inventions. If he should succeed in proving this with empirical material, then indeed I am a Gnostic. But in that case he will find himself in the uncomfortable position of having to dismiss all religious experiences as self-deception. Meanwhile I am of the opinion that Buber's judgment has been led astray. This seems especially evident in his apparent inability to understand how an "autonomous psychic content" like the God-image can burst upon the ego, and that such a confrontation is a living experience. It is certainly not the task of an empirical science to establish how far such a psychic content is dependent on and determined by the existence of a metaphysical deity. That is the concern of theology, revelation, and faith. My critic does not seem to realize that when he himself talks about God, his statements are dependent firstly on his conscious and then on his unconscious assumptions. Of *which* metaphysical deity he is speaking I do not know. If he is an orthodox Jew he is speaking of a God to whom the incarnation in the year 1 has not yet been revealed. If he is a Christian, then his deity knows about the incarnation of which Yahweh still shows no sign. I do not doubt his conviction that he stands in a

living relationship to a divine Thou, but now as before I am of
the opinion that this relationship is primarily to an autonomous
psychic content which is defined in one way by him and in another by the Pope. Consequently I do not permit myself the least
judgment as to whether and to what extent it has pleased a metaphysical deity to reveal himself to the devout Jew as he was
before the incarnation, to the Church Fathers as the Trinity, to
the Protestants as the one and only Savior without co-re-
demptrix, and to the present Pope as a Savior with co-re-
demptrix. Nor should one doubt that the devotees of other faiths,
including Islam, Buddhism, Hinduism, and so on, have the same
living relationship to 'God', or to Nirvana and Tao, as Buber has
to the God-concept peculiar to himself.

It is remarkable that he takes exception to my statement that
God cannot exist apart from man and regards it as a transcendental assertion. Yet I say expressly that everything asserted
about 'God' is a human statement, in other words a psychological
one. For surely the image we have or make for ourselves of God
is never detached from man? Can Buber show me where, apart
from man, God has made an image of himself? How can such a
thing be substantiated and by whom? Here, just for once, and as
an exception, I shall indulge in transcendental speculation and
even in 'poetry': God has indeed made an inconceivably sublime
and mysteriously contradictory image of himself, without the
help of man, and implanted it in man's unconscious as an archetype, an ἀρχέτυπον φῶς, archetypal light: not in order that
theologians of all times and places should be at one another's
throats, but in order that the unpresumptuous man might
glimpse an image, in the stillness of his soul, that is akin to him
and is wrought of his own psychic substance. This image contains everything he will ever imagine concerning his gods or concerning the ground of his psyche.

This archetype, whose existence is attested not only by ethnol-
ogy but by the psychic experience of individuals, satisfies me
completely. It is so humanly close and yet so strange and 'other';
also, like all archetypes, it possesses the utmost determinative
power with which it is absolutely necessary that we come to
terms. The dialectical relationship to the autonomous contents of

the collective unconscious is therefore, as I have said, an essential part of therapy.

Buber is mistaken in thinking that I start with a "fundamentally Gnostic viewpoint" and then proceed to "elaborate" metaphysical assertions. One should not misconstrue the findings of empiricism as philosophical premises, for they are not obtained by deduction but from clinical and factual material. I would recommend him to read some autobiographies of the mentally ill, such as John Custance's *Wisdom, Madness and Folly* (1951), or D. P. Schreber's *Memoirs of My Nervous Illness* (first published 1903), which certainly do not proceed from Gnostic hypotheses any more than I do; or he might try an analysis of mythological material, such as the excellent work of Dr. Erich Neumann, his neighbor in Tel Aviv: *Amor and Psyche* (1952). My contention that the products of the unconscious are analogous and related to certain metaphysical ideas is founded on my professional experience. In this connection I would point out that I know quite a number of influential theologians, Catholics as well as Protestants, who have no difficulty in grasping my empirical standpoint. I therefore see no reason why I should take my method of exposition to be quite so misleading as Buber would have us believe.

There is one misunderstanding which I would like to mention here because it comes up so often. This is the curious assumption that when a projection is withdrawn nothing more of the object remains. When I correct my mistaken opinion of a man I have not negated him and caused him to vanish; on the contrary, I see him more nearly as he is, and this can only benefit the relationship. So if I hold the view that all statements about God have their origin in the psyche and must therefore be distinguished from God as a metaphysical being, this is neither to deny God nor to put man in God's place. I frankly confess that it goes against the grain with me to think that the metaphysical God himself is speaking through everyone who quotes the Bible or ventilates his religious opinions. Faith is certainly a splendid thing if one has it, and knowledge by faith is perhaps more perfect than anything we can produce with our labored and wheezing empiricism. The edifice of Christian dogma, for instance, undoubtedly stands on a much higher level than the somewhat wild 'philosophoumena' of the Gnostics. Dogmas are spiritual structures of supreme beauty, and they possess a wonderful meaning which I have sought to fathom in my fashion. Compared with them our scientific endeavors to devise models of the objective psyche are unsightly in the extreme. They are bound to earth and reality, full of contradictions, incomplete, logically and aesthetically unsatisfying. The empirical concepts of science and particularly of medical psychology do not proceed from neat and seemly principles of thought, but are the outcome of our daily labors in the sloughs of ordinary human existence and human pain. They are essentially irrational, and the philosopher who criticizes them as though they were philosophical concepts tilts against windmills and gets into the greatest difficulties, as Buber does with the concept of the self. Empirical concepts are names for existing complexes of facts. Considering the fearful paradoxicality of human existence, it is quite understandable that the unconscious contains an equally paradoxical God-image which will not square at all with the beauty, sublimity, and purity of the dogmatic concept of God. The God of Job and of the 89th Psalm is clearly a bit closer to reality, and his behavior does not fit in badly with the God-image in the unconscious. Of course this image, with its Anthropos symbolism, lends support to the idea of the incarnation. I do not feel responsible for the fact that the history of dogma has made some progress since the days of the Old Testament. This is not to preach a new religion, for to do that I would have to follow the old-established custom of appealing to a divine revelation. I am essentially a physician, whose business is with the sickness of man and his times, and with remedies that are as real as the suffering. Not only Buber, but every theologian who balks at my odious psychology is at liberty to heal my patients with the word of God. I would welcome this experiment with open arms. But since the ecclesiastical cure of souls does not always produce the desired results, we doctors must do what we can, and at present we have no better standby than that modest 'gnosis' which the empirical method gives us. Or have any of my critics better advice to offer?

As a doctor one finds oneself in an awkward position, because unfortunately one can accomplish nothing with that little word 'ought'. We cannot demand of our patients a faith which they reject because they do not understand it, or which does not suit them even though we may hold it ourselves. We have to rely on the curative powers inherent in the patient's own nature, regardless of whether the ideas that emerge agree with any known creed or philosophy. My empirical material seems to include a bit of everything — it is an assortment of primitive, Western, and Oriental ideas. There is scarcely any myth whose echoes are not heard, nor any heresy that has not contributed an occasional oddity. The deeper, collective layers of the human psyche must surely be of a like nature. Intellectuals and rationalists, happy in their established beliefs, will no doubt be horrified by this and will accuse me of reckless eclecticism, as though I had somehow invented the facts of man's nature and mental history and had compounded out of them a repulsive theosophical brew. Those who possess faith or prefer to talk like philosophers do not, of course, need to wrestle with the facts, but a doctor is not at liberty to dodge the grim realities of human nature.

It is inevitable that the adherents of traditional religious systems should find my formulations hard to understand. A Gnostic would not be at all pleased with me, but would reproach me for having no cosmogony and for the cluelessness of my gnosis in regard to the happenings in the Pleroma. A Buddhist would complain that I was deluded by Maya, and a Taoist that I was too complicated. As for an orthodox Christian, he can hardly do otherwise than deplore the nonchalance and lack of respect with which I navigate through the empyrean of dogmatic ideas. I must, however, once more beg my unmerciful critics to remember that I start from *facts* for which I seek an interpretation.

Buber's Rejoinder to Jung

In the face of C. G. Jung's reply to my criticism of him in "Religion and Modern Thinking,"[1] it will be sufficient to clarify anew my position in regard to his arguments.

1. The chapter "Religion and Modern Thinking" appeared in German in the February 1952, issue of the periodical *Merkur.* The May issue carried an answer by Prof. C. G. Jung and my reply which follows here.

I have not, as he thinks, placed in question any essential part of his empirical psychiatric material. That would certainly be un-authorized. Nor have I criticized any of his psychological theses. This also is not my affair. I have merely pointed out that he makes assertions about religious subjects which overstep the realms of the psychiatric and the psychological — contrary to his assurance that he remains strictly inside them. Whether I have demonstrated this the conscientious reader can ascertain through checking my citations in their context. I have been at pains to facilitate this for him through careful statement of sources. Jung disputes my demonstration, and the method he uses to do so is made clear in his reply.

I have pointed out that Jung describes it as a "fact," "that the divine action arises from one's own inner self" and that he sets this fact in contrast to the "orthodox conception," according to which God "exists for Himself." He explains that God does not exist independent of the human subject. The controversial ques-tion is therefore this: Is God merely a psychic phenomenon or does He also exist independently of the psyche of men? Jung answers, God does not exist for Himself. One can also state the question in this way: Does that which the man of faith calls the divine action arise merely from his own inner self or can the action of a super-psychic Being also be included in it? Jung an-swers that it arises from one's own inner self. I have remarked in this regard that these are not legitimate assertions of a psycholo-gist who as such has no right to declare what exists beyond the psychic and what does not, or to what extent there are actions which come from elsewhere. But Jung now replies: "I have made judgments only about the unconscious!" He further states, "Why, I say explicitly that all, *simply all* [italics mine] that which is stated about God, is human statement, i.e. psychic." This view, strange to say, he again limits: He is of the opinion, he says, "that all statements about God proceed *first of all* [italics mine] from the soul."

Compare, to begin with, the first of these sentences with the theses of Jung which I have quoted above. To explain emphat-ically that the action of one of the powers of the unconscious arises from one's own inner self, or that it does not exist independent of the human subject, would be a nonsensical tautology once the terminology of the "unconscious" is laid down. It would simply mean that the psychic realm designated as the unconscious is psychic. The thesis first acquires a meaning through the fact that it reaches out with its No beyond the sphere of the powers of the unconscious and the psychic sphere in general. Jung now, to be sure, denies that it has this meaning. And he refers in this connection to the fact that all statements about God are "human statements, i.e. psychic." This sentence deserves a closer examination.

I see no possibility certainly of conducting a discussion otherwise than on the ground of this presupposition. (As a note, I do not bring my own beliefs into the discussion but hold them in check for the sake of human conversation. But it must be mentioned here for the sake of full clarity that my own belief in revelation, which is not mixed up with any "orthodoxy," does not mean that I believe that finished statements about God were handed down from heaven to earth. Rather it means that the human substance is melted by the spiritual fire which visits it, and there now breaks forth from it a word, a statement, which is human in its meaning and form, human conception and human speech, and yet witnesses to Him who stimulated it and to His will. We are revealed to ourselves — and cannot express it otherwise than as something revealed.) Not only statements about God, but all statements in general are "human." Yet is anything positive or negative thereby ascertained about their truth? The distinction which is here in question is thus not that between psychic and non-psychic statements, but that between psychic statements to which a super-psychic reality corresponds and psychic statements to which none corresponds. The science of psychology, however, is not authorized to make such a distinction; it presumes too much, it injures itself, if it does so. The only activity that properly belongs to the science of psychology in this connection is a reasoned restraint. Jung does not exercise such a restraint when he explains that God cannot exist independent of men. For, once again, if this is a statement about an archetype

called God, then the emphatic assurance that it is a psychic factor is certainly unnecessary. (What else could it be?) But if it is a
statement about some extra-psychical Being which corresponds
to this psychic factor, namely the statement that no such Being
exists, then we have here, instead of the indicated restraint, an
illicit overstepping of boundaries. We should at last extricate
ourselves from this ingenious ambiguity!

But Jung now brings to my attention that men do in fact have
many and different images of God, which they themselves make.
I think I was already aware of this and have many times stated
and explained it. But that which is essential is still the fact that
they are just images. No man of faith imagines that he possesses
a photograph of God or a reflection of God in a magic mirror.
Each knows that he has painted it, he and others. But it was
painted just as an image, a likeness. That means it was painted in
the intention of faith directed toward the Imageless whom the
image 'portrays', that is, means. This intention of faith directed
toward an existing Being, toward One Who exists, is common to
men who believe out of varied experience. Certainly "the modern
consciousness," with which Jung has identified himself in unmistakable places in his writing, "abhors" faith. But to allow this
abhorrence to affect statements which are presented as strictly
psychological will not do. Neither psychology nor any other science is competent to investigate the truth of the belief in God. It
is the right of their representatives to keep aloof; it is not, within
their disciplines, their right to make judgments about the belief
in God as about something which they know.

The psychological doctrine which deals with mysteries without
knowing the attitude of faith toward mystery is the modern manifestation of Gnosis. Gnosis is not to be understood as only a
historical category, but as a universal one. It — and not atheism,
which annihilates God because it must reject the hitherto existing images of God — is the real antagonist of the reality of faith.
Its modern manifestation concerns me specifically not only because of its massive pretensions, but also in particular because of
its resumption of the Carpocratian motif. This motif, which it
teaches as psychotherapy, is that of mystically deifying the in-

stincts instead of hallowing them in faith. That we must see C. G. Jung in connection with this modern manifestation of Gnosis I have proved from his statements and can do so in addition far more abundantly. His little "Abraxas" opus, which every unprejudiced reader will take to be not a poem as he says, but a confession, I have mentioned because here there is already proclaimed in all clarity the ambivalent Gnostic "God" who balances good and evil in Himself.

Elements of the Interhuman

The Social and the Interhuman

It is usual to ascribe what takes place between men to the social realm, thereby blurring a basically important line of division between two essentially different areas of human life. I myself, when I began nearly fifty years ago to find my own bearings in the knowledge of society, making use of the then unknown concept of the interhuman,[1] made the same error, From that time it became increasingly clear to me that we have to do here with a separate category of our existence, even a separate dimension, to use a mathematical term, and one with which we are so familiar that its peculiarity has hitherto almost escaped us. Yet insight into its peculiarity is extremely important not only for our thinking, but also for our living.

We may speak of social phenomena wherever the life of a number of men, lived with one another, bound up together, brings in its train shared experiences and reactions. But to be thus bound up together means only that each individual existence is enclosed and contained in a group existence. It does not mean that between one member and another or the group there exists any kind of personal relation. They do feel that they belong together in a way that is, so to speak, fundamentally differ-

Trans. by Ronald Gregor Smith.

1. "Das Zwischenmenschliche." See my introduction to Werner Sombart, *Das Proletariat,*, vol. 1 in *Die Gesellschaft: Sammlung sozialpsychologischer Monographien,* ed. Martin Buber, 1st ed. (Frankfurt am Main: Rütten & Loening, 1906).

ent from every possible belonging together with someone outside
the group. And there do arise, especially in the life of smaller
groups, contacts which frequently favor the birth of individual
relations, but, on the other hand, frequently make it more difficult. In no case, however, does membership in a group necessarily involve an existential relation between one member and
another. It is true that there have been groups in history which
included highly intensive and intimate relations between two of
their members — as, for instance, in the homosexual relations
among the Japanese Samurai or among Doric warriors — and
these were countenanced for the sake of the stricter cohesion of
the group. But in general it must be said that the leading elements
in groups, especially in the later course of human history, have
rather been inclined to suppress the personal relation in favor of
the purely collective element. Where this latter element reigns
alone or is predominant, men feel themselves to be carried by the
collectivity, which lifts them out of loneliness and fear of the
world and lostness. When this happens — and for modern man it
is an essential happening — the life between person and person
seems to retreat more and more before the advance of the collective. The collective aims at holding in check the inclination to
personal life. It is as though those who are bound together in
groups should in the main be concerned only with the work of
the group and should turn to the personal partners, who are
tolerated by the group, only in secondary meetings.

The difference between the two realms became very palpable
to me on one occasion when I had joined the procession through
a large town of a movement to which I did not belong. I did it
out of sympathy for the tragic development which I sensed was
at hand in the destiny of a friend who was one of the leaders of
the movement. While the procession was forming, I conversed
with him and with another, a goodhearted 'wild man', who also
had the mark of death upon him. At that moment I still felt that
the two men really were there, over against me, each of them a
man near to me, near even in what was most remote from me; so
different from me that my soul continually suffered from this
difference, yet by virtue of this very difference confronting me

with authentic being. Then the formations started off, and after a short time I was lifted out of all confrontation, drawn into the procession, falling in with its aimless step; and it was obviously the very same for the two with whom I had just exchanged human words. After a while we passed a café where I had been sitting the previous day with a musician whom I knew only slightly. The very moment we passed it the door opened, the musician stood on the threshold, saw me, apparently saw me alone, and waved to me. Straightway it seemed to me as though I were taken out of the procession and of the presence of my marching friends, and set there, confronting the musician. I forgot that I was walking along with the same step; I felt that I was standing over there by the man who had called out to me, and without a word, with a smile of understanding, was answering him. When consciousness of the facts returned to me, the procession, with my companions and myself at its head, had left the café behind.

The realm of the interhuman goes far beyond that of sympathy. Such simple happenings can be part of it as, for instance, when two strangers exchange glances in a crowded streetcar, at once to sink back again into the convenient state of wishing to know nothing about each other. But also every casual encounter between opponents belongs to this realm, when it affects the opponent's attitude — that is, when something, however imperceptible, happens between the two, no matter whether it is marked at the time by any feeling or not. The only thing that matters is that for each of the two men the other happens as the particular other, that each becomes aware of the other and is thus related to him in such a way that he does not regard and use him as his object, but as his partner in a living event, even if it is no more than a boxing match. It is well known that some existentialists assert that the basic factor between men is that one is an object for the other. But so far as this is actually the case, the special reality of the interhuman, the fact of the contact, has been largely eliminated. It cannot indeed be entirely eliminated. As a crude example, take two men who are observing one another. The essential thing is not that the one makes the other his object, but the fact that he is not fully able to do so and the reason for his failure. We have in common with all existing beings that we can be made objects of observation. But it is my privilege as man that by the hidden activity of my being I can establish an impassable barrier to objectification. Only in partnership can my being be perceived as an existing whole.

The sociologist may object to any separation of the social and the interhuman on the ground that society is actually built upon human relations, and the theory of these relations is therefore to be regarded as the very foundation of sociology. But here an ambiguity in the concept 'relation' becomes evident. We speak, for instance, of a comradely relation between two men in their work, and do not merely mean what happens between them as comrades, but also a lasting disposition which is actualized in those happenings and which even includes purely psychological events such as the recollection of the absent comrade. But by the sphere of the interhuman I mean solely actual happenings between men, whether wholly mutual or tending to grow into mutual relations. For the participation of both partners is in principle indispensable. The sphere of the interhuman is one in which a person is confronted by the other. We call its unfolding the dialogical.

In accordance with this, it is basically erroneous to try to understand the interhuman phenomena as psychological. When two men converse together, the psychological is certainly an important part of the situation, as each listens and each prepares to speak. Yet this is only the hidden accompaniment to the conversation itself, the phonetic event fraught with meaning, whose meaning is to be found neither in one of the two partners nor in both together, but only in their dialogue itself, in this 'between' which they live together.

Being and Seeming

The essential problem of the sphere of the interhuman is the duality of being and seeming.

Although it is a familiar fact that men are often troubled about

the impression they make on others, this has been much more
discussed in moral philosophy than in anthropology. Yet this is
one of the most important subjects for anthropological study.

We may distinguish between two different types of human existence. The one proceeds from what one really is, the other from
what one wishes to seem. In general, the two are found mixed
together. There have probably been few men who were entirely
independent of the impression they made on others, while there
has scarcely existed one who was exclusively determined by the
impression made by him. We must be content to distinguish between men in whose essential attitude the one or the other
predominates.

This distinction is most powerfully at work, as its nature indicates, in the interhuman realm — that is, in men's personal dealings with one another.

Take as the simplest and yet quite clear example the situation
in which two persons look at one another — the first belonging to
the first type, the second to the second. The one who lives from
his being looks at the other just as one looks at someone with
whom he has personal dealings. His look is 'spontaneous', 'without reserve'; of course he is not uninfluenced by the desire to
make himself understood by the other, but he is uninfluenced by
any thought of the idea of himself which he can or should
awaken in the person whom he is looking at. His opposite is
different. Since he is concerned with the image which his appearance, and especially his look or glance, produces in the other, he
'makes' this look. With the help of the capacity, in greater or
lesser degree peculiar to man, to make a definite element of his
being appear in his look, he produces a look which is meant to
have, and often enough does have, the effect of a spontaneous
utterance — not only the utterance of a psychical event supposed
to be taking place at that very moment, but also, as it were, the
reflection of a personal life of such-and-such a kind.

This must, however, be carefully distinguished from another
area of seeming whose ontological legitimacy cannot be doubted.
I mean the realm of 'genuine seeming', where a lad, for instance,
imitates his heroic model and while he is doing so is seized by

the actuality of heroism, or a man plays the part of a destiny and conjures up authentic destiny. In this situation there is nothing false: the imitation is genuine imitation and the part played is genuine; the mask, too, is a mask and no deceit. But where the semblance originates from the lie and is permeated by it, the interhuman is threatened in its very existence. It is not that someone utters a lie, falsifies some account. The lie I mean does not take place in relation to particular facts, but in relation to existence itself, and it attacks interhuman existence as such. There are times when a man, to satisfy some stale conceit, forfeits the great chance of a true happening between I and Thou.

Let us now imagine two men, whose life is dominated by appearance, sitting and talking together. Call them Peter and Paul. Let us list the different configurations which are involved. First, there is Peter as he wishes to appear to Paul, and Paul as he wishes to appear to Peter. Then there is Peter as he really appears to Paul, that is, Paul's image of Peter, which in general does not in the least coincide with what Peter wishes Paul to see; and similarly there is the reverse situation. Further, there is Peter as he appears to himself, and Paul as he appears to himself. Lastly, there are the bodily Peter and the bodily Paul. Two living beings and six ghostly appearances, which mingle in many ways in the conversation between the two. Where is there room for any genuine interhuman life?

Whatever the meaning of the word 'truth' may be in other realms, in the interhuman realm it means that men communicate themselves to one another as what they are. It does not depend on one saying to the other everything that occurs to him, but only on his letting no seeming creep in between himself and the other. It does not depend on one letting himself go before another, but on his granting to the man to whom he communicates himself a share in his being. This is a question of the authenticity of the interhuman, and where this is not to be found, neither is the human element itself authentic.

Therefore, as we begin to recognize the crisis of man as the crisis of what is between man and man, we must free the concept of uprightness from the thin moralistic tones which cling to it, and let it take its tone from the concept of bodily uprightness. If a presupposition of human life in primeval times is given in man's walking upright, the fulfillment of human life can only come through the soul's walking upright, through the great uprightness which is not tempted by any seeming because it has conquered all semblance.

But, one may ask, what if a man by his nature makes his life subservient to the images which he produces in others? Can he, in such a case, still become a man living from his being, can he escape from his nature?

The widespread tendency to live from the recurrent impression one makes instead of from the steadiness of one's being is not a 'nature'. It originates, in fact, on the other side of interhuman life itself, in men's dependence upon one another. It is no light thing to be confirmed in one's being by others, and seeming deceptively offers itself as a help in this. To yield to seeming is man's essential cowardice, to resist it is his essential courage. But this is not an inexorable state of affairs which is as it is and must so remain. One can struggle to come to oneself — that is, to come to confidence in being. One struggles, now more successfully, now less, but never in vain, even when one thinks he is defeated. One must at times pay dearly for life lived from the being; but it is never too dear. Yet is there not bad being, do weeds not grow everywhere? I have never known a young person who seemed to me irretrievably bad. Later indeed it becomes more and more difficult to penetrate the increasingly tough layer which has settled down on a man's being. Thus there arises the false perspective of the seemingly fixed 'nature' which cannot be overcome. It is false; the foreground is deceitful; man as man can be redeemed.

Again we see Peter and Paul before us surrounded by the ghosts of the semblances. A ghost can be exorcised. Let us imagine that these two find it more and more repellent to be represented by ghosts. In each of them the will is stirred and strengthened to be confirmed in their being as what they really are and nothing else. We see the forces of real life at work as they drive out the ghosts, till the semblance vanishes and the depths of personal life call to one another.

Personal Making Present

By far the greater part of what is today called conversation among men would be more properly and precisely described as speechifying. In general, people do not really speak to one another, but each, although turned to the other, really speaks to a fictitious court of appeal whose life consists of nothing but listening to him. Chekhov has given poetic expression to this state of affairs in *The Cherry Orchard*, where the only use the members of a family make of their being together is to talk past one another. But it is Sartre who has raised to a principle of existence what in Chekhov still appears as the deficiency of a person who is shut up in himself. Sartre regards the walls between the partners in a conversation as simply impassable. For him it is inevitable human destiny that a man has directly to do only with himself and his own affairs. The inner existence of the other is his own concern, not mine; there is no direct relation with the other, nor can there be. This is perhaps the clearest expression of the wretched fatalism of modern man, which regards degeneration as the unchangeable nature of *Homo sapiens* and the misfortune of having run into a blind alley as his primal fate, and which brands every thought of a breakthrough as reactionary romanticism. He who really knows how far our generation has lost the way of true freedom, of free giving between I and Thou, must himself, by virtue of the demand implicit in every great knowledge of this kind, practice directness — even if he were the only man on earth who did it — and not depart from it until scoffers are struck with fear, and hear in his voice the voice of their own suppressed longing.

The chief presupposition for the rise of genuine dialogue is that each should regard his partner as the very one he is. I become aware of him, aware that he is different, essentially different from myself, in the definite, unique way which is peculiar to him, and I accept whom I thus see, so that in full earnestness I can direct what I say to him as the person he is. Perhaps from time to time I must offer strict opposition to his view about the subject of our conversation. But I accept this person, the personal bearer of a conviction, in his definite being out of which his conviction has grown — even though I must try to show, bit by bit, the wrongness of this very conviction. I affirm the person I struggle with: I struggle with him as his partner, I confirm him as creature and as creation, I confirm him who is opposed to me as him who is over against me. It is true that it now depends on the other whether genuine dialogue, mutuality in speech arises between us. But if I thus give to the other who confronts me his legitimate standing as a man with whom I am ready to enter into dialogue, then I may trust him and suppose him to be also ready to deal with me as his partner.

But what does it mean to be 'aware' of a man in the exact sense in which I use the word? To be aware of a thing or a being means, in quite general terms, to experience it as a whole and yet at the same time without reduction or abstraction, in all its concreteness. But a man, although he exists as a living being among living beings and even as a thing among things, is nevertheless something categorically different from all things and all beings. A man cannot really be grasped except on the basis of the gift of the spirit which belongs to man alone among all things, the spirit as sharing decisively in the personal life of the living man, that is, the spirit which determines the person. To be aware of a man, therefore, means in particular to perceive his wholeness as a person determined by the spirit; it means to perceive the dynamic center which stamps his every utterance, action, and attitude with the recognizable sign of uniqueness. Such an awareness is impossible, however, if and so long as the other is the separated object of my contemplation or even observation, for this wholeness and its center do not let themselves be known to contemplation or observation. It is only possible when I step into an elemental relation with the other, that is, when he becomes present to me. Hence I designate awareness in this special sense as 'personal making present'.

The perception of one's fellow man as a whole, as a unity, and as unique — even if his wholeness, unity, and uniqueness are only partly developed, as is usually the case — is opposed in our time by almost everything that is commonly understood as specifically modern. In our time there predominates an analytical, reductive, and deriving look between man and man. This look is analytical, or rather pseudo-analytical, since it treats the whole being as put together and therefore able to be taken apart — not only the so-called unconscious which is accessible to relative objectification, but also the psychic stream itself, which can never, in fact, be grasped as an object. This look is a reductive one because it tries to contract the manifold person, who is nourished by the microcosmic richness of the possible, to some schematically surveyable and recurrent structures. And this look is a deriving one because it supposes it can grasp what a man has become, or even is becoming, in genetic formulae, and it thinks that even the dynamic central principle of the individual in this becoming can be represented by a general concept. An effort is being made today radically to destroy the mystery between man and man. The personal life, the ever near mystery, once the source of the stillest enthusiasms, is leveled down.

What I have just said is not an attack on the analytical method of the human sciences, a method which is indispensable wherever it furthers knowledge of a phenomenon without impairing the essentially different knowledge of its uniqueness that transcends the valid circle of the method. The science of man that makes use of the analytical method must accordingly always keep in view the boundary of such a contemplation, which stretches like a horizon around it. This duty makes the transposition of the method into life dubious; for it is excessively difficult to see where the boundary is in life.

If we want to do today's work and prepare tomorrow's with clear sight, then we must develop in ourselves and in the next generation a gift which lives in man's inwardness as a Cinderella, one day to be a princess. Some call it intuition, but that is not a wholly unambiguous concept. I prefer the name 'imagining the real', for in its essential being this gift is not a looking at the other, but a bold swinging — demanding the most intensive stir-ring of one's being — into the life of the other. This is the nature of all genuine imagining, only that here the realm of my action is not the all-possible, but the particular real person who confronts me, whom I can attempt to make present to myself just in this way, and not otherwise, in his wholeness, unity, and uniqueness, and with his dynamic center which realizes all these things ever anew.

Let it be said again that all this can only take place in a living partnership, that is, when I stand in a common situation with the other and expose myself vitally to his share in the situation as really his share. It is true that my basic attitude can remain un-answered, and the dialogue can die in seed. But if mutuality stirs, then the interhuman blossoms into genuine dialogue.

Imposition and Unfolding

I have referred to two things which impede the growth of life between men: the invasion of seeming, and the inadequacy of perception. We are now faced with a third, plainer than the others, and in this critical hour more powerful and more dan-gerous than ever.

There are two basic ways of affecting men in their views and their attitude to life. In the first a man tries to impose himself, his opinion and his attitude, on the other in such a way that the latter feels the psychical result of the action to be his own in-sight, which has only been freed by the influence. In the second basic way of affecting others, a man wishes to find and to further in the soul of the other the disposition toward what he has recog-nized in himself as the right. Because it is the right, it must also be alive in the microcosm of the other, as one possibility. The other need only be opened out in this potentiality of his; more-over, this opening out takes place not essentially by teaching, but by meeting, by existential communication between someone that is in actual being and someone that is in a process of becoming. The first way has been most powerfully developed in the realm of propaganda, the second in that of education.

The propagandist I have in mind, who imposes himself, is not in the least concerned with the person whom he desires to influence, as a person; various individual qualities are of importance only in so far as he can exploit them to win the other and must get to know them for this purpose. In his indifference to everything personal the propagandist goes a substantial distance beyond the party for which he works. For the party, persons in their difference are of significance because each can be used according to his special qualities in a particular function. It is true that the personal is considered only in respect of the specific use to which it can be put, but within these limits it is recognized in practice. To propaganda as such, on the other hand, individual qualities are rather looked on as a burden, for propaganda is concerned simply with *more* — more members, more adherents, an increasing extent of support. Political methods, where they rule in an extreme form, as here, simply mean winning power over the other by depersonalizing him. This kind of propaganda enters upon different relations with force; it supplements it or replaces it, according to the need or the prospects, but it is in the last analysis nothing but sublimated violence, which has become imperceptible as such. It places men's souls under a pressure which allows the illusion of autonomy. Political methods at their height mean the effective abolition of the human factor.

The educator whom I have in mind lives in a world of individuals, a certain number of whom are always at any one time committed to his care. He sees each of these individuals as in a position to become a unique, single person, and thus the bearer of a special task of existence which can be fulfilled through him and through him alone. He sees every personal life as engaged in such a process of actualization, and he knows from his own experience that the forces making for actualization are all the time involved in a microcosmic struggle with counterforces. He has come to see himself as a helper of the actualizing forces. He knows these forces; they have shaped and they still shape him. Now he puts this person shaped by them at their disposal for a new struggle and a new work. He cannot wish to impose himself, for he believes in the effect of the actualizing forces, that is, he

believes that in every man what is right is established in a single
and uniquely personal way. No other way may be imposed on a
man, but another way, that of the educator, may and must unfold
what is right, as in this case it struggles for achievement, and
help it to develop.

The propagandist, who imposes himself, does not really believe even in his own cause, for he does not trust it to attain its
effect of its own power without his special methods, whose symbols are the loudspeaker and the television advertisement. The
educator who unfolds what is there believes in the primal power
which has scattered itself, and still scatters itself, in all human
beings in order that it may grow up in each man in the special
form of that man. He is confident that this growth needs at each
moment only that help which is given in meeting, and that he is
called to supply that help.

I have illustrated the character of the two basic attitudes and
their relation to one another by means of two extremely antithetical examples. But wherever men have dealings with one another, one or the other attitude is to be found in more or less
degree.

These two principles of imposing oneself on someone and
helping someone to unfold should not be confused with concepts
such as arrogance and humility. A man can be arrogant without
wishing to impose himself on others, and it is not enough to be
humble in order to help another unfold. Arrogance and humility
are dispositions of the soul, psychological facts with a moral accent, while imposition and helping to unfold are events between
men, anthropological facts which point to an ontology, the ontology of the interhuman.

In the moral realm Kant expressed the essential principle that
one's fellow man must never be thought of and treated merely as
a means, but always at the same time as an independent end. The
principle is expressed as an 'ought' which is sustained by the idea
of human dignity. My point of view, which is near to Kant's in its
essential features, has another source and goal. It is concerned
with the presuppositions of the interhuman. Man exists anthropologically not in his isolation, but in the completeness of the

relation between man and man; what humanity is can be properly grasped only in vital reciprocity. For the proper existence of the interhuman it is necessary, as I have shown, that the semblance not intervene to spoil the relation of personal being to personal being. It is further necessary, as I have also shown, that each one means and makes present the other in his personal being. That neither should wish to impose himself on the other is the third basic presupposition of the interhuman. These presuppositions do not include the demand that one should influence the other in his unfolding; this is, however, an element that is suited to lead to a higher stage of the interhuman.

That there resides in every man the possibility of attaining authentic human existence in the special way peculiar to him can be grasped in the Aristotelian image of entelechy, innate self-realization; but one must note that it is an entelechy of the work of creation. It would be mistaken to speak here of individuation alone. Individuation is only the indispensable personal stamp of all realization of human existence. The self as such is not ultimately the essential, but the meaning of human existence given in creation again and again fulfills itself as self. The help that men give each other in becoming a self leads the life between men to its height. The dynamic glory of the being of man is first bodily present in the relation between two men each of whom in meaning the other also means the highest to which this person is called, and serves the self-realization of this human life as one true to creation without wishing to impose on the other anything of his own realization.

Genuine Dialogue

We must now summarize and clarify the marks of genuine dialogue.

In genuine dialogue the turning to the partner takes place in all truth, that is, it is a turning of the being. Every speaker 'means' the partner or partners to whom he turns as this personal existence. To 'mean' someone in this connection is at the same time to exercise that degree of making present which is possible to the speaker at that moment. The experiencing senses and the imagining of the real which completes the findings of the senses work together to make the other present as a whole and as a unique being, as the person that he is. But the speaker does not merely perceive the one who is present to him in this way; he receives him as his partner, and that means that he confirms this other being, so far as it is for him to confirm. The true turning of his person to the other includes this confirmation, this acceptance. Of course, such a confirmation does not mean approval; but no matter in what I am against the other, by accepting him as my partner in genuine dialogue I have affirmed him as a person.

Further, if genuine dialogue is to arise, everyone who takes part in it must bring himself into it. And that also means that he must be willing on each occasion to say what is really in his mind about the subject of the conversation. And that means further that on each occasion he makes the contribution of his spirit without reduction and without shifting his ground. Even men of great integrity are under the illusion that they are not bound to say everything 'they have to say'. But in the great faithfulness which is the climate of genuine dialogue, what I have to say at any one time already has in me the character of something that wishes to be uttered, and I must not keep it back, keep it in myself. It bears for me the unmistakable sign which indicates that it belongs to the common life of the word. Where the dialogical word genuinely exists, it must be given its right by keeping nothing back. To keep nothing back is the exact opposite of unreserved speech. Everything depends on the legitimacy of 'what I have to say'. And of course I must also be intent to raise into an inner word and then into a spoken word what I have to say at this moment but do not yet possess as speech. To speak is both nature and work, something that grows and something that is made, and where it appears dialogically, in the climate of great faithfulness, it has to fulfill ever anew the unity of the two.

Associated with this is that overcoming of semblance to which I have referred. In the atmosphere of genuine dialogue, he who is ruled by the thought of his own effect as the speaker of what he has to speak, has a destructive effect. If instead of what has to be said, I try to bring attention to my *I*, I have irrevocably miscarried what I had to say; it enters the dialogue as a failure, and the dialogue is a failure. Because genuine dialogue is an ontological sphere which is constituted by the authenticity of being, every invasion of semblance must damage it.

But where the dialogue is fulfilled in its being, between partners who have turned to one another in truth, who express themselves without reserve and are free of the desire for semblance, there is brought into being a memorable common fruitfulness which is to be found nowhere else. At such times, at each such time, the word arises in a substantial way between men who have been seized in their depths and opened out by the dynamic of an elemental togetherness. The interhuman opens out what otherwise remains unopened.

This phenomenon is indeed well known in dialogue between two persons; but I have also sometimes experienced it in a dialogue in which several have taken part.

About Easter of 1914 there met a group consisting of representatives of several European nations for a three-day discussion that was intended to be preliminary to further talks.[2] We wanted to discuss together how the catastrophe, which we all believed was imminent, could be avoided. Without our having agreed beforehand on any sort of modalities for our talk, all the presuppositions of genuine dialogue were fulfilled. From the first hour immediacy reigned between all of us, some of whom had just got to know one another; everyone spoke with an unheard-of unreserve, and clearly not a single one of the participants was in bondage to semblance. In respect of its purpose the meeting must be described as a failure (though even now in my heart it is still not a certainty that it had to be a failure); the irony of the situation was that we arranged the final discussion for the middle of August, and in the course of events the group was soon broken up. Nevertheless, in the time that followed, not one of

---

2. I have set down elsewhere an episode from this meeting. See my essay "Dialogue" in *Between Man and Man*, especially pp. 4–6.

the participants doubted that he shared in a triumph of the interhuman.

One more point must be noted. Of course it is not necessary for all who are joined in a genuine dialogue actually to speak; those who keep silent can on occasion be especially important. But each must be determined not to withdraw when the course of the conversation makes it proper for him to say what he has to say. No one, of course, can know in advance what it is that he has to say; genuine dialogue cannot be arranged beforehand. It has indeed its basic order in itself from the beginning, but nothing can be determined, the course is of the spirit, and some discover what they have to say only when they catch the call of the spirit.

But it is also a matter of course that all the participants, without exception, must be of such nature that they are capable of satisfying the presuppositions of genuine dialogue and are ready to do so. The genuineness of the dialogue is called in question as soon as even a small number of those present are felt by themselves and by the others as not being expected to take any active part. Such a state of affairs can lead to very serious problems.

I had a friend whom I account one of the most considerable men of our age. He was a master of conversation, and he loved it: his genuineness as a speaker was evident. But once it happened that he was sitting with two friends and with the three wives, and a conversation arose in which by its nature the women were clearly not joining, although their presence in fact had a great influence. The conversation among the men soon developed into a duel between two of them (I was the third). The other 'duelist', also a friend of mine, was of a noble nature; he too was a man of true conversation, but given more to objective fairness than to the play of the intellect, and a stranger to any controversy. The friend whom I have called a master of conversation did not speak with his usual composure and strength, but he scintillated, he fought, he triumphed. The dialogue was destroyed.

What Is Common to All

1

Among the sayings with which Heracleitus laid the foundation of
the edifice of Western thought, there is one of such great sim-
plicity, one which appears to us latecomers of the spirit so self-
evident that we are accustomed to understand it as only meant
metaphorically. What is more, Heracleitus himself in other sayings appears to relate to it in such a manner. But at this height
nothing concrete persists that is only metaphor, nothing that does
not also have a complete existence as the expression of the direct
contemplation of a perceived reality.

The saying reads, "The waking have a single cosmos in common," that is, a single world-shape in which they take part in
common. By this is already expressed what the later moral philosopher Plutarch, who preserved the fragment for us, pointed to
in his interpretation: In sleep each turns away from the common
cosmos and turns to something which belongs to him alone,
something thus which he does not and cannot share with any
other. That Heracleitus himself, on the contrary, understood this
less as the sleep of an individual, including the sphere of dreams,
than as a cosmos, one among numberless fleeting world-shapes,
in no way corresponds to what we know of his teachings.

The duality of sleeping and waking is not, as elsewhere in
Heracleitus, a symbol of the duality of that man who is aware of
his being and its meaning and all the others who live alienated
from it. There is here what is always necessary in order that a

Trans. by Maurice Friedman.

genuine symbol can take shape in the spirit — an existent corporeal reality which is grasped in a decisive vision. The philosopher
of Ephesus makes manifest for the Occident the fundamental
insight that the rhythmically regulated course of our daily existence does not mean an exchange of two states, but an exchange
of two spheres in which we find ourselves by turns, and one of
which Heracleitus calls a cosmos.

Heracleitus designates this one cosmos, which he as an eval-
uating thinker affirms, as one common to men. But it means
something other and greater than that they all dwell together in
the sphere that we call the world or that each of them is given
just this sphere to perceive. 'The common' is the sustaining category for Heracleitus. It enables him, despite men's want of understanding — so painfully suffered and so fiercely reproved by
him — to grasp and confirm as a spiritual reality their togetherness, the full mutuality of human being. When Heracleitus says
of the logos, the meaning of being that dwells in the substance of
the word, that it is common, he thereby asserts that all men in
the eternal originality of their genuine spoken intercourse with
one another have a share in the consummation of this indwelling.
This is the case with the world-shape which belongs to the whole
of the human race, the 'common cosmos'. The same meaning of
existence which holds sway in the coming-to-be of the words, the
same genuineness forever renewing itself in the fire of opposite-
ness is that which embodies itself in the world process. But this
world, which Heracleitus understands as the world of man,
never arises except out of the totality of the human race to which
it belongs. Men contribute to the cosmic process with all that
they are. Even in sleep, according to Heracleitus — no matter
though each is submerged in his private sphere — they are still, as
individuals, 'workers and co-workers in the world-happening',
passive workers. This means that there is no state in which the
individual merely leads his own existence without contributing
his part, just through living in this state, to the life of his human
environment and to the world in general. But waking men add in
common to the world-shape itself, which is just a human cosmos
recognizable as the cosmos of man as man. They associate with

one another in the world, helping one another through the power of the logos to grasp the world as a world order, without which ordering grasp it is not and cannot be a world. They can only do this, of course, if and in so far as they are truly awake, if they do not sleep while waking and spin dreamlike illusions which they call their own insight — if they exist in common.

"One must follow that which is common." This great saying of Heracleitus discloses its meaning to us only when we have considered his teaching of the community of the logos and the cosmos. Waking and sleeping are one of the pairs of opposites in which the unity of being fulfills itself, according to Heracleitus, swinging in them and bearing their tension. In each pair each of the two opposites has its own place and its own right. But the effacement of the tension and the mixture of the opposites is evil. This is also the case with waking and sleeping. In sleep there is no factual bond with others; each dreams of the others, but those of whom he dreams do not take part in his dream. Conversely, that dream condition in which each is to himself alone must not penetrate into the common world of waking. Here and only here are we 'We'. Here as men awake we may understand the logos by understanding one another in our truth, through whose voice the logos speaks. Here we are actively familiar with the cosmos through our co-operation, for it is a cosmos only to the degree in which we experience it together. Heracleitus places upon us the pure duty and responsibility of waking togetherness. He does not, of course, reject the dream, which has its place and its right in that withdrawnness inaccessible to the We. But he does reject that dreamlike refusal of the We through whose illusion the common day is broken asunder.

2

With his proclamation of the world-shape assigned to the waking and of the meaning of being which is represented in it as the common that we must follow, Heracleitus has indicated to the spirit the task of showing itself awake in the human world, and that means the task of establishing in common a common reality.

What that signifies in the history of the spirit can be made clear by two examples of the opposite.

In the same age in which the Asia Minor Greek, Heracleitus, established the right and duty of the waking spirit, China received, mostly through oral tradition, the decisive imprint of a teaching which was at once notably similar and notably dissimilar to his. This is the teaching of Tao, the Way, which is itself unconditional unity, yet bears, encompasses, and rhythmically regulates the alternation of the opposites and opposing processes, their correspondences and contradictions, their battles and their couplings. This happens in the world as in the spirit, for just as with Heracleitus, so here, they both belong to one order. But the opposites themselves do not stand here in the irreducible multiplicity of fire and water, day and night, life and death as they do for Heracleitus. Rather all these and their like are only appearances and acts of the two primal essences, yin and yang. These essences manifest themselves as the feminine and the masculine, the dark and the light, the loose and the fast, the yielding and the advancing, in short, as nonbeing and being. They supplement each other, wed each other; indeed, in the Tao Te King (which appears, despite the uncertainty of the traditions, to have preserved much of the oldest level of speech of the teaching) it is even said that being and nonbeing generate each other. Here, however, in contrast to Heracleitus, the passive principle is accorded the preeminence because it is the truly effective one. What this implies about the sphere of waking and that of dreams is shown with the utmost clarity in a text of Chuang Tzu, a thinker and poet of the fourth century who considered himself a late-born disciple of Lao Tze, the master by then wholly inwoven in legend.

Chuang Tzu reports a dream and its sequel. He speaks of himself in the third person.

> Chuang Tzu dreamed once that he was a butterfly, a butterfly fluttering hither and thither without care and desire, unconscious of his existence as Chuang Tzu. Suddenly he awoke, and he lay there, again the self-same Chuang Tzu. Now he does not know: is

he a man who dreamed that he was a butterfly or a butterfly who dreams that he is a man?[1]

This text is not isolated. Another Taoist book tells of a mythical realm at whose borders the play of the opposites grows lame. There is no difference between cold and hot, between night and day. The inhabitants, who need neither food nor clothing, sleep for seven weeks. When they then awaken, they hold what they have dreamed to be real and what they now experience to be only apparent.

In this teaching, obviously, no priority belongs to the waking existence; indeed, if one of the two spheres were to be claimed as world, it might much more easily be that of dreams, and this just for the reason that the awakened are able to recognize it as dream whereas the waker's circle of experience pretends to be simple reality without being able to support this claim.

Logos and cosmos are not valid here. But the common also is not valid here. The human person in his withdrawal obtains the full measure of his allotted existence.

In the same section in which the mythical realm is told of, we read how a frail servant was cruelly treated by his master, but dreamed night after night that he was a prince and lived in joy, and therefore was also content with his lot by day, whereas the opposite befell the master. And yet another story from the same section pictures Lao Tze as treating even madness with similar composure. "If the whole world were insane except for you," he says to the complaining father of a mentally ill son, "then it would be just you who would be the insane one."

Thus it stands here concerning the antithetical spheres in the life of man. What we wakers hold to be a dreamlike delusion is here valid as just as real as the waking world, indeed as more real. The other sphere stands ready to receive man, and even comfortingly and graciously. But just not us, rather only each individual among us separately. We, as We, cannot enter it; it

1. Martin Buber, *Reden und Gleichnisse des Tschuang-Tse* (Leipzig: Insel-Verlag, 1914).

receives no We. Each of us dreams that he associates with others; but none of these others experiences this in itself, none enters the dream sphere with us. The claim of the special realm to be a world is that against which Heracleitus poses his elemental saying: "One must follow that which is common."

3

The other manifestation out of the depths of the East is more far-reaching. It is a teaching of the oldest Upanishads, which means a teaching originally strictly esoteric, proceeding at times from the mouth of the master to the ears of the disciples who sit at his feet, the teaching of dream sleep and deep sleep.

The dream is generally regarded here as a first step. The spirit of the person is depicted as he, after entering into the dream sleep, roams all over the whole world and gathers his building materials which he 'splits up', that is, divides into their elementary parts in order to build out of them 'in his own light' what he can build, for 'he is a creator'. Verses, clearly of still older origin than the prose teaching, are quoted in which it is said:

> That lower nest, the breath must guard it,
> He springs away immortal from the nest,
> Immortal roves about, where he wills,
> The golden spirit, the solitary wandering goose.
> In the state of dreams he roves up and down
> And fashions for himself, godlike, all kinds of shapes.

The sovereign freedom of the dream is praised more strongly here than in the Taoist texts. All ties of the day are suspended. Self-glorious molder, the spirit fashions the whole world, subject to him as unresisting material. He needs for his work no other light than his own, and in divine power of transformation he clothes himself in shape after shape.

But now the sovereign spirit ascends beyond the sphere of dreams. He finds no more satisfaction in the play of transformations; he gives up the last tie with the world, that of the images taken from it, and enters into the fully dreamless, imageless, desireless deep sleep. "As in the air," continues that text, "a falcon or an eagle, weary of flight, folding its pinions, prepares to spiral down, thus the essential spirit hurries to that sleeping state where it wishes no wish and beholds no dream." Drawn forth from all shapes by which it was related to the material of the world, it has now attained a shapeless abiding in worldless being. Only then, enclosed and hidden in this state, is it, as is said further on, "beyond desire, untroubled by ills, free of anxiety," to all of which it was still exposed, in fact, in the dream world despite its absence of ties. He no longer experiences now what was separate from, separable from himself, for "there is no second outside of him." Another text, which stems out of the same oldest epoch of Upanishads, describes the same thing. "When it is said," we read here, "that a man sleeps" — by which it is just deep sleep that is meant — "he is united with being. He has entered into his self. Where one sees no other, hears no other, recognizes no other, this is the fullness."

We must pay close attention to what is said in this statement which in the West has had far-reaching effects in our age.

Sleep appears here as the way out of the sphere in which man is divided from the kernel of being to that in which he is united with it. The way leads beyond the freedom which unfolds in dreams to unity. This unity is that of the individual self with the Self of being: they are in reality a single self. Their disunion in the waking world is then the great illusion. We become independent of the waking world in dream and yet remain still imprisoned in it; in deep sleep we become free of it and thereby of illusion, which alone divides the personal self from the Self of being — an inference, to be sure, which was first conclusively drawn in later, more specifically philosophical teachings. According to them, the existence of man in the world is the existence of a world of appearance, a magical deception. But since the identity of the self can be reached only in an absolute solitude, such as deep sleep, the existence between man and man is also ultimately only appearance and illusion.

The saying "That art thou," which later ages have extended to the relation between man and man, is solely intended in the original teaching for the relation between Brahman and Atman, the

Self of being and the self of the human person. Even though each man experiences the identity of all selves in deep sleep, he cannot establish it in the waking world, in the world of appearance. In one of the Upanishadic texts cited here, being embraced by a beloved wife serves as a parable of unification; but considered as a fact of life, it is relegated to illusion. The man who adheres to the teaching of identity may, of course, when he says 'Thou' to a fellow man, say to himself in reference to the other, 'There are you yourself', for he believes the self of the other to be identical with his. But what the genuine saying of 'Thou' to the other in the reality of the common existence basically means — namely, the affirmation of the primally deep otherness of the other, the affirmation of his otherness which is accepted and loved by me — this is devalued and destroyed in spirit through just that identification. The teaching of identity not only stands in opposition to the belief in the true being of a common logos and a common cosmos; it also contradicts the arch reality of that out of which all community stems — human meeting.

When taken seriously in the factual, waking continuity of intercourse with one another, the ancient Hindu 'That art thou' becomes the postulate of an annihilation of the human person, one's own person as well as the other; for the person is through and through nothing other than uniqueness and thus essentially other than all that is over against it. And even if that supposed universal Self should remain in the ground of the I, it could no longer have intercourse with anyone. But we see in human existence, in the intercourse of men with one another that grows out of it, the chance for meeting between existing being and existing being. In this meeting each of the two certainly does not say to himself, 'He over there is you', but perhaps each says to the other, 'I accept you as you are'. Here first is uncurtailed existence.

4

The object of this juxtaposition of the sayings of Heracleitus with the sayings of the Taoist masters and of the early Upanishads is no historical one, but neither is it concerned with a

critical comparison of the Orient and the Occident. The stretch
of earth between the Black and the Red Seas in which, in the
same epoch, Anaximander and Heracleitus taught in Greek and
the Israelite prophets admonished and comforted in Hebrew,
must not be understood as a wall but as a bridge between East
and West. The teachings of those philosophers — the teaching
that all beings owe one another atonement, and the teaching of
the community of logos and cosmos — and the message of those
who proclaimed that all men owe help to one another and announced the task of communal life, both arose from the heart of
the East and both have contributed essentially to the foundation
of the spirit of the West.

If I appeal to the philosophy of Heracleitus, shot through with
contradictions as it appears, against the uniformly soaring wisdom of the Orient, it is for the sake of a specific need of our
time. I mean by this the confrontation of two points of view, the
first of which values the collectivity above all else, whereas the
second believes the meaning of existence to be disclosed or dis-
closable in the relation of the individual to his self. The first,
which is usually called the Eastern because it is today especially
at home in Eastern Europe, appears to be a travesty of the ancient idea of the common way; the second, represented by Western philosophy, psychology, and literature, readily invokes the
ancient Indian teaching and its offshoots. This latter I am discussing, and the reasons for this choice are weighty ones. The
modern collectivism does, in fact, place the collectivity above all,
but it does not ascribe to it the character of the absolute; it treats
the absolute in general as an inadmissible fiction. The modern
variety of individualism, in contrast, is inclined to understand the
individual self, which the I finds in its depth, as the self simply
and as the absolute. Despite all stress on the interest in the 'outer
world' or even a kind of cosmic sympathy, despite all reference
to the all-soul as the one that is really meant, what unmistakably
rules here is the tendency toward the primacy of the individual
existence and toward its self-glorification. And this individualism
is still more dangerous than collectivism, for the pretension of the
false absolute is more dangerous than the denial of the absolute.

Let us call to mind once more the vital originality of the three basic concepts of Heracleitus: the concept of the common, of the logos, and of the cosmos; and, starting from their originality, let us endeavor to penetrate into our situation. Heracleitus says of thinking that it is common to all, and he elucidates this by the statement that all men take part in thinking as well as in self-knowledge. The concreteness of his observation, which he preserves even in the highest abstractions, indicates that this does not mean the universally known fact that each of us possesses the capacity of thinking, but that when we know and think in accordance with the logos, we do so not in isolation but in common: we blend all our particular knowing and even in our knowledge of ourselves one person helps the other. This communality in which we participate, living with one another and acting on one another, this 'one must follow'.

Heracleitus always remained in accord with the thoroughly sensuous living speech of his time. For this reason the logos, even in its highest sublimation, does not cease to be for him the sensuous, meaningful word, the human talk which contains the meaning of the true. Meaning can be in the word because it is in being. Thus it stirs deep in the soul which becomes aware of the meaning; it grows in it and develops out of it to a voice which speaks to fellow souls and is heard by them, often, to be sure, without this hearing becoming a real receiving. And like the logos, so also the cosmos belongs to the common as to that in which men participate as in a common work. That it is common to them does not signify the likewise universally known fact that they find themselves together in the world; it signifies that their relationship to it is a common one. What is spoken of as the subjective side of our perceptions, however, is certainly not rendered uncertain by this insight of Heracleitus. For we can indeed show one another the things, describe for one another the things; each can, supplementing the other, help him to have a world-shape, a world.

There is more to be said about this. But first let us examine a variety of this individualism which is of interest as an example. The tendency to attain a higher side of existence, indeed the 'authentic' existence, through abandoning the communal finds here an especially drastic expression. The advocates of the undertaking intend, it is true, to be removed therein from what they call 'the world of selfhood', but in reality they are intent throughout upon isolating the sphere reserved for the individual and with it that of selfhood. The occurrences of this province are much more easily communicable than what takes place in the purely inward way, especially at its end, and thus there is some material available to us.

5

Not long ago the English novelist Aldous Huxley described and extolled the astonishing effects of mescalin intoxication. Mescalin is extracted from a cactus, the enjoyment of which so ravished and enraptured some ancient Mexican Indian tribes that they made the bounteous plant the center of an elaborate cult. Huxley reports the effects of the intoxication from his own experience, which took place under the watch of disciplined self-observation.

What he saw there with open eyes was not some sort of world-removed fantasy structure. It was his familiar domestic surroundings, loosened from their spatial limitations in undreamed-of brilliance of color and an overpowering presence of the individual object, which Huxley compares with the cubist way of seeing. But this radical aestheticizing of the relationship to things is only the first step toward a higher kind of vision which he describes as 'the sacramental vision of reality'. To the religions, sacrament means the participation, verified in life and death, of the whole person who has known the contact of the transcendent in his corporeal existence. But Huxley means by sacramental vision merely penetrating and being received into the depths of the world of the senses. In his view, the shadow realm, held together by concepts that we call reality, falls to pieces there, for it is unmasked as "the universe of a diminished consciousness," and this diminished consciousness is just that which comes to expression in speech. "Through the taking of a suitable chemical preparation," so Huxley says, everyone is enabled "to know from within of what the mystics speak"; the speechless primal ground of being opens itself to him in the objects. No distinction exists any longer between inner and outer, between subject and object. Naturally Huxley must avoid the eyes of those present in the room, people who are otherwise especially dear to him; they belong, indeed, to the "world of selfhood" that he has left.

With this concept he describes, without naming it, the common world. When he speaks of the mescalin trance as one of the different kinds of "flight out of selfhood and environment," to which flight the urge is "present in almost every man at almost every time," then he means again the common world from which the enjoyer of mescalin flees for the duration of his trance. Huxley calls it, to be sure, the "urge to go beyond the self," by which he means that here man escapes the entanglement in the net of his utilitarian aims. But in reality the consumer of mescalin does not emerge from this net into some sort of free participation in common being; rather merely into a strictly private special sphere given to him as his own for several hours. The "chemical holidays" of which Huxley speaks are holidays not only from the petty I, enmeshed in the machinery of its aims, but also from the person participating in the community of logos and cosmos — holidays from the very uncomfortable reminder to verify oneself as such a person.

Huxley speaks also of holidays from the possibly repugnant surroundings. But man may master as he will his situation, to which his surroundings also belong; he may withstand it, he may alter it, he may, when it is necessary, exchange it for another; but the fugitive flight out of the claim of the situation into situationlessness is no legitimate affair of man. And the true name of all the paradises which man creates for himself by chemical or other means is situationlessness. They are situationless like the dream state and like schizophrenia because they are in their essence uncommunal, while every situation, even the situation of those who enter into solitude, is enclosed in the community of logos and cosmos.

The men with whom we live also belong to that environment

from which, in Huxley's view, it is desirable and salutary to take holidays of the soul from time to time. If we have taken a sufficient dose of mescalin, then the objects of our environment are transformed into sheer glory; but the men who directly surround us are not transformed with them. It is logical therefore, as Huxley relates, that he now avoids their eyes; to regard each other means to recognize the common. It may be that the Indians who enjoyed the peyotl cactus looked at one another as much as before; the modern civilized man in this state turns his eyes away from the men of his surroundings since they belong to the world which formerly bound him.

We read something similar in many reports of experimental subjects about their mescalin trances. They relate how, "near to the 'thing in itself'" they found themselves floating above all, removed from the 'painful earthly world', and also experienced as 'kingly play' what they afterward determined to be 'hallucinations'. And it is only the other side of the same coin that they met their fellow men who were present with a deep mistrust, that the organs of strongest contact in their own body, such as the inner surface of the hand and the genital region, felt frozen; that hearing, the sense of mental communication, often seemed to be almost blocked out, that at times, indeed, they could not even succeed in picturing to themselves men in general. This 'feeling of being completely isolated' was once caught in the words, "There did not need to be any women and also no men." Many of these traits recall similar basic attitudes of schizophrenics, except that in the case of the latter we discover now and then the longing to alienate from the vile common world individual men who are of particular importance to them and to carry them off into the special world which is alone reliable and meaningful to them.

6

Huxley distinguishes, as mentioned, two stages within the trance.

In the first, one sees the things from within, as the creating artist sees them, at once objectively deepened and transfigured by an inner light. In the second, from which he looks down almost scornfully on his beloved art as on an *ersatz*, one experiences to some degree what the mystics experience.

In fact, the artist too is removed from the common seeing in his decisive moments and raised into his special formative seeing; but in just these moments he is determined through and through, to his perception itself, by the drive to originate, by the command to form. Huxley understands this manner of seeing everything in brilliant coloration and penetrating objectivity not only as 'how one should see', but also as 'how things are in reality'. What does that mean concretely? What we call reality always appears only in our personal contact with things which remain unperceived by us in their own being; and there exists personal contact which, freer, more direct than the ordinary, represents things with greater force, freshness, and depth. This is true of creative states and it is also true of toxic states, but the fundamental distinction between the former and the latter is that the enjoyer of mescalin, for instance, produces the alteration of his consciousness arbitrarily; the vocation of the artist, in contrast, sets him in his unarbitrary special relation to existing being, and from there, willing what he should, he does his work in conscious realization. Where arbitrariness interferes, the art becomes illegitimate.

The same problem comes to light in the second of the stages described — or rather indicated — by Huxley. He says that the mescalin trance enables one "to know from within of what the visionary, the medium, yes even the mystic speaks." Let us leave to one side the problematic medium and content ourselves with the observation of the great visions and mystical experiences of human history so far as they are accessible to our observation. One thing is common to all of them: He to whom this happens is overtaken by something from a sphere in which he does not dwell and could not dwell, a 'face', a 'hand', a 'word', a 'mystery'. He is not in accord with it; indeed, he often enough resists what accosts him. He clings to the common world until he is torn from it. And that is by no means a secondary trait, it is the essence of the occurrence itself. The shaman, the yogi have their methods through whose practice they acquire, or imagine they acquire, power of magic and power of absorption; the man of whom we speak has nothing other than his way on which he is assaulted, on which he is led. What takes place here is no flight: one is seized, one is overpowered, one is called.

Neither the artist nor the mystic transposes himself into the condition in which, from time to time, he beholds the vision; he receives it. They do not take themselves out of the communality, they are taken out. And they must deliver up not less than themselves, the whole living person and his whole personal life, in order to withstand what has taken possession of them.

7

The great teachings from which we have proceeded, that of the Asia Minor bridge and that of the Far East, resemble each other in that in both of them the spirit places its claim on the whole of the personal existence, and this claim is only seemingly separable from the teaching. They demand without remainder the life of him who hears it. The early Upanishads point to the objective unification of the self of the soul and the Self of being which arises out of the cessation of consciousness in deep sleep. This unity, the claim is made, shall be fulfilled afterward by the waking, fully conscious, knowing person out of conscious existence, through identifying his own self with that of the world.

The teaching of Lao tze points to the Tao of heaven, which governs the swinging cosmic opposites, as to the primal image that man shall imitate and can imitate if he is aware of the Tao that dwells in himself, the Tao of man. He shall and can reconcile and wed with each other the conflicting opposites of existence without neutralizing them. For this teaching, too, no less than the whole personal existence will do: the existence which does not interfere but radiates. Both teachings wish to lead men out of the entanglement in the common to the freedom of detachment, that of the Upanishads into the solitude above the world, that of Taoism into the solitude in the midst of the world.

In contrast to both of them stands Heracleitus's teaching that
bids one follow that which is common; but the existential claim
of the spirit on the person is here actually of still greater weight.
Just because, unlike those Indians, Heracleitus's teaching accepts the being of what is in all its manifoldness and knows no
other harmony than that which arises out of its tensions, and just
because, unlike those Chinese, he finds the meaning of being not
in the ground of separateness but in what is common to all, the
existential claim is here so direct. Heracleitus's angry reprimand
is aimed at the man who hears his word but does not yet truly
understand it. It is not he himself that men must understand, he
says, but the logos that is common to them all and that makes
use of the man Heracleitus in order to enter between them into
the spokenness. The logos is certainly not alien to them: indeed,
as Heracleitus says, they continually have the closest intercourse
with it, with the word, in that they always, in fact, take it in their
mouth; and yet they live in discord with it because they always
misuse the meaningful word and pervert its sense into nonsense.

For, it must be emphasized yet again, the Heracleitian concept
of logos cannot be understood otherwise than from the primal
establishment of the wedding between meaning and speech. It is
hammered at us three and four times in the fragments that have
been preserved: logos is something that is to be heard but is
misheard and that should be heard in the right way, as word-
with-meaning. It seems incorrect to me to translate logos in over-
simplified fashion as "meaning" whereby its original concreteness
is given up; nor can I agree when, from an especially competent
quarter, it is interpreted, "Not with me, rather with the logos in
yourselves, must you agree," whereas Heracleitus simply says,
"Do not listen to me but to the logos." Each soul does, of course,
have its logos deep in itself, but the logos does not attain to its
fullness in us but rather between us; for it means the eternal
chance for speech to become true between men. Therefore, it is
common to them.

To man as man belongs the ever renewed event of the entrance of meaning into the living word. Heracleitus demands of
the human person that he preserve this occurrence in life in such

a way that it can legitimately take part in the reality of the common logos, in a genuine service of meaning. Out of such persons alone can circles be formed that follow the logos. These are they who genuinely think with one another because they ʹgenuinely talk to one another. All men, according to Heracleitus, have an essential share in self-knowledge and sensible thinking. That is naturally something that each person can only fulfill personally; but while they fulfill it and in so far as they fulfill it, they take part in the self-knowledge of man and in his common thinking. And again, no matter how numberless are the people of whom Heracleitus says that they understand neither how to listen nor how to talk, no aberration, no perversion of thought can undermine the fact that such communal guarding of meaning is existentially effected.

But there is also in the Heracleitian idea of the common cosmos an existential demand to be disclosed. The logos that becomes known as meaningful word between men is the same as that which immutably governs the swinging opposites of our cosmos. Indeed, without this lightninglike rudder, "the most beautiful world order," according to Heracleitus, would be "like a heap of chaotically spilled-out refuse." But we ourselves too, as the ready and obedient bearers of the word of the logos, accord to the cosmos its reality which consists in being our world. Through us it becomes the shaped world of man, and only now does it deserve the name of cosmos as a total order, formed and revealed. Only through our service to the logos does the world become "the same cosmos for all." Thus and only thus do the waking, just in so far as they are awake, have in truth a single common world whose unity and community they work on in all real waking existence. For in sleep we are also, of course, as Heracleitus says, "workers and co-workers" in the world happening, passive workers; but only awake, only working together awake, do we allow the totality of this happening to become manifest as cosmos. For then we experience with one another, help one another experience, and supplement one another in our experience: the living working together with the other living, and all the living with all the dead. "Not as men asleep," says Heracleitus, "must we act and speak." For in sleep appearance reigns, but reality exists only in waking and, in fact, only to the degree of our working together. However, this working together is in no way to be conceived of as a team hitched to the great wagon; it is a strenuous tug of war for a wager, it is battle and strife. But in so far as it lets itself be determined by the logos it is a common battle and produces the common: out of the extremest tension, when it takes place in the service of the logos, arises ever anew the harmony of the lyre. Here the second existential demand of Heracleitus is comprehensible: that the person disengage himself from the great indolence, which Heracleitus calls a cowlike satiety, and that he realize in the common logos what is unique to him without curtailing its uniqueness, and that he work thereby on the common cosmos. This cosmos from which we come and which comes from us is, understood in its depth, infinitely greater than the sum of all special spheres of dreams and intoxication into which man flees before the demand of the We.

8

Heracleitus does not say 'We'. He would not have denied, nonetheless, that one cannot follow the logos more adequately than by saying 'We' — by saying it not frivolously and not impudently, but in truth. Since then the genuine saying of We has been manifest ever again in the way of life of the human race though also, of course, more and more endangered. What was and is said thereby is directly opposite to what Kierkegaard designates as the 'crowd' — opposite as the clear shape is to its caricature.

The genuine We is to be recognized in its objective existence, through the fact that in whatever of its parts it is regarded, an essential relation between person and person, between I and Thou, is always evident as actually or potentially existing. For the word always arises only between an I and a Thou, and the element from which the We receives its life is speech, the communal speaking that begins in the midst of speaking to one another.

Speech in its ontological sense was at all times present wherever men regarded one another in the mutuality of I and Thou; wherever one showed the other something in the world in such a way that from then on he began really to perceive it; wherever one gave another a sign in such a way that he could recognize the designated situation as he had not been able to before; wherever one communicated to the other his own experience in such a way that it penetrated the other's circle of experience and supplemented it as from within, so that from now on his perceptions were set within a world as they had not been before. All this flowing ever again into a great stream of reciprocal sharing of knowledge — thus came to be and thus is the living We, the genuine We, which, where it fulfills itself, embraces the dead who once took part in colloquy and now take part in it through what they have handed down to posterity.

The We of which I speak is no collective, no group, no objectively exhibitable multitude. It is related to the saying of 'We' as the I to the saying of 'I'. Just as little as the I does it allow itself to be carried over factually into the third person. But it does not have the comparative constancy and continuity that the I has. As potentiality it lies at the base of all history of spirit and deed; it actualizes itself and is no longer there. It can actualize itself within a group which then consists of just a fiery core and a drossy crust, and it can flare up and burn outside of all collectives. In the atmosphere of debates it cannot breathe, and no multitude of the so-called like-minded can legitimately say 'We' in the midst of debate; but it also happens even today that people are speaking in many tongues and suddenly the genuine We lives and moves in their speech.

Man has always had his experiences as I, his experiences with others, and with himself; but it is as We, ever again as We, that he has constructed and developed a world out of his experiences. A band, say of the same age, in which the overwhelming new experience had by the individuals becomes speech in animated shouting and immediately finds confirming and supplementing echo — a band and again a band; thus was originally obtained, I suppose, out of the abyss of being the common cosmos, the shaped order of what is experienced by man and what is known as experienceable, a shape that grows and changes. And thus also, in the midst of precipitous being, the human cosmos is preserved, guarded by its molder, the human speech-with-meaning, the common logos. Thus the cosmos is preserved amid the changes of the world images.

Man has always thought his thoughts as I, and as I he has transplanted his ideas into the firmament of the spirit, but as We he has ever raised them into being itself, in just that mode of existence that I call 'the between' or 'betweenness'. That is the mode of existence between persons communicating with one another, which we cannot co-ordinate with either the psychic or the physical realms. It is to this that the seventh Platonic epistle points when it hints at the existence of a teaching which attains to effective reality not otherwise than in manifold togetherness and living with one another, as a light is kindled from leaping fire. Leaping fire is indeed the right image for the dynamic between persons in We.

The flight from the common cosmos into a special sphere that is understood as the true being is, in all its stages, from the elemental sayings of the ancient Eastern teachings to the arbitrariness of the modern counsel to intoxication, a flight from the existential claim on the person who must verify himself in We. It is flight from the authentic spokenness of speech in whose realm a response is demanded, and response is responsibility.

The fleeing man acts as if speech were nothing but the temptation to falsehood and convention, and it can, indeed, become temptation; but it is also our great pledge of truth.

For the typical man of today the flight from responsible personal existence has singularly polarized. Since he is not willing to answer for the genuineness of his existence, he flees either into the general collective which takes from him his responsibility or into the attitude of a self who has to account to no one but himself and finds the great general indulgence in the security of being identical with the Self of being. Even if this attitude is turned into a deepened contemplation of existing being, it remains a flight from the leaping fire.

The clearest mark of this kind of man is that he cannot really listen to the voice of another; in all his hearing, as in all his seeing, he mixes observation. The other is not the man over against him whose claim stands over against his own in equal right; the other is only his object. But he who existentially knows no Thou will never succeed in knowing a We.

In our age, in which the true meaning of every word is encompassed by delusion and falsehood, and the original intention of the human glance is stifled by tenacious mistrust, it is of decisive importance to find again the genuineness of speech and existence as We. This is no longer a matter which concerns the small circles that have been so important in the essential history of man; this is a matter of leavening the human race in all places with genuine We-ness. Man will not persist in existence if he does not learn anew to persist in it as a genuine We.

We had to confront the degenerate Western spirit with its origin and have therefore summoned the help of Heracleitus. But now he parts from us in our need or we part from him. For what he designates as the common has nothing that is over against it as such: logos and cosmos are, to him, self-contained; there is nothing that transcends them. And even when Heracleitus bears witness to the divine as at once bearing a name and being nameless, even then there is no real transcendence. No salvation is in sight for us, however, if we are not able again 'to stand before the face of God' in all reality as a We — as it is written in that faithful speech that once from Israel, the southern pillar of the bridge between the East and the West, started on its way.

In our age this We standing before the divine countenance has attained its highest expression through a poet, through Friedrich Hölderlin (1770–1843). He says of the authentic past of man as man, "since we have been a dialogue and have been able to hear from one another." And after that comes the words, "But we are soon song." The self-contained communality of Heracleitus that overspans the opposites has here become the choral antiphony which, as we know from Hölderlin, is directed upward.

Guilt and Guilt Feelings

1

At the London International Conference for Medical Psycho-therapy of 1948,[1] "The Genesis of Guilt" was fixed as the theme of the first plenary session. The first speaker, a Hollander, began with the announcement that in his special group the question had been discussed as to whether the genesis of guilt or the genesis of guilt feelings was meant. The question remained unclarified. But in the course of the discussion it was left to the theologians to speak of guilt itself (by which, indeed, they did not actually mean personal guilt, but the original sin of the human race). The psychologists concerned themselves merely with guilt feelings.

This distribution of themes, through which the factual occur-rences of guilt in the lives of 'patients', of suffering men, hardly enters into view, is characteristic of most of what one calls the psychotherapeutic discipline. Only in the most recent period have some begun to complain that both in the theory and in the practice of this science the psychic 'projection' of guilt is afforded room, the real events of guilt are not. This omission has not been been presented and methodologically grounded as such. It has been treated as a limitation that follows as a matter of course from the nature of psychology.

Nothing of the kind is self-evident, however; indeed, nothing

Trans. by Maurice Friedman.

1. International Congress of Mental Health, *Proceedings of the International Conference on Medical Psychotherapy*, vol. 3 (London: International Congress of Mental Health, 1948).

of the kind by right exists. Certainly, in the course of the history of the spirit each science that has detached itself from a comprehensive context and ensured for itself the independence of its realm has just thereby severely and ever more severely limited its subject and the manner of its working. But the investigator cannot truthfully maintain his relationship with reality — a relationship without which all his work becomes a well-regulated game — if he does not again and again, whenever it is necessary, gaze beyond the limits into a sphere which is not his sphere of work, yet which he must contemplate with all his power of research in order to do justice to his own task. For the psychotherapist this sphere is formed from the factual course of the so-called external life of his patients and especially the actions and attitudes therein, and again especially the patient's active share in the manifold relation between him and the human world. Not only his decisions are included in this share, but also his failures to come to a decision when, in a manner perceptible to him, they operate as decisions.

To the valid scientific realm of psychotherapy belong the 'inner' reactions of the individual to his passive and active life-experience, the psychic elaboration of the biographical events, whether it takes place in conscious or in unconscious processes. The relationship of the patient to a man with whom he stands in a contact that strongly affects his own life is for the psychologist important as such only in so far as its effects on the psyche of the patient can serve the understanding of his illness. The relationship itself in its reciprocal reality, the significant actuality of what is happening and has happened between the two men, transcends his task as it transcends his method. He limits himself to those of its inner connections that his work of exploring the mind of the patient makes accessible to him. And yet, if he wishes to satisfy not merely what he owes to the laws of his discipline and their application, but also what he owes to the existence and the need of man, he may, in fact he must, go beyond that realm where an existing person merely relates to himself. He must cast his glance again and again to where existing person relates to existing person — this person, the 'patient', to another living being who is not 'given' to the doctor and who may be completely unknown to him. The psychotherapist cannot include this other person, these other persons in his work. It is not for him to concern himself with them. And yet he may not neglect them in their reality; he must succeed in grasping their reality as adequately as possible in so far as it enters into the relationship between them and his patient.

This state of affairs manifests itself with the greatest intensity in the problem that occupies us here. Within his methods the psychotherapist has to do only with guilt feelings, conscious and unconscious (Freud was already aware of the contradiction that lies in the concept of unconscious feelings). But within a comprehensive service to knowledge and help, he must himself encounter guilt as something of an ontic character whose place is not the soul but being. He will do this, to be sure, with the danger that through his new knowledge the help which he is obliged to give might also be modified so that something uncustomary will be demanded of his method; indeed, he must be ready even to step out of the established rules of his school. But a 'doctor of souls' who really is one — that is, who does not merely carry on the work of healing but enters into it at times as a partner — is precisely one who dares.

2

The boundaries set by the psychotherapist's method do not, in any case, suffice to explain the negative or indifferent attitude that psychotherapy has so long taken toward the ontic character of guilt. The history of modern psychology shows us that here deeper motives are at work that have also contributed to the genesis and development of the methods. The two clearest examples of it are provided us by the two most noteworthy representatives of this intellectual tendency: Freud and Jung.

Freud, a great, late-born apostle of the enlightenment, presented the naturalism[2] of the enlightenment with a scientific sys-

2. Freud himself described psychoanalysts as "incorrigible mechanists and

tem and thereby with a second flowering. As Freud himself recognized with complete clarity,[3] the struggle against all metaphysical and religious teachings of the existence of an absolute and of
the possibility of a relation of the human person to it had a great
share in the development of psychoanalytic theory. As a result of
this basic attitude, guilt was simply not allowed to acquire an
ontic character; it had to be derived from the transgression
against ancient and modern taboos, against parental and social
tribunals. The feeling of guilt was now to be understood as essentially only the consequence of dread of punishment and censure by this tribunal, as the consequence of the child's fear of
'loss of love' or, at times when it was a question of imaginary
guilt, as a 'need for punishment' of a libidinal nature, as 'moral
masochism'[4] which is complemented by the sadism of the superego. "The first renunciation of instinctual gratification," Freud
stated in 1924, "is enforced by external powers, and it is this that
creates morality which express itself in conscience and exacts a
further renunciation of instinct."[5]

Of an entirely different, indeed diametrically opposed, nature
is the teaching of Carl Jung, whom one can describe as a mystic
of a modern, psychological type of solipsism. The mystical and
religio-mystical conceptions that Freud despised are for Jung the
most important subject of his study; but they are such merely as
'projections' of the psyche, not as indications of something extra-
psychic that the psyche meets. For Freud the structure of the
psyche culminates in the superego, which represents, with its
censory function, only the authoritative tribunals of family and
society; for Jung it culminates or rather is grounded in the self,

---

materialists" (Sigmund Freud, "Psycho-analysis and Telephathy," in *The Standard Edition of the Complete Psychological Works of Sigmund Freud*, vol. 18 (London:
Hogarth Press, 1955), 177–93.

3. See, for example, "A Philosophy of Life," chap. 7 in Sigmund Freud, *New
Introductory Lectures on Psycho-Analysis* (London: Hogarth Press; New York: W.
W. Norton, 1933).

4. Sigmund Freud, "The Economic Problem in Masochism," in *Collected Papers* (London: Hogarth Press, 1948), 255, 268.

5. Ibid., 267.

which is "individuality in its highest meaning"[6] and forms "the most immediate experience of the divine which can be grasped at all psychologically."[7] Jung does not recognize at all any relationship between the individual soul and another existing being which oversteps the limits of the psychic. But to this must be added the fact that the integration of evil as the unification of the opposites in the psyche is put forward as a central motif in the process of "individuation," of the "realization of self."[8] Seen from this vantage point, there is in Jung's panpsychism, as in Freud's materialism, no place for guilt in the ontological sense, unless it be in the relationship of man to himself — that is, as failure in the process of individuation. In fact, in the whole great work of Jung we learn nothing of guilt as a reality in the relation between the human person and the world entrusted to him in his life.

With the other psychoanalytic doctrines it stands, in general, much the same. Almost everyone who seriously concerns himself with the problem of guilt proceeds to derive the guilt feelings that are met with in analysis from hidden elements, to trace them back to such elements, to unmask them as such. One seeks the powerful repressions in the unconscious as those that hide behind the phenomena of illness, but not also the live connection the image of which has remained in the living memory, time and again admonishing, attacking, tormenting, and, after each submersion in the river of no-longer-thinking-about-that, returning and taking up its work anew.

A man stands before us who, through acting or failing to act, has burdened himself with a guilt or has taken part in a community guilt, and now, after years or decades is again and again visited by the memory of his guilt. Nothing of the genesis of his illness is concealed from him if he is only willing no longer to conceal from himself the guilt character of that active or passive

6. Carl Jung, *Von den Wurzeln des Bewusstseins*, Psychologische Abhandlungen, IX (Zurich: Rascher, 1954), 296 f.

7. Ibid., 300.

8. Ibid.

occurrence. What takes possession of him ever again has nothing to do with any parental or social reprimand, and if he does not have to fear an earthly retribution and does not believe in a heavenly one, no court, no punishing power exists that can make him anxious. Here rules the one penetrating insight — the one insight capable of penetrating into the impossibility of recovering the original point of departure and the irreparability of what has been done, and that means the real insight into the irreversibility of lived time, a fact that shows itself unmistakably in the starkest of all human perspectives, that concerning one's own death. From no standpoint is time perceived so like a torrent as from the vision of the self in guilt. Swept along in this torrent, the bearer of guilt is visited by the shudder of identity with himself. I, he comes to know, I, who have become another, am the same.

I have seen three important and, to me, dear men fall into long illnesses from their failing to stand the test in the days of an acute community guilt. The share of the psychogenic element in the illness could hardly be estimated, but its action was unmistakable. One of them refused to acknowledge his self-contradiction before the court of his spirit. The second resisted recognizing as serious a slight error he remembered that was attached to a very serious chain of circumstances. The third, however, would not let himself be forgiven by God for the blunder of a moment because he did not forgive himself. It now seems to me that all three needed and lacked competent helpers.

The psychotherapist into whose field of vision such manifestations of guilt enter in all their forcefulness can no longer imagine that he is able to do justice to his task as doctor of guilt-ridden men merely through the removal of guilt feelings. Here a limit is set to the tendency to derive guilt from the taboos of primeval society. The psychologist who sees what is here to be seen must be struck by the idea that guilt does not exist because a taboo exists to which one fails to give obedience, but rather that taboo and the placing of taboo have been made possible only through the fact that the leaders of early communities knew and made use of a primal fact of man as man — the fact that man can become guilty and know it.

Existential guilt — that is, guilt that a person has taken on himself as a person and in a personal situation — cannot be comprehended through such categories of analytical science as 'repression' and 'becoming conscious'. The bearer of guilt of whom I speak remembers it again and again by himself and in sufficient measure. Not seldom, certainly, he attempts to evade it — not the remembered fact, however, but its depths as existential guilt — until the truth of this depth overwhelms him and time is now perceived by him as a torrent.

Can the doctor of souls function here as helper, beyond professional custom and correct methods? May he do so? Is he shown at times another and higher therapeutic goal than the familiar one? Can and may he try his strength, not with conscious or unconscious, founded or unfounded guilt feelings, but with the self-manifesting existential guilt itself? Can he allow himself to recognize, from this standpoint, that healing in this case means something other than the customary, and what it means in this case?

The doctor who confronts the effects on the guilty man of an existential guilt must proceed in all seriousness from the situation in which the act of guilt has taken place. Existential guilt occurs when someone injures an order of the human world whose foundations he knows and recognizes as those of his own existence and of all common human existence. The doctor who confronts such a guilt in the living memory of his patient must enter into that situation; he must lay his hand in the wound of the order and learn: this concerns you. But then it may strike him that the orientation of the psychologist and the treatment of the therapist have changed unawares and that if he wishes to persist as a healer he must take upon himself a burden he had not expected to bear.

One could protest that an existential guilt is only the exception and that it is not proper to frighten the already overburdened therapist with the image of such borderline cases. But what I call existential guilt is only an intensification of what is found in some measure wherever an authentic guilt feeling burns, and the authentic guilt feeling is very often inextricably mingled with the problematic, the 'neurotic', the 'groundless'. The therapist's methods, naturally, do not willingly concern themselves with the authentic guilt feeling which, in general, is of a strictly personal character and does not easily allow itself to be imprisoned in general propositions. It lies essentially nearer to the doctrine and practice to occupy itself with the effects of repressed childhood wishes or youthful lusts gone astray, than with the inner consequences of a man's betrayal of his friend or his cause. And for the patient it is a great relief to be diverted from his authentic guilt feeling to an unambiguous neurotic one that, favored within this category by the school of his doctor, allows itself to be discovered in the microcosmos of his dreams or in the stream of his free associations. To all this the genuine doctor of souls stands opposed with the postulative awareness that he should act here as at once bound and unbound. He does not, of course, desist from any of his methods, which have in fact become adaptable. But where, as here, he becomes aware of a reality between man and man, between man and the world, a reality inaccessible to any of the psychological categories, he recognizes the limits that are set here for his methods and recognizes that the goal of healing has been transformed in this case because the context of the sickness, the place of the sickness in being, has been transformed. If the therapist recognizes this, then all that he is obliged to do becomes more difficult, much more difficult — and all becomes more real, radically real.

3

I shall clarify this statement through the example of a life history that I have already made use of before, although all too briefly.[9] I select it from among those at my disposal because I was a witness, sometimes more distant, sometimes nearer, to the happenings, and I have followed their sequence. The life course I

9. See my preface to Hans Trüb's posthumous work, *Heilung aus der Begegnung: Eine Auseinandersetzung mit der Psychologie C. G. Jungs* (E. Klett: Stuttgart, 1965).

have in mind is that of a woman — let us call her Melanie — of more intellectual than truly spiritual gifts, with a scientific education, but without the capacity for independent mastery of her knowledge. Melanie possessed a remarkable talent for good comradeship which expressed itself, at least from her side, in more or less erotically tinged friendships that left unsatisfied her impetuous rather than passionate need for love. She made the acquaintance of a man who was on the point of marriage with another, strikingly ugly, but remarkable woman. Melanie succeeded without difficulty in breaking up the engagement and marrying the man. Her rival tried to kill herself. Melanie soon afterward accused her, certainly unjustly, of feigning her attempt at suicide. After a few years Melanie herself was supplanted by another woman. Soon Melanie fell ill with a neurosis linked with disturbances of the vision. To friends who took her in at the time, she confessed her guilt without glossing over the fact that it had arisen not out of a passion, but out of a fixed will.

Later she gave herself into the care of a well-known psychoanalyst. This man was able to liberate her in a short while from her feelings of disappointment and guilt and to bring her to the conviction that she was a 'genius of friendship' and would find in this sphere the compensation that was due her. The conversion succeeded, and Melanie devoted herself to a rich sociality which she experienced as a world of friendship. In contrast to this, she associated in general with the men with whom she had to deal in her professional 'welfare work' not as persons needing her understanding and even her consolation, but as objects to be seen through and directed by her. The guilt feelings were no longer in evidence; the apparatus that had been installed in place of the paining and admonishing heart functioned in model fashion.

Now that is certainly no extraordinary fate. We recognize again the all too usual distress of human action and suffering, and there can be no talk here of existential guilt in the great sense of the term. And yet, the guilt feeling that grew up at that time in the illness and that so fused with the illness that no one could say which of the two was the cause and which the effect, had throughout an authentic character. With the silencing of the

guilt feeling there disappeared for Melanie the possibility of reconciliation through a newly won genuine relationship to her environment in which her best qualities could at the same time
unfold. The price paid for the annihilation of the sting was the
final annihilation of the chance to become the being that this
created person was destined to become through her highest
disposition.

Again one may raise the objection that it cannot be the affair
of the psychotherapist to concern himself about this kind of
thing. His task is to investigate malady and to heal it, or rather to
help it toward healing, and it is just this that the doctor who had
been called in had done. But here lies an important problem.
Stated generally, one can formulate it somewhat as follows: Shall
a man who is called upon to help another in a specific manner
merely give the help for which he is summoned or shall he also
give the other help that, according to the doctor's knowledge of
him, this man objectively needs?

However, what is the meaning here of the help that one objectively needs? Clearly this, that his being follows other laws than
his consciousness. But also quite other ones than his 'unconscious'. The unconscious is still far less concerned than the conscious about whether the essence of this man thrives. Essence —
by this I mean that for which a person is peculiarly intended,
what he is called to become. The conscious, with its planning and
its weighing, concerns itself with it only occasionally; the unconscious, with its wishes and contradictions, hardly ever. Those are
great moments of existence when a man discovers his essence or
rediscovers it on a higher plane; when he decides and decides
anew to become what he is and, as one who is becoming this, to
establish a genuine relation to the world; when he heroically
maintains his discovery and decision against his everyday consciousness and against his unconscious. Should the helper, can
the helper, may the helper now enter into an alliance with the
essence of him who summoned him, across this person's conscious and unconscious will, provided that he has really reliably
recognized the need of this essence? Is something of this sort at
all his office? Can it be his office? Particularly where the helping

profession is so exactly circumscribed by principles and methods as in modern psychotherapy? Does not the danger threaten here of pseudo-intuitive dilettantism that dissolves all fixed norms?

An important psychologist and doctor of our time, the late Viktor von Weizsaecker, laid down, in very precise language, a sober admonition on this point. There the "treatment of the essential in man" is simply excluded from the realm of psychotherapy. "Just the final destiny of man," he writes, "must not be the subject of therapy."[10] And my lay insight must concur with this declaration. But there is an exceptional case — the case where the glance of the doctor, the perceiving glance that makes him a doctor and to whom all his methods stand in a serving relation, extends into the sphere of the essence, where he perceives essential lapse and essential need. There, to be sure, it is still denied him to treat 'the essential' in his patients, but he may and should guide it to where an essential help of the self, a help till now neither willed nor anticipated, can begin. It is neither given the therapist nor allowed to him to indicate a way that leads onward from here. But from the watchtower to which the patient has been conducted, he can manage to see a way that is right for him and that he can walk, a way that it is not granted the doctor to see. For at this high station all becomes personal in the strictest sense.

The psychotherapist is no pastor of souls and no substitute for one. It is never his task to mediate a salvation; his task is always only to further a healing. But it is not merely incumbent upon him to interest himself in that need of the patient which has become symptomatically manifest in his sickness — to interest himself in it as far as the analysis conducted according to the therapist's method discloses to him the genesis of this illness. That need is also confided to him which first allows itself to be recognized in the immediacy of the partnership between the patient who is having recourse to the doctor and the doctor who is concerned about the recovery of the patient — although occasionally this need remains veiled, even then.

10. *Äratliche Fragen* (1934) p. 9.

I have already pointed to the fact that the doctor, in order to be able to do this adequately, must for the time being lift himself off the firm ground of principles and methods on which he has learned to walk. One must not, of course, understand this to mean that he now soars in the free ether of an unrestrained 'intuition'. Now too, and only now really, he is obliged to think consistently and to work exactly. And if he may now surrender himself to a more direct vision, it can still only be one that realizes its individual norms in each of its insights — norms that cannot be translated into general propositions. In this sphere of action, too, even though it seems left to his independent direction, the man of the intellectual profession learns that a true work is an affair of a listening obedience.

But in order that the therapist be able to do this, he must recognize just one thing steadfastly and recognize it ever again: there exists real guilt, fundamentally different from all the anxiety-induced bugbears that are generated in the cavern of the unconscious. Personal guilt, whose reality some schools of psychoanalysis contest and others ignore, does not permit itself to be reduced to the trespass against a powerful taboo.

We cannot now content ourselves, however, with allowing this knowledge, which was long under a ban, to be conveyed to us by this or that tradition which is holy to us. It must arise anew from the historical and biographical self-experience of the generation living today. We who are living today know in what measure we have become historically and biographically guilty. That is no feeling and no sum of feelings. It is, no matter how manifoldly concealed and denied, a real knowledge about a reality. Under the schooling of this knowledge, which is becoming ever more irresistible, we learn anew that guilt exists.

In order to understand this properly we must call to mind one fact, no accessory fact but the basic one. Each man stands in an objective relationship to others; the totality of this relationship constitutes his life as one that factually participates in the being of the world. It is this relationship, in fact, that first makes it at all possible for him to expand his environment (*Umwelt*) into a world (*Welt*). It is his share in the human order of being, the share for which he bears responsibility. An objective relationship in which two men stand to one another can rise, by means of the existential participation of the two, to a personal relation; it can be merely tolerated; it can be neglected; it can be injured. Injuring a relationship means that at this place the human order of being is injured. No one other than he who inflicted the wound can heal it. He who knows the fact of his guilt and is a helper can help him try to heal the wound.

4

One last clarification is still necessary. When the therapist recognizes an existential guilt of his patient, he cannot — that we have seen — show him the way to the world, which the latter must rather seek and find as his own personal law. The doctor can only conduct him to the point from which he can glimpse his personal way or at least its beginning. But in order that the doctor shall be able to do this, he must also know about the general nature of the way, common to all great acts of conscience, and about the connection that exists between the nature of existential guilt and the nature of this way.

In order not to fall into any error here, however, we must bear in mind that there are three different spheres in which the reconciliation of guilt can fulfill itself and between which noteworthy relations often establish themselves. Only one of these spheres, that which we shall designate as the middle one, directly concerns the therapist whom I have in mind.

The first sphere is that of the law of the society. The action begins here with the demand, actually made or latent, which society places on the guilty man according to its laws. The event of fulfillment is called confession of guilt. It is followed by penalty and indemnification. With this sphere the therapist, naturally, has nothing to do. As doctor, an opinion is not even accorded him as to whether the demand of the society is right or not. His patient, the guilty man, may be guilty toward the society or he may not be; its judgment over him may be just or it may not be. This does not concern the doctor as doctor; he is incompetent here. In his relation to the patient this problematic theme can find no admission, with the exception of the unavoidable occupation with the anxiety of the patient in the face of the punishments, the censure, the boycotts of society.

But the third and highest sphere, that of faith, also cannot be his affair. Here the action commences within the relation between the guilty man and his God and remains therein. It is likewise consummated in three events which correspond to the three of the first sphere, but are connected with each other in an entirely different manner. These are the confession of sin, repentence, and penance in its various forms. The doctor as such may not touch on this sphere even when he and the patient stand in the same community of faith. Here no man can speak unless it be one whom the guilty man acknowledges as a hearer and speaker who represents the transcendence believed in by the guilty man. Also when the therapist encounters the problem of faith in the anxiety concerning divine punishment that is disclosed in the patient's analysis, he cannot interfere here — even if he possesses great spiritual gifts — without falling into a dangerous dilettantism.

The middle sphere, as we have said, is one to the sight of which the therapist may lead — up to it, but no farther. This sphere, about which he must *know* for this purpose, we may call that of conscience, with a qualification which I shall shortly discuss. The action demanded by the conscience also fulfills itself in three events, which I call self-illumination, perseverance, and reconciliation, and which I shall define more exactly still.

Conscience means to us the capacity and tendency of man radically to distinguish between those of his past and future actions which should be approved and those which should be disapproved. The disapproval, in general, received far stronger emotional stress, whereas the approval of past actions at times passes over with shocking ease into a most questionable self-satisfaction. Conscience can, naturally, distinguish and if necessary condemn in such a manner not merely deeds but also omissions, not merely decisions but also failures to decide, indeed even images and wishes that have just arisen or are remembered.

In order to understand this capacity and tendency more exactly, one must bear in mind that among all living beings known to us man alone is able to set at a distance not only his environment, but also himself. As a result, he becomes for himself a detached object about which he can not only 'reflect', but which he can, from time to time, confirm as well as condemn. The content of conscience is in many ways determined, of course, by the commands and prohibitions of the society to which its bearer belongs or those of the tradition of faith to which he is bound. But conscience itself cannot be understood as an introjection of either the one authority or the other, neither ontogenetically nor phylogenetically. The table of shalts and shalt-nots under which this man has grown up and lives determines only the conceptions which prevail in the realm of the conscience, but not its existence itself, which is grounded in just that distancing and distinguishing — primal qualities of the human race. The more or less hidden criteria that the conscience employs in its acceptances and rejections only rarely fully coincide with a standard received from the society or community. Connected with that is the fact that the guilt feeling can hardly ever be wholly traced to a transgression against a taboo of a family or of society. The totality of the order that a man knows to be injured or injurable by him transcends to some degree the totality of the parental and social taboos that bind him. The depth of the guilt feeling is not seldom connected with just that part of the guilt that cannot be ascribed to the taboo-offence, hence with the existential guilt.

The qualification of which I spoke, accordingly, is that our subject is the relation of the conscience to existential guilt. Its relation to the trespassing of taboos concerns us here only in so far as a guilty man understands this trespassing more strongly or weakly as real existential guilt which arises out of his being and for which he cannot take responsibility without being responsible to his relationship to his own being.

The vulgar conscience that knows admirably well how to torment and harass, but cannot arrive at the ground and abyss of guilt, is incapable, to be sure, of summoning to such responsibility. For this summoning a greater conscience is needed, one that has become wholly personal, one that does not shy away from the glance into the depths and that already in admonishing envisages the way that leads across it. But this in no way means that this personal conscience is reserved for some type of 'higher' man. This conscience is possessed by every simple man who gathers himself into himself in order to venture the breakthrough out of the entanglement in guilt. And it is a great, not yet sufficiently recognized, task of education to elevate the conscience from its lower common form to conscience-vision and conscience-courage. For it is innate to the conscience of man that it can elevate itself.

From what has been said it already follows with sufficient clarity that the primeval concept of conscience, if only it is understood as a dynamic one rather than as a static, judging one, is more realistic than the modern structural concept of the superego. The concept of the superego attains only an orienting significance and one, moreover, which easily orients the novice falsely.

If we now wish to speak of actions in the sphere of conscience in this high and strict sense, we do not mean thereby the well-known synthesis out of the internalization of censure, torment, and punishment that one customarily regards as the proper factual content of conscience — that pressuring and oppressing influence of an inner high court on an 'ego' that is more or less subject to it. Rather this tormenting complex has, for our consideration, only the character of an angelic-demonic intermezzo on which the high dramatic or tragicomic act of neurosis may follow, and the whole affair may end with a therapy that passes for successful. What concerns us here is another possibility, whether it be the true process of healing after the neurosis, or whether it be without a neurosis preceding it. It is that possible moment when the whole person who has become awake and unafraid ascends from the anguishing lowland of the conscience to its heights and independently masters the material delivered to him by it.

From this position a man can undertake the threefold action to which I have referred: first, to illuminate the darkness that still weaves itself about the guilt despite all previous action of the conscience — not to illuminate it with spotlights but with a broad and enduring wave of light; second, to persevere, no matter how high he may have ascended in his present life above that station of guilt — to persevere in that newly won humble knowledge of the identity of the present person with the person of that time; and third, in his place and according to his capacity, in the given historical and biographical situations, to restore the order-of-being injured by him through the relation of an active devotion to the world — for the wounds of the order-of-being can be healed in infinitely many other places than those at which they were inflicted.

In order that this may succeed in that measure that is at all attainable by this man, he must gather the forces and elements of his being and ever again protect the unity that is thus won from the cleavage and contradiction that threaten it. For, to quote myself, one cannot do evil with his whole soul, one can do good only with the whole soul.[11] What one must wrest from himself, first, is not yet the good; only when he has first attained his own self does the good thrive through him.

5

The event of illumination corresponds on the plane of the law to the legal confession of guilt, on the plane of faith to the confession of sin. As a social concept, confession of guilt is naturally the most familiar of the three; what takes place here takes place in public in the legal institutions of society.

The confession of sin is spoken by a man when, seeking reconciliation with God, he directly or indirectly steps before the absolute judgment. That may happen in the chorus of the community, as at the Jewish Day of Atonement, or in the whispers of the confessing man into the ear of the confessor, or even in solitude by those who feel themselves as standing before God and their speech as addressing God: the confessing one is always removed from the anonymous publicity of society, but by no means referred to himself. He has one over against him who receives his

11. See page 27 above.

confession, answers it, 'forgives' him — for the Jews, in a significant co-operation with him toward whom the confessing one has become guilty.

The matter is otherwise with the first of the three events in the action of the great conscience, the event of illumination. Here a man ventures to illuminate the depths of a guilt which he has certainly recognized as what it is, but not yet in its essence and its meaning for his life. What he is now obliged to do cannot be accomplished in any other place than in the abyss of I-with-me, and it is just this abyss that must be illuminated.

Legal confession of guilt means a dialogue with the representatives of society who rejoin as judges according to the penal law. Religious confession means a dialogue with the absolute divine person who replies in mysterious fashion out of his mystery. As for the illumination of essence, it is in its most real moments not even a monologue, much less a real conversation between an ego and a superego: all speech is exhausted; what takes place here is the mute shudder of self-being. But without this powerful wave of light which illuminates the abyss of mortality, the legal confession of guilt remains without substance in the inner life of the guilty man, no matter how weighty its consequences may be, and the religious confession is only a pathetic prattle that no one hears.

We must not fail to recognize that it has become more difficult for the man of our age than any earlier one to venture self-illumination with awake and unafraid spirit, although he imagines that he knows more about himself than did the man of any earlier time. The inner resistance which shows itself here — a deeper one than all that discloses itself to the genetic investigation of the analyst — has found so valid a representation in two of the characteristic forms of the epic literatures of the nineteenth and twentieth centuries that we cannot do better than to turn to them in order to supplement our understanding of the problem. I mean Nikolai Stavrogin in Dostoevski's novel *The Possessed* and Joseph K in Kafka's narrative *The Trial*. In our discussion of this subject, the second of these books, as little as it is comparable to the first in artistic power, must still be the more important because in it the present stage of the human problem of guilt has found expression. But in order to see how this later stage is connected with that which preceded it, we must turn our attention first to Dostoevski.

For our formulation of the question it is necessary to proceed from the complete text of the novel, that which contains the chapter of Stavrogin's confession later expunged by the author on external grounds, and some related material.

Stavrogin was thought of by Dostoevski as the man on the outermost rim of the age who dissolves the meaning of existence through denying it and who manages to destroy himself through the destruction of all over whom he gets power. In the omitted chapter it is told how Stavrogin visits a holy man and brings to him the record of a confession which he declares he wishes to publish. In it he confesses how he raped a little girl. Later he disavows the confession, evidently because he knows from the reaction of the priest as soon as it has been made that it cannot accomplish what he has expected it to. The content of the confession is true, but the act of making it is fictitious. It has nothing at all to do with Stavrogin's self-illumination, with persevering self-identification, with reconciling renewed relationship with the world. Thus even his "unfeigned need for a public execution" (as Dostoevski states in explanation) is permeated with the fictitious. What Stavrogin desires is "the leap." A fragmentary sketch by Dostoevski informs us unambiguously about this. It says, clearly in this connection, that the priest opposed Stavrogin's intention to publish the confession: The high priest pointed out that a leap was not necessary, that the man must rather set himself to rights from within — through long work; only then could he complete the leap. "And would it be impossible to do it suddenly?" Stavrogin asks. "Impossible?" rejoins the priest. "From the work of an angel it would become the work of a devil." "Ah," exclaims Stavrogin, "that I already knew myself."

Stavrogin 'commits' the confession as he commits his crimes: as an attempt to snatch the genuine existence which he does not possess, but which — nihilist in practice but (in anticipation) existentialist in views — he has recognized as the true good. He is full of 'ideas' (Dostoevski even lends him his own!), full of 'spirit', but he does not exist. Only after Dostoevski's time, only in our own, will this type of man discover the basic nihilism in existential form after he has learned that he cannot attain to existence by the ways corresponding to his kind of person. Only this is now left to him: to proclaim the spiritful *nihil* as existence and himself as the new man. Stavrogin is not yet so 'advanced'. All he can do is to kill himself; after all, the 'demonic' game with ideas, crimes, and confessions — this game that has a goal — has proved itself powerless. The decisive moment, excised in the usual version of the novel as abridged by the author, is precisely the failure of the confession: Stavrogin has wanted the holy man to believe in its existential character and thereby help him, Stavrogin, to existence. But existential confession is possible only as a breaking-through to the great action of the high conscience in self-illumination, persevering self-identification, and a reconciling relationship to the world. This possibility, however, is in Stavrogin's eyes one of two things: either essentially not accorded to him or destroyed by him through his life-game. In Dostoevski's own eyes, however, man is redeemable when he wills redemption *as such* and thereby also his share in it — the great act of the high conscience.

6

The Possessed was written in 1870, Kafka's *Trial* in 1915. The two books represent two basically different but closely connected situations of human history from which their authors suffered: the one the uncanny negative certainty, "Human values are beginning to shatter," and the other the still more uncanny uncertainty, "Do world-meaning and world-order still have any connection at all with this nonsense and this disorder of the human world?" — an uncertainty that appears to have arisen out of that negative certainty.

Everything in Kafka's book is intended to be uncertain and indefinite, at times to the point of an absurdity, which always remains artistically mastered. This court of justice before which

Joseph K is unexpectedly cited because of an unnamed and to him unknown guilt is at once prosaically real and of ghostly indefiniteness, wild, crude, and senselessly disordered through and through. But Joseph K is himself, in all his actions, of hardly less indefiniteness — merely a different kind — as, charged with guilt, he confusedly carries on day after day a life as directionless as before. Directionless, that is, except for the one aim he now pursues, sometimes busily, sometimes incidentally: namely, that of getting free of the court. To this end he occupies himself with indefinite advocates, indefinite women, and other indefinite human instruments in order that they may provide him, in the face of the peculiar ways of this peculiar court, with the protection that he imagines is all he needs. The indefinite guilt with which he is charged occupies him only in so far as he thinks from time to time of composing a written defense in the form of a short description of his life which will explain, in connection with each more important event, on what grounds he then acted thus and not otherwise, and whether he now approves or condemns his manner of acting at that time. Finally there happens what is reported in an unfinished chapter: "From then on K forgot the court."

All this is not to be called chaotic, for in a chaos is hidden a world that shall emerge out of it; here there is no trace of a cosmos that wills to come into being. But one may well call all this taken together — the court, the accused, and the people around him — labyrinthine. The disorder, mounting to absurdity, points toward a secret order, one, however, which nowhere shows itself except by way of a hint, which apparently would first become manifest only if Joseph K did what until the end he does not do — make "the confession" that is demanded of him. But he cannot, as he says, discover the least guilt on account of which one could accuse him. Indeed, he ends later — clearly without quite knowing what he is saying — by uttering the presumptuous words that are not proper to any human mouth: "I am completely guiltless." The thread that leads out of the labyrinth is not to be found in the book; rather this thread exists only when just that happens which did not happen, the "confession of guilt."

But what can be meant here, under the given presuppositions, by making a confession? This question hovers in a strange, altogether intentional paradox. A well-informed young woman says to Joseph K, leaning on his shoulder, "One cannot, in fact, defend oneself against this court; one must make the confession. Make it therefore at the first opportunity. Only then is there any possibility of escaping." And he answers, "You understand much about this court and about the deceit that is necessary here." Since Kafka himself says nothing like this, it can only mean that Joseph, who holds himself, in fact, to be "entirely guiltless," understands that he should make a false confession, and at this moment he does not seem disinclined to do so. Later, however, a painter, who is likewise, as we hear, well-acquainted with the ways of this court, advises him thus: "Since you are guiltless, it is really possible for you to rely on your innocence." Note well: In the same speech the same speaker declares that he has never yet witnessed a single acquittal, but immediately afterwards he says that the decisions of the court were not published, that there exist, however, "legends" of actual acquittals, and that these legends probably contain "a certain truth."

In this atmosphere the action moves forward, and it clearly seems as though the accusation and with it the encouragement to confession are a senseless absurdity, as Joseph K has declared them to be in his speech before the court: "And the meaning of this great organization, gentlemen? It consists in the fact that innocent persons are arrested, and against them a senseless and for the most part, as in my case, inconsequential proceedings are instituted." Some Kafka interpreters take these words to express the essential message of the book. This position is refuted through the further course of the action and through notes in Kafka's diaries relating to it.

I have in mind the chapter, "In the Cathedral," in which is told how Joseph K comes by accident into a church and is here addressed by name by a clergyman unknown to him, the prison chaplain, who also belongs to the organization of the court, but does not act by order of the court. This chapter corresponds exactly to the one excised by Dostoevski from *The Possessed*, in which Stavrogin hands over his confession to the high priest (a chapter which Kafka, moreover, could have known only in an incomplete version, not including the text of the confession). In both a priest is the antagonist, in both it is a matter of a confession of guilt; however, in Dostoevski it is furnished undemanded while in Kafka it is demanded. For it is this demand that the chaplain wishes to convey by the information that the case is going badly, since the court holds the guilt to be proved. "But I am not guilty," answers K, "it's a misunderstanding. And, if it comes to that, how can any man be called guilty? We are all simply men here, one as much as the other." One must listen closely: What is denied here is the ontic character of guilt, the depth of existential guilt beyond all mere violations of taboos. It is just this that Freud wished to deny when he undertook to relativize guilt feeling genetically. And to Joseph K's reply the priest answers, "That is true," which means: Indeed we are all men, and should not overestimate the difference between men. He continues, however, "But that's how all guilty men talk," which means: He who is in question gets off by talking about the others, instead of occupying himself with himself.

Now the priest asks, "What is the next step you propose to take in the matter?" "I'm going to seek more help," answers K. "You cast about too much for outside help," he now hears. And when he still will not understand, the chaplain shrieks at him, "Can't you see two steps in front of you?" He speaks like one who sees a man, still standing there before him, as already fallen. What he wants to say with his words, without directly saying it, is that the verdict, "into which the proceedings gradually pass over," now stands at hand, and the verdict itself already means death.

And now, as the last and most extreme effort, the chaplain tells the man, for whose soul and destiny he wrestles in one, the parable of the doorkeeper who stands, as one of countless men, "before the Law," before one of the countless doors leading into the interior of the Law, and of the man who desires entrance here. This man is frightened by the difficulties that await him who dares entrance, according to the information imparted to him by the doorkeeper. He now passes days and years, the entire remainder of his life, sitting sideways before this one out of innumerably many doors, until shortly before his end the keeper discloses to him that his doorway was destined for him alone and now is going to be shut. Joseph K listens to the parable and does not understand it: What then could the man have done to manage to get in? The clergyman does not tell him. Kafka himself, as he records in his diaries, first understood the significance of the story when he read it aloud to his fiancée. On another occasion, he clearly expressed this significance himself in an unforgettable passage in his notebooks: "Confession of guilt, unconditional confession of guilt, door springing open, it appears in the interior of the house of the world whose turbid reflection lay behind walls." The confession is the door springing open. It is the true "breakthrough," by which word Joseph K is falsely accustomed to describe the aspired-for escape from the law.

What does the legal concept of confession of guilt become here? What is so named here is self-illumination, the first and opening event in the action of the great conscience.

Stavrogin makes a confession in words. He describes therein in horrible detail the course of his crime, but both in remembering it and in recording it he remains incapable of self-illumination. He lacks the small light of humility that alone can illuminate the abyss of the guilty self in broad waves. He seeks for some kind of foothold, no matter how meagre; then he gives up and kills himself.

Joseph K makes no confession; he refused to understand that it is necessary for him to do so. In distinction from Stavrogin he is not proud; unlike the latter, he does not distinguish himself from other men. But by that very fact, with his, "We are all simply men here," he escapes the demand to bear into his inner darkness (of which Kafka speaks in his diaries) the cruel and salutary light. He insists that there is no such thing as personal existential guilt. His innermost being knows otherwise — because Kafka, who is closely connected with Joseph K, knows otherwise — but he shuns penetrating to this innermost being until it is too late. At this point Franz Kafka and Joseph K seem to have to part company. Kafka had imparted to him something of his own name, he had given him to bear (as he gave to 'K' in *The Castle*) his own suffering from a senselessly acting environment; with humorous caricature he had endowed him with his own traits. But now in the decisive hour, according to the logic of the fiction, he lets him say, "How can any man be called guilty?" and lets him lengthily and ingeniously dispute over the story of the doorkeeper, Kafka's most concentrated statement of his life-view, instead of accepting its teaching. As a result, Kafka, who understands the depth of existential guilt, must separate himself at this point from Joseph K.

He attains connection with him again, however, through the fact that soon afterwards, when the executioners are already leading Joseph K to his death, Kafka lets him concentrate himself in a strong, although still rational, self-recollection. He lets Joseph, who now knows that and how the trial is going to end, say to himself, "I always wanted to snatch at the world with twenty hands, and not for a very laudable motive, either." Joseph K has recognized that he has projected on the disordered human world only his own disorder. His self-recollection is not, of course, the beginning of a self-illumination, but it is a first step toward it, without the man who does it knowing it. And now, before the end, Kafka may again take the foolish man to his heart, although at the very end, before the knife falls on Joseph K, Kafka lets the old foolish notions of some still forgotten objections come into his mind. Perhaps Kafka meant himself by the man whom Joseph K glimpses at the last standing in a window, "a man faint and insubstantial at that distance and at that height": he wants to help his creature and may not.

It might still be asked how the absurd confusion that rules in the court is to be reconciled with the justice of the accusation and the demand. The question places before us a central problem of Kafka's that we find in the background of this novel and of the related novel *The Castle*, where an inaccessible power governs by means of a slovenly bureaucracy. We can extract the answer from an important note in Kafka's diary, from the time of the genesis of *The Trial*, in which he speaks of being occupied with the biblical figure of the unjust judges. It reads, "I find, there-

fore, my opinion, or at least the opinion that I have formerly
found in me." Psalm 82, of which he is clearly speaking here, has
as its subject God's judgment over those "sons of God," or angels, to whom He had entrusted the regimen over the human
world and who had vilely misused their office and "judged
falsely." The content of this late psalm is connected with that of
the oriental myth, elaborated by the Gnostics, of the astral spirits
who fatefully determine the destiny of the world, but from whose
power that man may become free who dedicates himself to the
concealed highest light and enters into rebirth. I have reason to
assume that Kafka also knew this myth at that time.[12] In *The Trial*
he modified it, in accord with his own contemplation of the
world, through letting the just accusation of an inaccessible highest judgment be conveyed by a disorderly and cruel court. Only
that man can escape the arm of this court who, out of his own
knowledge, fulfills the demand for confession of guilt according
to its truth through executing the primal confession, the self-
illumination. Only he enters the interior of the Law.

7

The destiny of both men, that of Stavrogin and that of Joseph
K, is determined by their false relationship to their guiltiness.

Stavrogin, of course, plays with the thought of bearing before
him like a banner the confession of his most shameful guilt, but
he does not bring forth the greater courage to understand in self-
illumination his essential being and the origin of his guilt. His
feeling, as he says in his last letter, is "too weak and too shallow,"
his wish "too little strong; it cannot lead me." He declares himself
unable to kill himself, for "vexation and shame can never exist in
me, and consequently no despair." But immediately thereafter
despair overwhelms him and he gives himself up to death.

Joseph K belongs to another, essentially later, more 'advanced'
generation. Not merely before the world, but also before himself,

12. I refer to a question concerning this myth that Kafka put to me at the
time of his visit to my house in Berlin in 1911 or 1912.

he refuses to concern himself with an ostensible state of guilt. He refuses to find and illuminate in himself the cause of this indictment which this questionable society casts on him from somewhere — say, from an invisible, unknowable 'highest court'. Indeed, it now passes as proved, in this his generation, that no real guilt exists; only guilt feeling and guilt convention. Until the last moment he refuses to enter through the door that still stands open and is only apparently shut; thus the verdict overtakes him.

Both Stavrogin and Joseph K have not taken the crucial hour of man upon themselves, and now have lost it.

It is the crucial hour of man of which we speak. For, to use Pascal's language, the greatness of man is bound up with his misery.

Man is the being who is capable of becoming guilty and is capable of illuminating his guilt.

I have illustrated through two examples from epic literature the manifold resistance of the human being against self-illumination. But this inner resistance is entirely different from the patient's struggle, well known to the psychoanalyst, against his efforts to convey from the unconscious into the conscious[13] a repressed state of facts of a guiltlike nature. For the guilt which is in question here is not at all repressed into the unconscious. The bearer of existential guilt remains in the realm of conscious existence. This guilt is not one that allows itself to be repressed into the unconscious. It remains in the chamber of memory, out of which it can at any moment penetrate unexpectedly into that of consciousness, without it being possible for any barriers to be erected against this invasion. The memory receives all experiences and actions without the assistance of man. It may, however, retain the ingredients of what is remembered in such a manner that what ascends into the actual remembering does not enter it in its original character. The existential guilt, therefore, does not enter it as such. Only when the human person himself overcomes his inner resistance can he attain to self-illumination.

13. Sigmund Freud, *A General Introduction to Psychoanalysis* (New York: Liveright, 1920), see lecture 19.

The 'opening door' of self-illumination leads us into no place beyond the law, but into the interior of the law. It is the law of man in which we then stand: the law of the identity of the human person as such with himself, the one who recognizes guilt with the one who bears guilt, the one in light with the one in darkness. The hard trial of self-illumination is followed by the still harder, because never ceasing, trial of persevering in this self-identification. But by this is not meant an ever renewed scourging of the soul with its knowledge of its abyss understood as something inevitably allotted to it. What is meant is an upright and calm perseverance in the clarity of the great light.

If a man were only guilty toward himself, in order to satisfy the demanding summons that meets him at the height of conscience, he would only need to take this one road from the gate of self-illumination, that of persevering. But a man is always guilty toward other beings as well, toward the world, toward the being that exists over against him. From self-illumination he must, in order to do justice to the summons, take not one road but two roads, of which the second is that of reconciliation. By reconciliation is understood here that action from the height of conscience that corresponds on the plane of the law to the customary act of reparation. In the realm of existential guilt one cannot, of course, 'make reparation' in the strict sense — as if the guilt with its consequences could thereby be recalled, as it were. Reconciliation means here, first of all, that I approach the man toward whom I am guilty in the light of my self-illumination (in so far as I can still reach him on earth) acknowledge to his face my existential guilt and help him, in so far as possible, to overcome the consequences of my guilty action. But such a deed can be valid here only as reconciliation if it is done not out of a premeditated resolution, but in the unarbitrary working of the existence I have achieved. And this can happen, naturally, only out of the core of a transformed relationship to the world, a new service to the world with the renewed forces of the renewed man.

This is not the place to speak of the events in the sphere of faith that correspond to the events in the sphere of the high conscience that we have just discussed. For the sincere man of faith, the two spheres are so referred to each other in the practice of his life, and most especially when he has gone through existential guilt, that he cannot entrust himself exclusively to either of them. Both, the human faith not less than the human conscience, can err and err again. And knowing about this their erring, both — conscience not less than faith — must place themselves in the hands of grace. It is not for me to speak in general terms of the inner reality of him who refuses to believe in a transcendent being with whom he can communicate. I have only this to report: that I have met many men in the course of my life who had told me how, acting from the high conscience as men who had become guilty, they experienced themselves as seized by a higher power. These men grew into an existential state to which the name of rebirth is due.

8

With all this, I repeat, the psychotherapist in his medical intercourse with his patients has nothing directly to do, not even when he ventures in a particular case to set for himself the goal of an existential healing. The utmost that can be expected of him, as I have said, is only this: that, reaching out beyond his familiar methods, he conduct the patient, whose existential guilt he has recognized, to where an existential help of the self can begin. But to do this, he must know about the reality toward which I have tried to point in this chapter.

Afterword to I and Thou

1

When I drafted the first sketch of this book (more than forty years ago), I felt impelled by an inner necessity. A vision that had afflicted me repeatedly since my youth but had always been dimmed again, had now achieved a constant clarity that was so evidently supra-personal that I soon knew that I ought to bear witness of it. Some time after I had earned the appropriate diction that permitted me to write the book in its definitive form,[1] it appeared that a good deal remained to be added — but in its own place, independently. Thus several shorter works came into being:[2] I found occasions to clarify the crucial vision by means of examples, to elaborate it by refuting objections, and to criticize views to which I owed something important but which had missed the central significance of the close association of the relation to God with the relation to one's fellowmen, which is my most essential concern. Later other discussions were added: of the anthropological foundations[3] and of the sociological implications.[4] Nevertheless it has become plain that by no means has

Translated by Walter Kaufmann.

1. It appeared in 1923.

2. *Zwiesprache* (1930); *Die Frage an den Einzelnen* (1936); *Über das Erzieherische* (1926); *Das Problem des Menschen* (Hebrew, 1943). All included in Martin Buber, *Werke,* vol. 1: *Schriften zur Philosophie* (1962) and in *Between Man and Man* [1937]).

3. *Urdistanz und Beziehung* (1950). Also in *Werke,* vol. 1 (also in this volume).

4. *Elemente des Zwischenmenschlichen* (1954). Also in *Werke,* vol. 1 (also in this volume).

everything been clarified sufficiently. Again and again readers have asked me what I might have meant here or there. For a long time I answered each individually, but gradually I saw that I could not do justice to these demands, and moreover I surely must not restrict the dialogical relationship to those readers who decide to speak up: perhaps some of those who remain silent deserve special consideration. Hence I resolved to answer publicly — first of all a few essential questions that are interrelated.

2

The first question might be formulated like this, with reasonable precision: The book speaks of our I-You relation not only to other men but also to beings and things that confront us in nature; what, then, constitutes the essential difference between the former and the latter? Or, still more precisely: if the I-You relation entails a reciprocity that embraces both the I and the You, how can the relationship to something in nature be understood in this fashion? Still more exactly: if we are to suppose that the beings and things in nature that we encounter as our You also grant us some sort of reciprocity, what is the character of this reciprocity, and what gives us the right to apply to it this basic concept?

Obviously, no sweeping answer can be given to this question. Instead of considering nature as a single whole, as we usually do, we must consider its different realms separately. Man once 'tamed' animals, and he is still capable of bringing off this strange feat. He draws animals into his own sphere and moves them to accept him, a stranger, in an elementary manner and to accede to his ways. He obtains from them an often astonishing active response to his approach, to his address — and on the whole this response is the stronger and more direct, the more his relation amounts to a genuine You-saying. Not infrequently animals, like children, see through feigned tenderness. But outside the tamed circle, too, we occasionally encounter a similar contact between men and animals: some men have deep down in their being a potential partnership with animals — most often persons who are by no means 'animalic' by nature but rather spiritual.

Animals are not twofold, like man: the twofoldness of the basic words I-You and I-It is alien to them although they can both turn toward another being and contemplate objects. We may say that in them twofoldness is latent. In the perspective of our You-saying to animals, we may call this sphere the threshold of mutuality.

It is altogether different with those realms of nature which lack the spontaneity that we share with animals. It is part of our concept of the plant that it cannot react to our actions upon it, that it cannot 'reply'. Yet this does not mean that we meet with no reciprocity at all in this sphere. We find here not the deed of posture of an individual being but a reciprocity of being itself — a reciprocity that has nothing except being. The living wholeness and unity of a tree that denies itself to the eye, no matter how keen, of anyone who merely investigates, while it is manifest to those who say You, is present when *they* are present: they grant the tree the opportunity to manifest it, and now the tree that has being manifests it. Our habits of thought make it difficult for us to see that in such cases something is awakened by our attitude and flashes toward us from that which has being. What matters in this sphere is that we should do justice with an open mind to the actuality that opens up before us. This huge sphere that reaches from the stones to the stars I should like to designate as the pre-threshold, meaning the step that comes before the threshold.

3

Now we come to the questions posed by that sphere which might be called, sticking to the same sort of image, the 'over-threshold' (*superliminare*), meaning the lintel that is above the door: the sphere of the spirit.

Here, too, we must separate two realms, but the distinction cuts deeper than that within nature. On the one side is the spirit that has already entered the world and now can be perceived in it by means of our senses; on the other, the spirit that has not yet entered the world but is ready to do so and now becomes present to us. This distinction is founded on the fact that I can show you, more or less, my reader, the spiritual forms that have already entered the world, but not the others. The spiritual forms that are "at hand" in our common world, no less than a thing or a natural being, I can point out to you as something actually or potentially accessible to you. But what has not yet entered the world I cannot point out to you. If I am asked here, too, in the case of this borderland, where one is supposed to find mutuality, I can only point indirectly to certain scarcely describable events in human life where spirit was encountered; and if this indirect procedure proves inadequate, nothing remains to me in the end but an appeal to the testimony of your own mysteries, my reader, which may be buried under debris but are presumably still accessible to you.

Let us now return to the first realm, to that which is 'at hand'. Here it is possible to adduce examples.

Let those who ask about this realm call to mind one of the traditional sayings of a master who died thousands of years ago. Let them try, as best they can, to receive this saying with their ears — as if the speaker had said it in their presence, addressing them. To this end they must turn with their whole being toward the speaker, who is not at hand, of the saying that is at hand. In other words, they must adopt toward the master who is dead and yet living that attitude which I call You-saying. If they succeed (and will and effort are not sufficient, but now and then it can be undertaken), they will hear a voice, perhaps none too clearly at first, that is identical with the voice that speaks to them through other genuine sayings of the same master. Now they will not be able any longer to do what they did as long as they treated the saying as an object: they will not be able to separate out content and rhythm; they receive nothing but the indivisible wholeness of something spoken.

But here we are still dealing with a person and the manifestation of a person in his words. What I have in mind, however, is not limited to the continued presence of some personal existence in words. Hence I must supplement this account by pointing to an example in which there is no longer anything personal. As always, I choose an example that is associated with strong memories at least for some people. Take the Doric column, wherever it appears to a man who is able and ready to turn toward it. It confronted me for the first time out of a church wall in Syracuse into which it had been incorporated: secret primal measure presenting itself in such a simple form that nothing individual could be seen or enjoyed in it. What had to be achieved was what I was able to achieve: to confront and endure this spiritual form there that had passed through the mind and hand of man and become incarnate. Does the concept of mutuality disappear here? It merely merges into the darkness behind it — or it changes into a concrete state of affairs, coldly rejecting concepthood, but bright and reliable.

From here we may also look across into that other realm where that which is 'not at hand' belongs, the contact with 'spiritual beings,' the *genesis* of word and form.

Spirit become word, spirit become form — whoever has been touched by the spirit and did not close himself off knows to some extent of the fundamental fact: neither germinates and grows in the human world without having been sown; both issue from encounters with the other. Encounters not with Platonic Ideas (of which I have no direct knowledge whatever and which I am incapable of understanding as having any being) but with the spirit that blows around us and inspires us. Again I am reminded of the strange confession of Nietzsche who circumscribed the process of inspiration by saying that one accepts without asking who gives. That may be so — one does not ask, but one gives thanks.

Those who know the spirit's breath commit a transgression if they wish to gain power over the spirit or to determine its nature. But they are also unfaithful if they ascribe this gift to themselves.

4

Let us consider once more what has here been said about encounters with what is natural and with what is spiritual.

The question may be asked at this point whether we have any right to speak of a 'reply' or 'address' that comes from outside the sphere to which in our consideration of the orders of being we ascribe spontaneity and consciousness as if they were like a reply or address in the human world in which we live. Is what has here been said valid except as a 'personalizing' metaphor? Are we not threatened by the dangers of a problematic 'mysticism' that blurs the borderlines that are drawn, and necessarily have to be drawn, by all rational knowledge?

The clear and firm structure of the I-You relationship, familiar to anyone with a candid heart and the courage to stake it, is not mystical. To understand it we must sometimes step out of our habits of thought, but not out of the primal norms that determine man's thoughts about what is actual. Both in the realm of nature and in the realm of spirit — the spirit that lives on in sayings and works and the spirit that strives to become sayings and works — what acts on us may be understood as the action of what has being.

5

The next question no longer concerns the threshold, pre-threshold, and over-threshold of mutuality, but mutuality itself as the gate of entry into our existence.

People ask: What about the I-You relationship between men? Is this always entirely reciprocal? Could it be, is it permitted to be? Is it not, like everything human, subject to the limitations of our inadequacy, and is it not limited further by the inner laws that govern our life with one another?

The first of these two obstacles is surely familiar enough. Everything, from your own experience of looking day after day into the eyes of your 'neighbor' who needs you after all but responds with the cold surprise of a stranger, to the melancholy of the holy men who repeatedly offered the great gift in vain — everything tells you that complete mutuality does not inhere in men's life with one another. It is a form of grace for which one must always be prepared but on which one can never count.

Yet there are also many I-You relationships that by their very nature may never unfold into complete mutuality if they are to remain faithful to their nature.

Elsewhere[5] I have characterized the relationship of a genuine educator to his pupil as being of this type. The teacher who wants to help the pupil to realize his best potentialities must intend him as this particular person, both in his potentiality and in his actuality. More precisely, he must know him not as a mere sum of qualities, aspirations, and inhibitions; he must apprehend him, and affirm him, as a whole. But this he can only do if he encounters him as a partner in a bipolar situation. And to give his influence unity and meaning, he must live through this situation in all its aspects not only from his own point of view but also from that of his partner. He must practice the kind of realization that I call embracing. It is essential that he should awaken the I-You relationship in the pupil, too, who should intend and affirm his educator as this particular person; and yet the educational relationship could not endure if the pupil also practiced the art of embracing by living through the shared situation from the educator's point of view. Whether the I-You relationship comes to an end or assumes the altogether different character of a friendship, it becomes clear that the specifically educational relationship is incompatible with complete mutuality.

Another, no less instructive example of the normative limits of mutuality may be found in the relationship between a genuine psychotherapist and his patient. If he is satisfied to 'analyze' his patient — that is, to bring to light unconscious factors from his microcosm and to apply to a conscious project the energies that have been transformed by this emergence — he may successfully accomplish some repairs. At best, he may help a diffuse soul that is poor in structure to achieve at least some concentration and order. But he cannot absolve his true task, which is the regeneration of a stunted personal center. That can be brought off only by a man who grasps with the profound eye of a physician the buried, latent unity of the suffering soul, which can be done only

5. *Über das Erzieherische:* see note 2 above.

if he enters as a partner into a person-to-person relationship, but never through the observation and investigation of an object. In order to promote coherently the liberation and actualization of this unity in a new situation in which the other person comes to terms with the world, the therapist, like the educator, must stand not only at his own pole of the bipolar relationship but also at the other pole, experiencing the effects of his own actions. Again the specific 'healing' relationship would end as soon as the patient decided to practice the art of embracing and actually succeeded in experiencing events also from the doctor's point of view. Healing, like educating, requires that one lives in confrontation and is yet removed.

The most striking example of the normative limits of mutuality could probably be found in the work of those charged with the spiritual well-being of their congregation: here any attempt at embracing from the other side would violate the consecrated authenticity of the mission.

Every I-You relationship in a situation defined by the attempt of one partner to act on the other one so as to accomplish some goal depends on a mutuality that is condemned never to become complete.

6

In this context only one more question can be discussed, but this has to be taken up because it is incomparably the most important of all.

How — people ask — can the eternal You be at the same time exclusive and inclusive? How is it possible for man's You-relationship to God, which requires our unconditional turning toward God, without any distraction, nevertheless to embrace all the other I-You relationships of this man and to bring them, as it were, to God?

Note that the question is not about God but only about our relationship to him. And yet in order to be able to answer, I have to speak of him. For our relationship to him is as supra-contradictory as it is because he is as supra-contradictory as he is.

Of course, we shall speak only of what God is in his relationship to a human being. And even that can be said only in a
paradox; or more precisely, by using a concept paradoxically; or
still more precisely, by means of a paradoxical combination of a
nominal concept with an adjective that contradicts the familiar
content of the concept. The insistence on this contradiction must
give way to the insight that thus, and only thus, the indispensable designation of this object by this concept can be justified.
The content of the concept undergoes a revolutionary transformation and expansion, but that is true of every concept that,
impelled by the actuality of faith, we take from the realm of
immanence and apply to transcendence.

The designation of God as a person is indispensable for all
who, like myself, do not mean a principle when they say 'God',
although mystics like Eckhart occasionally equate 'Being' with
him, and who, like myself, do not mean an idea when they say
'God', although philosophers like Plato could at times take him
for one — all who, like myself, mean by 'God' him that, whatever
else he may be in addition, enters into a direct relationship to us
human beings through creative, revelatory, and redemptive acts,
and thus makes it possible for us to enter into a direct relationship to him. This ground and meaning of our existence establishes each time a mutuality of the kind that can obtain only
between persons. The concept of personhood is, of course, utterly incapable of describing the nature of God; but it is permitted and necessary to say that God is *also* a person. If for once I
were to translate what I mean into the language of a philosopher,
Spinoza, I should have to say that of God's infinitely many attributes we human beings know not two, as Spinoza thought, but
three: in addition to spiritlikeness — the source of what we call
spirit — and naturelikeness, exemplified by what we know as nature, also thirdly the attribute of personlikeness. From this last
attribute I should then derive my own and all men's being persons, even as I should derive from the first two my own and all
men's being spirit and being nature. And only this third attribute,
personlikeness, could then be said to be known directly in its
quality as an attribute.

But now the contradiction appears, appealing to the familiar content of the concept of a person. A person, it says, is by definition an independent individual and yet also relativized by the plurality of other independent individuals; and this, of course, could not be said of God. This contradiction is met by the paradoxical designation of God as the absolute person, that is one that cannot be relativized. It is as the absolute person that God enters into the direct relationship to us. The contradiction must give way to this higher insight.

Now we may say that God carries his absoluteness into his relationship with man. Hence the man who turns toward him need not turn his back on any other I-You relationship: quite legitimately he brings them all to God and allows them to become transfigured 'in the countenance of God'.

One should beware altogether of understanding the conversation with God — the conversation of which I had to speak in this book and in almost all of my later books — as something that occurs merely apart from or above the everyday. God's address to man penetrates the events in all our lives and all the events in the world around us, everything biographical and everything historical, and turns it into instruction, into demands for you and me. Event upon event, situation upon situation is enabled and empowered by this personal language to call upon the human person to endure and decide. Often we think that there is nothing to be heard as if we had not long ago plugged wax into our own ears.

The existence of mutuality between God and man cannot be proved any more than the existence of God. Anyone who dares nevertheless to speak of it bears witness and invokes the witness of those whom he addresses — present or future witness.

Jerusalem
October 1957

Martin Buber

The Word That Is Spoken

2

Against the insight into the dialogical character of speech, it will probably be pointed out that thinking is essentially a man's speaking to himself. A reality is doubtless touched on here, but it is only touched on, not grasped. The so-called dialogue with one-self is possible only because of the basic fact of men's speaking with each other; it is the 'internalization' of this capacity. But he who does not shun the difficult task of reflecting on a past hour of his thinking — not according to its outcome, but fundamentally, according to its events, beginning with the beginning — may thrust inward to a primal level through which he can now wander without meeting a word. One notices that one has got hold of something without perceiving any conceptuality that wishes to come into being. In such a backward glance the second level allows itself to be seen more clearly, dominated by precisely this wishing to come into being. We may designate it as that of striving toward language. What is within strives over and over again toward becoming language, thought language, conceiving language. And only now in our work of memory do we enter into the true level of language. Here, indeed, language, even when still soundless, is already recognizably spoken. But does the thinker speak to himself as to the one thinking? In speaking the inner word he does not want to be heard by himself, for he knows it already as the person uttering it. Rather he wants to be heard by the nameless, unconceived, inconceivable other, by

Trans. by Maurice Friedman.

whom he wants to be understood in his having understood. The thinker is originally more solitary than the poet, but he is not more solitary in terms of his goal. Like the poet he is turned toward without turning himself. Certainly it is a court of his own through which he makes the competent examination of his world of concepts, but this world is not intended for this court, not dedicated to it. Many modern — and that means often de-Socratizing — philosophers have fallen, with the totality of their thought world, into a monologizing hubris, something which rarely happens to a poet. But this monologism, which, to be sure, is well acquainted with the existentialist but not with the existential, means in all its conjuring force the starkest menace of disintegration.

Every attempt to understand monologue as fully valid conversation, which leaves unclear whether it or dialogue is the more original, must run aground on the fact that the ontological basic presupposition of conversation is missing from it, the otherness, or more concretely, the moment of surprise. The human person is not in his own mind unpredictable to himself as he is to any one of his partners: therefore, he cannot be a genuine partner to himself, he can be no real questioner and no real answerer. He always 'already knows somewhere' the answer to the question, and not, to be sure, in the 'unconscious' of modern psychology, but rather in a sphere of conscious existence, a sphere which, although not present at the moment of the question, can in the very next moment flash up into presentness.

In philosophical discussions of language, speaking has occasionally been described as 'monadic through and through'. This interpretation may not validly appeal to Wilhelm von Humboldt's givenness of the Thou in the I; for Humboldt knew exactly through what process the fact of the Thou in the I is established: through the I becoming a Thou to another I. "From where else could the fundamental possibility of misunderstanding or being misunderstood originate?" asks the philosopher Hönigswald, mistakenly appealing to Humboldt in this connection. But what if precisely this possibility belongs essentially to speaking because language by its nature is a system of possible tensions — and thinking is just for this reason not a 'speaking with oneself' because it lacks the real tension? It is not true that a dialogue in which two speakers aim at an understanding of the meaning of an event must presuppose, as John Locke thought, an already existing understanding on the meaning of the words employed. When two friends discuss, say, the concept of thought, then the concept of the one and that of the other may be very similar in meaning; but we are not allowed to regard them as identical in meaning. This does not cease to be true even when the two of them begin by agreeing on a definition of the concept: the great fact of personal existence will penetrate even into the definition unless the two 'fellows in speech' join in betraying the logos for logical analysis. If the tension between what each means by the concept becomes too great, there arises a misunderstanding that can mount to destruction. But below the critical point the tension need by no means remain inoperative; it can become fruitful, it always becomes fruitful where, out of understanding each other, genuine dialogue unfolds.

From this it follows that it is not the unambiguity of a word but its ambiguity that constitutes living language. The ambiguity creates the problematic of speech, and it creates its overcoming in an understanding that is not an assimilation but a fruitfulness. The ambiguity of the word, which we may call its aura, must to some measure already have existed whenever men in their multiplicity met each other, expressing this multiplicity in order not to succumb to it. It is the communal nature of the logos as at once 'word' and 'meaning' which makes man man, and it is this which proclaims itself from of old in the communalizing of the spoken word that again and again comes into being.

I recall how about forty-five years ago, I received from an International Institute for Philosophy in Amsterdam, at whose head stood the mathematician Brouwer, the plan of an academy whose task it should be "to create words of spiritual value for the language of the western peoples," that is, words freed from ambiguity. I answered that in my judgment one should fight the misuse of the great old words rather than teach the use of new, manufactured ones. For in language, as in general, the *set* community kills the living. Certainly modern science has the great right to create for its purposes a medium of understanding that may be employed without remainder, but modern science knows that the word that is spoken can never arise in this way.

3

If, as we have seen, a monological primal character of language cannot be proved from the self-experience of thinking men, still less can it be discovered in the realm of phylogenesis. Certainly, it is an imperatively valid symbol when the Biblical narrative shows God as leaving to man the naming of the animals that He leads past him, but this happens to man as a being already standing in an adequate communication: it is through God's addressing man — Franz Rosenzweig's *Stern der Erlösung* teaches us — that He establishes man in speech. A precommunicative stage of language is unthinkable. Man did not exist before having a fellow being, before he lived over against him, toward him, and that means before he had dealings with him. Language never existed before address; it could become monologue only after dialogue broke off or broke down. The early speaker was not surrounded by objects on which he imposed names, nor did adventures befall him which he caught with names: the world and destiny became language for him only in partnership. Even when in a solitude beyond the range of call the hearerless word pressed on his throat, this word was connected with the primal possibility, that of being heard.

I will explain what I mean by an ethnological state of facts: by citing those remarkable word-compounds, adequately comprehensible to our thinking only as a residue of an early stage of language, which are preserved in the languages of many societies unrelated to one another — in particular those of the Eskimo and the Algonquin. In these so-called polysynthetic or holophrastic languages, the unit of speech with which one builds is not the word but the sentence. This is a structure that in its fully developed form exhibits components of three different kinds.[1] Two of

---

1. I follow here almost throughout the formulation of Edward Sapir, without being able to go along with his general basic view.

them, the so-called core element and the formal elements both the modal as well as the personal, can also emerge as independent. Not so the element of the third kind, which might be designated as preponderantly suffixes: they appear exclusively in their serving function, but it is they that properly make possible the form of the sentence.

It would, to be sure, be presumptuous to connect our ideas about the origin of language with an attempted reconstruction of the genesis of that particular form of the sentence, but at any rate one is reminded of J. G. Hamann's bold statement that at first the word probably "was neither a noun nor a verb but at the least a whole period." We do not find as decisive man confronting things that he undertakes to put into words and only in this way bringing them to their full status as things. As important as this act is, we still find as decisive men with one another who undertake to come to an understanding over situations. Not things but situations are primary. If Stefan George's saying that no thing exists for which the word is wanting may hold true for things, it is inapplicable to the situations that man is given to know before he comes to know the things. Out of different situations of different kinds that early man experiences emerge similar, so to speak similar-remaining, things and beings, events and states that want to be conceived as such, named as such.

In the early period, which we seek to disclose in this way, language presents itself to us above all as the manifestation and apprehension of an actual situation between two or more men who are bound together through a particular being-directed-to-each-other. This moment may, for example, be grounded in work in which the labor is shared, work in which the participants are often separated from each other, yet not so far that each is unable to hear clearly the articulated utterances of the other. If one man finds himself in a new, unforeseen situation, though not one unknown in its nature — for example, that of a threatening danger the like of which has already existed — then he calls to his comrade something that can be understood by the latter, but not by the members of an unfriendly neighboring clan that might be in the vicinity. What I speak of is in no way to be compared with a 'cry for help' or a 'signal', as they are known to us from the life of animals, the first as improvised, the second as an utterance returning in unchanged form under similar circumstances. We can derive it from neither of the two, for even the most un-differentiated word designating a primordial situation must, just as a word, already have brought to sound that sudden and dis-covering freedom, alien to the animal, in which one man turns to the other in order to lead him to take notice of something exist-ing or happening. Every genetic investigation which preserves its disinterestedness confirms for us the old insight which cannot be referred to often enough: that the mystery of the coming-to-be of language and that of the coming-to-be of man are one.

I have already drawn attention to the fact that the solitary category 'man' is to be understood as a working together of dis-tance and relation (see "Distance and Relation," 3–16). Unlike all other living beings, man stands over against a world from which he has been set at a distance, and, unlike all other living beings, he can again and again enter into relationship with it. This fundamental double stance nowhere manifests itself so com-prehensively as in language. Man — he alone — speaks, for only he can address the other just as the other being standing at a distance over against him; but in addressing it, he enters into relationship. The coming-to-be of language also means a new function of distance. For even the earliest speaking does not, like a cry or a signal, have its end in itself; it sets the word outside itself in being, and the word continues, it has continuance. And this continuance wins its life ever anew in true relation, in the spokenness of the word. Genuine dialogue witnesses to it, and poetry witnesses to it. For the poem is spokenness, spokenness to the Thou, wherever this partner might be.

But — so it may be asked — if this is so, if it is not a metaphor but a fact that the poem is a spokenness, then does that not necessarily mean that not merely the dialogue but also the poem can be regarded according to its content of truth? This question can only be answered with Yes and No at once. Every authentic poem is also true, but its truth stands outside all relation to an expressible What. We call poetry the not very frequently appearing verbal form that imparts to us a truth which cannot come to words in any other manner than just in this one, in the manner of this form. Therefore, every paraphrase of a poem robs it of its truth. I say, The poem speaks; one may also say: The poet speaks—if one does not mean by that the subject of a biography and the author of many works, but just the living speaker of this very poem. The speaker is as poet the speaker of a truth. Nietzsche's jest, "The poets lie too much," misses the depth of this truth, which is submerged in the mystery of the witnessing How. Also bound up with these facts is the problematic of the interpretation of poetry in so far as it seeks anything further than that the word-compound be more adequately perceived. The conceptuality that sets as its goal bringing a knowable What to clarity and value, diverts us from the genuine understanding of the poem and misses the truth borne by it.

But if the name of truth really belongs to both, the conceptual and the poetic, how can one lay hold of one truth that embraces both? For a first answer to this question about the two truths and the one, an ancient text which points to the primal phenomenon of language may help us.

A holy scripture of India, the Brahmana of the Hundred Paths, relates that the gods and the demons both sprang from the self-sacrifice of the primal creator and entered into his heritage. Then it says:

> The heritage, that was the word: truth and falsehood, at once truth and falsehood. Now this and that one spoke the truth, this and that one spoke the falsehood. Since they spoke the same, they were like one another. But now the gods rejected the falsehood and accepted the truth alone; but now the demons rejected the truth and accepted the falsehood alone. Then that truth that was with the demons pondered: "Well, the gods have rejected the falsehood and have accepted the truth alone. So I shall go thither." And it came to the gods. But that falsehood that was with the gods pondered: "Well, the demons have rejected the truth and have accepted the falsehood alone. So I shall go thither." And it went to the demons. Now the gods spoke the

whole truth, the demons spoke the whole falsehood. Since the gods spoke only the truth, they became weaker and poorer, therefore, whoever speaks only the truth always becomes weaker and poorer. But in the end he endures, and in the end the gods endured. And the demons, who only spoke the falsehood, grew and thrived; therefore, whoever speaks only the falsehood grows and thrives. But in the end he cannot endure, and the demons could not endure.

It is worth noticing how here the fate of being is determined through the speaking of the word, and, indeed, through the speaking of the true and of the false word. But what can 'true' and 'false' mean to us when we transpose the myth into our human reality? Clearly not something that can be grasped only through the relation to a reality existing outside the speaking. The myth knows only the totality of the one, still undivided sphere. When we shift from the myth into our world, therefore, we can turn toward no other sphere commensurate with that one. 'One speaks the truth' may, accordingly, be paraphrased by: 'One says what he means.' But what meaning does 'mean' have here? In our world and in our language this obviously signifies that just as the speaker, because he is who he is, means what he means, so also because he is who he is, he says what he means. The relation between meaning and saying points us to the relation between the intended unity of meaning and saying, on the one side, and that between meaning and saying and the personal existence itself, on the other side.

In this myth an especially strong accent falls on the establishment of the fact that expressed in our language — the truth, chemically purified, as it were, of its content of falsehood, is ineffectual in the course of history. Everything depends here on interpreting correctly the words, 'But in the end he endures'. This is no expression of an optimistic view of history, nor is it an eschatological saying. 'In the end' means for us: in the pure reckoning of the personal existence. In the language of religion it is expressed thus: 'When the books are opened'; that is not there and then, however, but here and now.

The truth that is concerned in this fashion is not the sublime 'unconcealment' suitable to Being itself, the *aletheia* of the Greeks; it is the simple conception of truth of the Hebrew Bible, whose *etymon* means 'faithfulness', the faithfulness of man or the faithfulness of God. The truth of the word that is genuinely spoken is, in its highest forms — in poetry and incomparably still more so in that messagelike saying that descends out of the stillness over a disintegrating human world — indivisible unity. It is a manifestation without a concomitant diversity of aspects. In all its other forms, however, three different elements must be distinguished in it. It is, in the first place, faithful truth in relation to the reality which was once perceived and is now expressed, to which it opens wide the window of language in order that it may become directly perceptible to the hearer. It is, second, faithful truth in relation to the person addressed, whom the speaker means as such, no matter whether he bears a name or is anonymous, is familiar or alien. And to mean a man means nothing less than to stand by him and his insight with the elements of the soul that can be sent forth, with the 'outer soul', even though at the same time one fundamentally remains and must remain with oneself. Third, it is the truth of the word that is genuinely spoken, faithful truth in relation to its speaker, that is, to his factual existence in all its hidden structure. The human truth of which I speak — the truth vouchsafed men — is no pneuma that pours itself out from above on a band of men now become super-personal: it opens itself to one just in one's existence as a person. This concrete person, in the life-space allotted to him, answers with his faithfulness for the word that is spoken by him.

Letters

Correspondence with Hans Trüb

1. Martin Buber to Hans Trüb[1]

Heppenheim
18 October 1923

Sehr geehrter Herr,

After reading your letter I think that I can imagine more or less accurately what you expect for your circle.[2] Only I am not quite clear about the question, whether a scientific or a more immediate formulation of the theme is more desirable. In the first case I would call the lecture "Psychology and Ontology" or such, otherwise "On the Psychologizing of the World." Please let me know which one you prefer. I agree to the date you have suggested.

2. Martin Buber to Hans Trüb

Heppenheim
14 August 1925

Lieber Dr. Trüb,

Your good words gladdened my heart. I too like to remember Amersfoort[3] like a young tree which one can trust. I want to add

1. Hans Trüb (1889–1949), psychoanalyst and psychotherapist from C. G. Jung's school, a close friend of Buber since the middle 1920s. Under Buber's influence, he increasingly detached himself from Jung and developed an independent psychotherapeutic method. His last work, *Healing Through Meeting*, was published posthumously in 1951, with a preface by Buber.
2. Refers to the lecture Buber was planning to give, "On the Psychologizing of the World" at the Psychology Club in Zürich on 1 Dec. 1923.
3. Between 20 and 25 July 1925, Buber gave a course of lectures in Amersfoort on "Faith in Rebirth."

161

today only that I shall be presumably for a few hours in Zürich in the first week of September; it is not yet completely certain. I shall let you know.

I could speak only shortly to the Jungs[4] in Heidelberg. There was a conference atmosphere[5] that I could only overcome during the discussion at my lecture.

3. Hans Trüb to Martin Buber

Zürich
3 February 1926

Lieber, verehrter Freund,

. . . Since Gandria[6] I had a surprising amount of work in my practice. Indeed, every week a new case was added, which is quite enough in our kind of work. When I look back on this period of time, I notice how since Gandria, I must always and constantly heed the one and only question which you put to me. When I told you about this particular case you asked me at the end, if the female patient did in fact try to avoid "responsibility." This word, spoken at that moment by you has not let me rest since then. Indeed, so many other expressions and passages from your books come often into my mind and help me here and there. But with the word "responsibility" it was quite different at that moment. Somehow it was quite central. Through it and my daily personal experience with it, I can today recall the thought of "Amersfoort" completely. When one is aware of the depth of meaning of this word, e.g. when one tries every moment, in

4. Carl Gustav Jung (1875–1961), Swiss psychologist, psychiatrist, and professor in Zürich, then living exclusively as a physician and a researcher. He was originally a disciple and collaborator of Sigmund Freud, from whom he distanced himself increasingly and developed his own "analytical (complex) psychology."

5. The Third International Conference on Education in Heidelberg. Buber gave the main lecture, "Über das Erzieherische" (On education).

6. Buber and Trüb met in Gandria on Lake Lugano in the first week of October 1925, according to a card of Buber from 6 Sept. 1925.

which one feels the inevitability of one's existence, to be aware of one's meaning, then one reaches necessarily the central formulation of the question as you expounded it at the close of your lecture in Holland. "Are you ready with your whole being to persevere in your vocation? Are you ready, with nothing else but your own person, with your 'here I am' to justify your existence?" You won't believe how great is this given aim and your help for me in my daily work. Surely, I have always instinctively groped in this direction. But your many hints have illuminated long stretches of the way which I have chosen and they were of invaluable help to me.

Have I ever told you how I tried already five or six years ago to free myself from the established psychological in-content-based analysis of the patient? I had no other possibility. I discovered one day the ultimate meaning of the a priori reality of relationship. I don't have to create it myself, i.e. we only have to become aware of it. It lies in the dark. I saw it as a way which (because of its unknown darkness) is binding us together while lying between us. It is illuminated through the event of the encounter. I imagined this event as being something "not psychological," i.e. not something "inside" the human being. It is something between us. *Therefore*, I kept away from the systematic psychological analysis *on* the patient and conducted the treatment giving the patient the analysis of my "own experience with him." Which means I let him go as an object and used myself, i.e. "my experience with him" as object of the examination. I said to myself: The point is to travel the way which lies between us. The obstacles from here and from there are the same, the distance is the same from me to him, as from him to me. If I want to remove his difficulties with him, then I can recognize them from what *I* myself experience with him, when I acknowledge my experience honestly and unreservedly. I always added to my confession the question: "and how does it appear to you?" I gave it the name "analysis of relationship"; about four years ago I gave a few short lectures about it in the Club. Thus it started to become clear to me that we should not start from the "other" but from our own person, that the subject of our consideration should not be the "other" but the reality of the relationship. I felt psychological considerations more and more as something "penultimate," as something which we only take seriously in order to be able to "let it go."

Every day I must perform a kind of translation from the material I received through you, across into the daily experience and then back, which is no easy task because every moment I feel how great a responsibility I carry. I cannot rest until I have verified everything that I heard and received from you first and foremost. These are not perceptions taken up, gathered and classified from a higher standpoint and spread out over reality, as I have so often encountered in books and with people. I acknowledge your work as a true and honest report of that which your good and loyal eyes [see], on which you rely with complete confidence even in the most startling moment. Your gaze is unforgettable to me. It is penetrating but in no way offensive, strict, unrelenting and nevertheless of unflinching goodness! . . .

4. Martin Buber to Hans Trüb

Heppenheim,
2 October 1928

Lieber Hans,

The difficulty seems to me to be, first and foremost that you are too much concerned with the composition, and the uniform context.[7] Do proceed — without consideration of this — to draw the "images of the situation," and you will, when you are finished with it, have gathered all the significant material together; then you will miss only the putting in order and the interpretation which is still somewhat weird for you. The best way to put things in the right order is that, in the sequence of the images, the experience of the limits becomes ever more explicit, more

---

7. Hans Trüb had had difficulties with an essay that he wanted to write for the periodical *Die Kreatur* about his experiences with his patients. Compare *Die Kreatur* 3: Hans Trüb, a "A Scene in the Doctor's Consulting Room," page 53ff., and "From a Corner of My Consulting Room," page 403ff.

serious, more instructive, so that the reader, by absorbing the reported events, already takes the proper path of cognition step by step. If such an arrangement is successful then little more discussion is necessary, since the genuine reader himself contributes the interpretation; what is only needed then are the introductory explanation of the problem, the connecting text which is necessary for the understanding of the various situational problems, and a short final observation. So you can confidently do your own thing, just from your close point of view, just to do justice to the brief span of the moment, not to write 'about' but what is 'there', yes — even from the 'inside', and don't be shy once and again to testify to the actuality what happened to your 'patient' and to you the 'agent', together. . . .

5. Hans Trüb to Martin Buber

Zürich,
5 October 1928

Lieber Martin,

. . . I don't want to say everything. I must concentrate on that which is really near to my heart, which needs me, which I can here and now free from its ties. Only now am I able to comprehend the meaning of your words, that you gave me then in Heppenheim, when I confided this difficulty of mine to you. You said: take your thoughts like your patients. Take them to you in their lack of salvation. They need you to become free. Take them like beings, like humans.

I must and want to be satisfied to acknowledge the one scene I depicted, and will try to work out what it wants to tell me with its paradoxical content. I think you also will recognize this scene as one belonging to the 'essential' of the sickness report. It is the threshold I am standing on. Behind us the old day, in front of us the new day and in between — the here and now — the night, the present. I and the Other. I and the creature. I and the soul which has been entrusted to me. Not voluntarily but reluctantly, I let it fall into His hand. From now on is this the soul in which I will be able to confide? Will it be the one that can take my part? Did not always all the help that I extended to it point to this threshold where this soul — beyond failure — will instead of me step in and act? It, which recognizes the call that reaches its ear. It, that knows the way to the Father, the way of being His child?

I feel driven to pose these questions, to give account to myself. But I will make an effort to stay close to the fact that this scene took place in the doctor's consulting room, that on no account I vanish altogether. . . .

I thank you from the bottom of my heart for your good letter. You support me in daring to cross a threshold, in front of which I would still stand thinking that only others may cross it. Certainly, to do this still appears to me even today as fraught with consequences. I am still trembling and advancing with groping feet. Yet perhaps also this is part of it. Be thanked for your help! . . .

6. Martin Buber to Hans Trüb

Heppenheim
30 September 1935

Lieber Hans,

'Individuation' is in my opinion to begin with a wrong term:[8] we *begin as* individuals and we become *persons*. The principle of individuation is known in philosophy, since it exists, namely as the reason for the existence of the plurality of individuals, each of whom is single and unique: already Anaximander[9] saw the metaphysical problem which is posed here, because he saw individuation as guilt — toward undivided One — and death as repentance. This individuation is, of course, not an anthropological but a cosmological principle. Jung's opinion is different, namely the personation, the becoming a person. This also is a very old problem. In our time it was dealt with most significantly by Kier-

8. Trüb had asked Buber what meaning the principle of individuation has for him.

9. Anaximander von Milet (ca. 610–540 B.C.), Ionic philosopher of nature and pupil of Thales. His literary work "About Nature" is only preserved in fragments. It was the first philosophical work of the Greeks.

kegaard[10] mainly as a problem of *existence*. For Jung it is a problem of *psychological development*; he does not deal at all with the dimension of existence, it is as if instead of a body its projection onto a screen becomes a thing. Concerning myself, as you know, for a long time already I do not concern myself much with psychological projection, only with existential corporeality. Actually, I talk about it all the time, without saying that I am talking about personation or such like. One should not talk about it expressis verbis — as Kierkegaard already knew — better not to talk, because in reality it is not a subject, but only the veiled premise of the subject. Besides, already in the fifth Daniel-dialogue you can find something about this, although in a still unfinished way.

7. Martin Buber to Hans Trüb
(Archive No. 138)

Heppenheim
7 June 1936

Lieber Hans,

. . . What you report to me about your lecture and what you sent me made me very glad for you. At the same time the whole thing makes me think; Jung's answer (is this an answer?) opened for me a new and big problem. The relation between analysis and synthesis is *after all* a different one. But this should still be discussed thoroughly another time. . . .

8. Martin Buber to Hans Trüb

Heppenheim
13 June 1936

Lieber Hans,

The sentence about analysis and synthesis in my letter did not refer to your own thoughts about this but to the problem of the

10. Sören Kierkegaard (1813–55) Danish author and philosopher of religion. He had a profound influence on the dialectic theology and the existential philosophy of our century.

balance between the two. It appears to me that these two are just not quite on the same level. Every synthetic act is a *factual* process against the demand of analysis, it states the right of reality against that of its symbolic substitute, and that claim is after all the higher one — reality must grant space to symbolicalness and not the other way around. Synthesis represents the whole, analysis the inroad. The first represents being and the other its becoming questionable.

I am *very* much in favor of publication.[11] will do the notes as soon as possible.

9. Hans Trüb to Martin Buber

Zürich
17 June 1936

Lieber Martin,

I am very happy about your detailed explanation concerning analysis and synthesis. Has not the analytical quite an analogous position to that of the state = status? The way you once talked about it? The analytical advances as much as the synthetical recedes and "grants it space." Yet I ask you: How far is this "granting space" conscious? Does the synthetical become conscious of itself as being the positive — only through the advance of the analytical which is its negative? — I have sent Jung and Pannwitz each a copy of my "corrected copy." Pannwitz replied to me: "If Jung, Buber and I make notes — I, of course, will do it — then you yourself will have the opportunity to remain standing upright. At least something very uniquely interesting is developing! Hopefully not each of the three will take away another piece of you! But seriously: I believe that this way it will be best!" — Does Pannwitz think the notes will also be published? Would that perhaps be desirable? What do you think?

---

11. Hans Trüb, "Psychosynthese als seelischgeistiger Heilungsprozess" (Psychosynthesis as psychic-mental process of healing) (Zürich/Leipzig, 1936).

10. Martin Buber to Hans Trüb

Heppenheim
25 June 1936

Lieber Hans,

Only now do I arrive at answering your letter of the seventeenth.

Your comparison of the analytical to the "state" is very fitting. The question about the synthetical becoming conscious is a rather delicate one. All becoming conscious is split into two, dangerous, and can be turned toward salvation only out of the depth of responsibility; nevertheless, the road has to lead through this crisis. In fact, the synthetical becomes conscious of itself only through the pressing forward of its counterpart, but just because of this it has to happen.

I cannot make the notes before the vacation — but if you are in a hurry, I shall undertake it nevertheless: I am just now loaded down with work. The easiest would be if I could learn from Jung's and Pannwitz's notes if you already have them. I do not think that publication of the notes is advisable; mine certainly will not be suitable for it. . . .

11. Martin Buber to Hans Trüb

Heppenheim
31 October 1936

Lieber Hans,

. . . Which kind of setback in your practice has this been? Can you say something about it? Perhaps I could give you a "hint": I know something, of course in other areas, about the possible uses of setbacks.

My "annoyance"[12] still continues, but there is some hope for a speedy solution.

The problem that I mean for my book, is the relation between

12. The Nazi authorities had taken away Buber's passport.

special world and common world, for instance for the schizophrenic, the double line of consciousness etc. I suppose that the
best is still in Bleuler[13]; yet it does not satisfy me. . . .

12. Hans Trüb to Martin Buber

Zürich
3 November 1936

Lieber Martin,

I want to try and tell you something about the "setback in my
practice." First a general observation: maybe it was always like
that, in any case I notice for some years that the work in my
practice is growing by leaps and bounds; I am able to cope with
the fullness of the task before me for some time, until it is suddenly falling apart and lies about in pieces. It is a desperate business. In a fresh starting situation I attract people, they come
from near and far, and at once my weekly schedule is full and
there is much to listen to, to answer and much to do. At the start
I am wholly focused on myself and therefore unintentionally
oblige the other to find himself. Then everything falls into place
and much help is being given and I can be whole-heartedly
happy with the objective result of my efforts.

I am sure that this falling to pieces is not only the result of
fatigue. I want to tell you straightforward where I suspect the
trouble lies, and it is surely right that I turn to you in this difficulty; because I know that you overcame this difficulty in your
own way of work and life in a creative manner and can undoubtedly give me a hint. I see only now where I want to give you an
account of myself, my situation is crystal clear: the kind of effort
and my attitude during work with the patient is completely correct. Nothing is missing. On the contrary: in my actual performance and doing I am far in advance of myself, e.g. my intellectual
grasp. In my daily meetings with the sufferers, small miracles of

---

13. Eugen Bleuler (1857–1939), psychiatrist and professor of psychiatry at
the University of Zürich. He is the author of *Lehrbuch der Psychiatrie* (Textbook
of psychiatry) (Berlin, 1916).

real recognition, real determination, repentence and probation occur, and it is just this abundance of positive events, which then
leads to my downfall.

At times I suffocate on the growing abundance of positive experience. Day in and day out I am part of the secrecy of the
exclusive meeting with the individual other, a blood witness to
the renewal that occurred, and as an individual who has experienced this with many, I suddenly experience the "setback." I cannot want to keep to myself that mass of experience that is
bursting to be known and that in its significance much surpasses
the tolerance of the single person. It eventually chokes me and
then comes the change in the internal power balance. Suddenly I
become powerless and all the events I lived through do not make
sense anymore, and this lasts a long time. In fact, during this
period I do not actually experience *anything anymore,* because I
am completely shut off and excluded.

I presume that my skin disease is the result of this complica-
tion. I have called it the "tunnel disease." I think that people who
all the time work "underground" are more liable to get this illness — oversensitivity to sun and light. I see my way of life for
the last twelve years: I have, under great renunciation of the
spiritual general context, reached the lonely and hidden place of
the isolated person — hoping for the best, if I ever find my way
back — and now that I really can communicate with the single,
isolated individual, I don't find my way back. I am afraid of
indiscretion. I avoid the light of day and am frightened of my
own word, which wants to break out from the 'exclusive two-
some' into the big space of the general world (by the way, this is
connected with my [being] hard of hearing, which is only functional, as my ear doctor told me — I necessarily must make myself deaf against the word of my own innermost depth, because it
threatens to burst out into the big space).

This is my sore spot. Only slowly can I again get used to the
light and move carefully forward with voice and ear. I know very
well that the echo is there, but I must take my being frightened
of it seriously in order not to lose the "proper proportions"

In other words: I know now that it is in the interest of my

work, performed in quietude, and even the patients too, that I now find the way and form of generally understood communication. What goes on in the discreet meetings in the consulting room wants eventually to also verify itself and to prove itself in the eyes of this world. I have been caught and made to keep silent by the 'special world of the many'. But now I see that I really should — for the sake of those many — unlock my own special world toward the common world or let it be disclosed as the common world. Here also purely technical questions become acute. How to divide the day to create a rhythm? How do I learn to switch over, lead over: from the special experience and communication to the general comprehension. I now must almost protect myself from too many positive things happening, which I then may neglect until it affects *me*. I must learn to absorb and shape it daily, otherwise it will follow me and eventually hit me on the head for my being blind and deaf. So I gladly take you as my model in a concrete and everyday manner: I must first work to get rid of what has accumulated so that I don't get under it and suffocate — with the excuse that I am overtired. Well, now you have a point of reference and I am already now grateful to you for your penetrating questions and consequently also for each word that gives me "a hint." . . .

13. Martin Buber to Hans Trüb

Heppenheim
7 November 1936

Lieber Hans,

You write: ". . . as a Single One who has so much experience with the Many . . .". I emphasize "the Many." Somebody like you who has (on a daily basis putting your person on the line) to deal with many, must, if it is impossible to draw them together into a uniform world (and in this case this cannot be done), objectify each single one — without regard to all subjective ties — in order not to become "buried." As examples of such technical objectifying I mention: the opening of a file for each single person, the writing down of all details, separating the materials; but within each file a division into two: material and interpretation, and in the interpretation writing down continuously each new insight. This sounds badly technical, but it means simply an orderly spiritual and work world. Of course you keep an account on everybody; but I assume that something is wrong and that because of that the soul is being overtaxed, because it has to deliver something for which it is not needed at all. First I have given you just a proven home-remedy; further treatment will follow after information about the situation. . . .

14. Martin Buber to Hans Trüb

Jerusalem
4 August 1946

Dear Hans,

Your letter of 28 July arrived surprisingly fast, almost "normally", and despite the news about your illness — may it promptly become but a constructive memory! — it gratified me. What you write about your breakthrough regarding expression was particularly valuable to me. The fundamentally important thing for you now is to stand up to the expectable whisperings of the evil spirit Undone and of course also to the real, also expectable difficulties. Your practice will benefit even more from the experience of holding out than from the substance derived from intellectual work.

In recent times, I have moved even closer to the problems that occupy me. As I have already indicated, it is a matter of the relationship between the 'cosmic' material world with which we are so familiar and the 'chaotic' world that is experienced in dreams, intoxication, and psychosis. Note that this is not a question of experiencing, but one, as momentous as it is uncanny, of existence itself. Thus, everything psychological can be only an aid here, albeit an indispensable one. I need it far more for this second and apparently last part of my philosophy than I needed it for the first part.[14]

---

14. This second part of Buber's view of psychology was never completed.

In the meantime, I have established contact with Binswanger[15] and received some information as well as an essay from him. Since I would like to complete the book for all practical purposes by the end of the winter, I ask you to send me your notes on the subject as soon as possible — just as they are; I shall make sense of them. I am certain that you have a specific understanding of the basic problem — the breakdown of cosmic security in the literal sense of the term. . . .

P. S. A younger philosopher living here has written an interesting work about Jung and myself. I shall send you the German manuscript soon.[16]

15. Martin Buber to Hans Trüb

Jerusalem
27 August 1946

Lieber Hans,

Your letter of the nineteenth which contains the crucial questions, makes me strongly aware that in such cases written advice can only be a substitute for spoken advice. But I want in this way to do my best to facilitate clarification for you, since it is vital for me, that you will find the simple major outlines of this matter.

. . . 'World' is evidently *first of all* that which the soul 'stubs' itself against. For the infant 'world' is not the mother's breast

---

In it, he planned to develop his thoughts on the borderline states of the human soul, which he frequently discussed in his correspondence with Trüb. Only "Guilt and Guilt Feelings," the subject of his lectures at the Washington, D.C., School of Psychiatry in 1957, was published, in Buber, *Knowledge of Man: A Philosophy of the Interhuman,* ed. and trans. Maurice Friedman and Ronald Gregor Smith (New York: Harper & Row, 1965), 121–46.

15. Ludwig Binswanger; see correspondence with Binswanger.

16. Arië Sborowitz, "Beziehung und Bestimmung. Die Lehren von Martin Buber und C. G. Jung in ihrem Verhältnis zueinander" (Relation and intention: The teachings of Martin Buber and C. G. Jung and their mental relation) (Darmstadt, 1955). Erstdruck in: Psyche. Eine Zeitschrift für Tiefenpsychologie und Menschenkunde in Forschung und Praxis, Bd.II, Heidelberg 1948, S.9 ff.

that belongs to him, but the edge of the table that causes him
pain. 'World' is first of all, i.e. from a man's 'starting point' that
which is so emphatically documented as 'different from me', that
which I cannot enclose into my soul, cannot 'include'. Perception
of world *as world* occurs again and again through adversity,
through resistance, through contradiction, through 'absurdity' —
which must be overcome before it can come to an understanding
or even to a friendship, or to a love relationship with the world.
Before the world becomes actual to me as not-mine, it cannot
become mine. This fact, that the world 'is not mine but can 'become' mine (of course, not automatically so, but only now and
then in genuine encounters), and that even then, when in this
way the world becomes mine, it is not mine as in-me but mine as
with-me; this fact, has — like some other modern concepts — also
been obscured through the concept of the 'unconscious'. As an
auxiliary psychological concept — that must always be treated
with caution and reservation, must always be confronted with
reality, must be understood constantly as dynamic and not as
static, as a process and not as an existence — as such the unconscious should be accepted; yet it pretends to be much much
more, it aims to conceal the possibility of the 'life of the soul with
the world', hence the appearance at each time of a world that
is mine-with-me, through the fiction of the 'world within the
soul' — hence through a world that is mine-in-me.

I cannot advise you to use theological terms in your work.
'Inhabiting' (more correct than 'inhabiting glory')[17] presumes an
inhabitant or at least something inhabiting in the sense of: taking
up residence. But with this you would open the door to objections which can be avoided. In a basic *psychological* work, theological terms should only be used marginally, to some extent as a
last regard into a sphere which is no more psychologically determined; but a psychotherapeutic work is necessarily a psychological one *in this sense*. In such a work one can speak only of the
existential secret or of the substantial secret, i.e. of the secret as
not being a function of our way of perception (so that it would

17. The Schechina (God's presence).

be less secret to a more complete perception), but as a secret in itself, according to its nature (so that — in a way — it would remain an undiminished secret also for the most complete understanding that comes from outside itself). Facing this secret apperception is impossible, but contact with it, meeting with it, communication with it are possible, and just in that way the life of the soul with the world establishes itself. The way all this becomes possible to us, this then may be called the inborn Thou. So far as a beginning. Write to me as precisely as possible, about what you would wish to have more exact information. Unfortunately, I have sent pages 1–13 back already. I leave it entirely to you what more you want to send; but you should know that here there are for you two ears (represented more or less through the reading eyes) and a mouth (poorly represented through the writing hand).[18]

P.S. I presume that the work of Sborowitz, which you probably received in the meantime, is of use to you, although in my opinion it inclines too much to the side of Jung: it avoids the real problems.

16. Martin Buber to Hans Trüb

Jerusalem
9 September 1946

Lieber Hans,

. . . I hope I shall be able to write to you soon in detail; but I want to say to you already today something more in regard to your work. Have you read the book of Jung and Kerenyi *Introduction into the Nature of Mythology* [Einführung in das Wesen der Mythologie]?[19] The unbiased reader can learn a lot from it. Pre-

18. In the introduction to his book *Vom Selbst zur Welt. Der zweifache Auftrag des Psychotherapeuten* (From the Self to the world. The two-fold mission of the psychotherapist) (Zürich, 1947), Trüb dealt with the relation of man to the world, and he had asked for Buber's opinion.
19. First edition, Amsterdam/Leipzig, 1941.

sumably the two authors are concerned with the same thing but from different aspects; but in truth myths are for K. something which emerge from the contact with the reality of the world, as unlocking and imaging of secrets of this world-reality, whereas J. understands the myth as something which is created in a seemingly parthenogenetic way within the soul and ultimately can say nothing, can mean nothing more than just principles and mysteries of the soul itself. J.'s view means — at least practically — the immanence of the soul. More about this another time. Incidentally have you received Sborowitz's essay and what do you think about it?[20]

17. Hans Trüb to Martin Buber

Zürich
10 October 1948

Lieber Martin,
. . . About a week ago I sent to Sborowitz my first two chapters by airmail. I hope that they have arrived safely. I asked that should this be possible, he bring them to you for reading soon. . . . I am very eager to know what you two have to say about what I have elaborated so far. It certainly will help me to advance some more. Now I labor on the last, the 'casuistic' chapter: Anthropological Psychotherapy. After long efforts I found a good start. In the framework of this study 'casuistics' cannot be dealt with thoroughly. This would lead too far. I can only make a start by describing small characteristic situations in order to illustrate thus the fundamental shift in psychotherapy. Incidentally I would like to give this little book[21] the title "Psychotherapy at the Turning?" What do you think?

20. See note 16, this chapter.
21. This book was published only in 1951, after Trüb's death; it was edited by Ernst Michel and Arië Sborowitz, with an introduction by Buber with the title "Heilung aus der Begegnung" (Healing through meeting). This also became the title of Trüb's book.

18. Hans Trüb to Martin Buber

Zürich
2 October 1949

Lieber Martin,

Do receive my heartfelt thanks for your good, beautiful birthday letter that made me extremely happy. This year has brought me much good, amongst which I count the visit of Arië Sborowitz who came to my spiritual aid by his deep interest in my intellectual attempts at giving shape. He is a dear person and as such I became rather fond of him. Since he has left I am at work uninterruptedly as never before. I have reworked all previous material for a last time, and after I had titled the chapters, transfers and additions became necessary according to these titles. Sbor. will explain to you everything eventually. Now I start the completion of the last concluding part and hope to finish it about the end of October or November. . . . You will hear from me again as soon as I am done working on the book.[22]

22. On 8 Oct. 1949 Hans Trüb died unexpectedly of a heart attack.

Correspondence with
Hermann Menachem Gerson,
Ronald Gregor Smith,
Rudolf Pannwitz, and Ernst Michel

19. Martin Buber to Hermann Menachem Gerson[1]

Engadin
30 August 1928

Dear Mr. Gerson,

I cannot write any letters at the moment, and therefore only tell you in the meantime, that in cases like the one mentioned by you, it is important to force upon the ratio of the experience of its own unchangeable limits with rational methods — more than that is neither necessary nor possible here. I hope soon to find some time to answer Freud's paper.[2] I intended to do it for quite a while but have not had the time yet.

1. Hermann Menachem Gerson (1908–84), youth leader, educator, and writer. He studied simultaneously at the Academy for Jewish Studies and at the University of Berlin. Together with a group from the German Jewish youth club Kameraden, he founded the Zionist youth movement Werkleute. Gerson emigrated to Palestine with Werkleute in 1934 and founded the kibbutz Hazorea, which in 1938 joined the Marxist Hashomer Hatzair movement. For Gerson, who had had close personal contact with Buber since late 1926, this meant turning away from Buber's religious socialism and dialogical principle, and led to a personal estrangement for a time. In later years, Gerson was active in the teacher-training program of the kibbutz movement and directed its research institute.

2. Buber did not do so at this time. In a previous letter, Gerson had discussed Freud's paper, "Zukunft einer Illusion" (The future of an illusion) (Vienna, 1927).

179

20. Martin Buber to Hermann Menachem Gerson

Heppenheim
23 April 1937

Lieber Hermann Gerson,

Naturally, I am not "against analysis as a therapeutic means"[3] —
that would not make sense! But, for instance, what matters is the
question that in diseases of the 'soul' the concept of therapy itself
becomes ambiguous and problematic and needs clarification.
When X instead of his 'heart-of-flesh'[4] which pained and tor-
mented him terribly (and this means admonished and goaded
him, etc.) would receive a reliable clockwork which would not
hurt him at all, would he be 'cured'?

My dear, let us make room for all critical questions on all subjects,
then it's all right with me. But also make room for critique of the
critic. There is nothing more dogmatic than the critic who acts dogmatically. And some (not all) psychoanalysis is doing this already,
treating the psyche like a 'spatiality' (Raumding).[5] Yet I am particularly concerned with criticism of concepts and premises in use.

21. Martin Buber to Ronald Gregor Smith[6]

Heppenheim
28 December 1936

Dear Mr. Smith,

. . . Some applications to psychological problems may be
found in two works by Hans Trüb, "Individuation, Guilt, and

3. From a discussion with Gerson about the significance of psychoanalysis.
4. Allusion to Ezekiel (Jecheskel) 11:19; 36:26 as contradiction to "Stein-
herz" (heart of stone).
5. Greek: dissolve.
6. Ronald Gregor Smith (1913–68), professor of theology at Glasgow, Scotland, contributor to various theological and philosophical journals. Smith was
the first English translator of *I and Thou* (1937) and, after World War II, of
several other works by Buber. Smith had asked Buber for bibliographical information on the impact of the *I and Thou* on philosophy in general, on Protestant theology in particular, and also on its applications to psychological
problems. This letter is Buber's answer to that last request.

Decision: On the Boundaries of Psychology"[7] (in the Festschrift for C. G. Jung that appeared in 1935 under the title *The Cultural Significance of Analytical Psychology*)[8] and *Psychosynthesis* [1936][9]

22. Martin Buber to Rudolf Pannwitz[10]

Heppenheim
1 January 1937

Dear Friend,

. . . I will start the year with this letter. . . . You are surely right in what you say about Trüb,[11] but he now seems to be overcoming his dependence on Jung after all. What seems to me the important thing about him, which always goes beyond the defects of his conceptualization, is the fact that, as far as his life is concerned, he had already achieved more than he promises after the fact. This places an aura around the idea that is in itself inadequate. Your review[12] is revealing . . .

7. "Individuation, Schuld und Entscheidung:Über die Grenzen der Psychologie."

8. Psychology Club of Zürich, *Die kulturelle Bedeutung der komplexen Psychologie* (Berlin, 1935).

9. Trüb, *Psychosynthese als seelisch geistiger Heilungsprozess* (Psychosynthesis as a psychical-spiritual process of healing) (Zürich, 1936).

10. Rudolf Pannwitz (1881–1969), writer and cultural philosopher. He contributed *Die Erziehung* (On education) to Buber's series *Die Gesellschaft*.

11. In two letters dated 2 and 5 December 1936, Pannwitz had expressed himself in detail on Hans Trüb, asserting that as a pragmatist Trüb would not be able to accomplish the attempted theoretical-systematic elaboration of his thought that was intended to go beyond the psychoanalysis of C. G. Jung, vis-à-vis whom Trüb had a sort of Oedipus complex.

12. Probably a review of Trüb's *Psychosynthesis as a Psychical-Spiritual Process of Healing*.

23. Martin Buber to Ernst Michel[13]

Jerusalem
23 September 1949

Lieber Ernst Michel,

Many thanks for sending your new works, which I have read with great interest and profit. I have to mention only one reservation, albeit a weighty one as it seems to me, concerning your very valuable study on hysteria.[14] As far as I understand, this study is meant for neurologists and psychotherapists in general, not only for those who are believers; yet how can it be demanded of the nonbelievers to accept the being called by the Transcendence as something that is included in the premises of the elucidation — since these premises should after all be shared by them, the author, as well as by his believing readers? You — E. M. — say that this assertion had been reached by experience — albeit not by *their* experience; that it has been confirmed by daily reality — albeit not by their reality! Yet their experience is not soon becoming an experience of faith and their reality a reality of faith; the being called by the Transcendence however is experienced only by faith and is found in reality again and again anew. The nonbelievers understand their individuation from completely different premises. However when you say that they are not truly individuated ("in a life that passes in a stereotyping

13. Ernst Michel (1889–1964), sociologist concerned with social and cultural policy, leading figure in progressive Catholicism. From 1922 to 1933 he served as a lecturer at the Academy of Labor founded in Frankfurt by Eugen Rosenstock-Huessy; from 1931 to 1933 he was an adjunct professor at the University of Frankfurt from which he was retired compulsorily in 1933. He trained as a psychotherapist and opened a practice of "personal psychotherapy" in the spirit of Buber's dialogical thought. Since 1946 he also wrote and published on psychotherapy and corresponded and exchanged publications with Buber. Later he was again a professor at the University of Frankfurt.

14. "Zur anthropologischen Deutung der Hysterie. Ein Beitrag zur Neurosenlehre" (On the anthropological interpretation of hysteria). *Studium Generale* 3.Jg., Heft 6 (1950).

way"), then you destroy the basis of mutual understanding. This difference between those hearing the call and those not hearing it, does not lie in the realm of the will (James's "Will to Believe"),[15] but is a basic fact of humanity. On the other hand: is it not the essential duty of the researcher and interpreter of diseases of the soul to present his insights to *all* those competent believers just as well as nonbelievers. Or is it meant by any chance, that the nonbelievers are not competent? Yet this would open an abyss between them and the believers, and would have disastrous consequences for the entire sphere of coming to an understanding of disease and healing of the soul. It can also not be denied that human beings who are nonbelieving in this sense of hearing the call (although they believe in another sense — they may "believe in God") can have a healing influence on neurotics.

Moreover, to what extent is it at all acceptable to include the Transcendence into an exposition that is not just ontological but essentially anthropological-psychological? You will say to me that not [the Transcendence] itself will be included but what comes from it. But how far is this possible without including itself? Already by your naming it the Transcendence, by your claiming that it is just that and nothing that can be found in the Immanence, you include just that which exists for us only in faith, yet not in our observation of the life of sick or healthy human beings. Certainly I may and should bear witness to God's call as to that what happens from Him; moreover, I may and should bear witness to it as the truth, but may I in a research of human situations and their treatment draw conclusions from this as from a proven statement? These questions of mine are not rhetorical, I am concerned with real problems, with serious, very serious problems, that should be taken by us as seriously as they are. . . .

15. William James, *The Will to Believe and Other Essays in Popular Philosophy,* New York, 1897.

Correspondence with Ludwig Binswanger

24. Ludwig Binswanger[1] to Martin Buber

Kreuzlingen
7 February 1933

Sehr verehrter Herr Professor!

My sincere thanks for sending me your *Dialogue* (Zwiesprache) which I read in one go. As I know *I and Thou* very well it was not difficult for me to read. I was most impressed by the second paragraph, and here once again the paragraphs on Thinking, Eros, and the Community. I wholly agree with it, the same is true for the conversation with the adversary. As I was called upon to be in charge of a 'big enterprise' early in life but am a physician at the same time, and would like more and more to become a full human being, this is the indicated way, the way of my total existence, hence not only my thinking and striving existence but also of what I experience each day personally. . . .

---

1. Ludwig Binswanger (1881–1966), Swiss psychiatrist and head of Kreuzlingen Mental Hospital, who was influenced by Dilthey, Husserl, and Heidegger in developing his own method of psychotherapeutic treatment, "existential analysis." Buber's call for a dialogical encounter between the physician and his patient was important for his theory.

25. Martin Buber to Ludwig Binswanger

Heppenheim
23 October 1936

Dear Mr. Binswanger,

I am especially grateful for your latest gift.[2] The 'anthropological critique' namely, what you say on page 295, at last presents that exact justice which I was missing up to now with regard to Freud.

I shall soon send you a little book of mine which is meant to contribute something to Kierkegaard's critique; it deals with the category of the 'Single One'.

In another book on which I am working, one paragraph deals with the metaphysics of insanity. Is there in the newest psychiatric literature anything which could be of use to me in regard to concrete material or otherwise? What I am interested in chiefly is the relationship of the 'unreal' and the 'real', more accurately between the special and the common world in the schizophrenic and the paranoid. There are several problems that I would love to have opportunities to discuss with you.

26. Ludwig Binswanger to Martin Buber

Kruezlingen
17 November 1936

Lieber Herr Professor!

Many thanks for kindly sending me your new book[3] which I read immediately with great joy and interest. I not only go along with you everywhere but see in you also an ally not only against Kierkegaard but also against Heidegger,[4] to whom I am deeply

2. Compare: Ludwig Binswanger, Freud's perception of the human being in light of anthropology, *Netherlands tijdschrift voor de psychologie en haar grensgebieden*, Jahrgang IV (1936), Nr.5/6.

3. *Die Frage an den Einzelnen* (The question to the Single One).

4. Martin Heidegger (1889–1976), philosopher, professor in Marburg and

indebted as to method. His concept of existence (existence *ever mine*), although secularized is still completely in line with Kierkegaard. It is very important that you want the public to be understood, not only in the sense of a mass or of 'One'. Stirner's[5] illustration of the Sophist is so beautiful and true. Of course, I also found a great deal that is beautiful in the text. I again thank you most sincerely.

27. Martin Buber to Ludwig Binswanger

Jerusalem
4 June 1946

Verehrter Herr Binswanger,

The chance reading of the advertisement of a book by you about anthropology[6] (the book itself is not yet available here although during the last few weeks, after a long interval, the first Swiss books have arrived) gives me the outward impetus to renew the personal contact with you which is always so important to me. We had found, especially at the time of my unforgettable visit with you, many things in common, which now, when we have again — even if only in a sketchy way — a 'world', should be further clarified and fostered. But I also have a special request. In connection with a philosophical work (I have worked more than ever during these years) I am engaged with the problem of the world becoming chaotic through various abnormal circumstances. Would you be prepared to help me in acquiring relevant material? These should be fairly reliable descriptions. Whatever is available through the literature known to me (for the last eight years I have had no information because nothing reached us

Freiburg i. Br. He gained great influence starting out from the phenomenology of Edmund Husserl, through his major work, "Sein und Zeit" (Being and time) (First half, Hall/Saale, 1927), that presents existentialist philosophy.

5. Max Stirner, pseudonym of Kaspar Schmidt (1806–56), philosopher, representative of Sophist anarchism.

6. *Grundformen und Erkenntnis menschlichen Daseins* (Basic forms and knowledge of human existence) (Zurich, 1942).

here) are mostly descriptions of case histories, whereas I am interested in descriptions of the states of mind themselves (dreams
and related phenomena, intoxication, mental diseases), in which
the outer world is experienced differently from our ordinary
world, especially regarding its coherence, order, etc. I would be
very grateful for any suggestion regarding literature, hints about
possible connections, methodological advice, etc. Due to the situation, I have published in the meantime only in Hebrew, but now
some of my work will soon appear in English, and I shall send
you those books which might be of interest to you.

28. Ludwig Binswanger to Martin Buber

Kruezlingen
10 January 1952

Sehr verehrter, lieber Herr Professor!

I was not feeling well over the end of the year, otherwise I
would have thanked you earlier for your kindness of having your
new book *Images of Good and Evil* sent to me by the publishers.
But then, I had leisure to read your new, for me most welcome
work, with great attention. I saw that one can learn only from
you how one should read the Bible, but noticed also again that
there is no other person nowadays from whom we could get
more and better advice about the problem of Good and Evil.
This is probably also true because your sphere of influence, at
least as far as I can see from my own circle and that of my
acquaintances, is getting bigger and deeper. I could notice this
particularly with regard to *The Way of Man*. Dr. Sborowitz — to
whom I send my best regards — will have told you that I redis-
covered in *The Way of Man* the basic tenets which I have used
therapeutically all along, as long it was not a specialist treatment.
You may understand that I acquired the book at once for our
patient's library, as it provides wonderful support to my treatment, whereas I must, of course, point out that I do not have at
my disposal either your knowledge, or your power of description, or the depth with which you view all these problems.

Are you coming to Switzerland again this summer? In case
you cannot come to me — you are welcome to be my guest at any
time for as long as you wish — I would like to meet you in
Zürich, as I did last time.

Lately, I have occupied myself much with Kafka and Kierkegaard, whereby I often thought of you, and in my mind asked
you many a question. Besides, I have now finished my fourth
study of schizophrenia[7] (serious form of persecution mania). Unfortunately, it will take some time until I will be able to send it to
you. This reminded me of Kierkegaard's saying, that the cowardice of humankind cannot bear what death and madness have to
say about life.

29. Ludwig Binswanger to Martin Buber

Kruezlingen
8 October 1957

Sehr verehrter, lieber Herr Professor!

Many thanks for kindly sending me your lecture that appeared in *Merkur*,[8] which I received during my holidays. At the
end of these I was in Brissago and also met there Professor
Scholem one afternoon. Your ears must have been ringing because you were the subject of our conversation most of the time.
I, of course, agree with your distinction between guilt and guilt
feelings, as well as your distinction between healing and salvation, or between therapy and spiritual care, but the last distinction more for reasons of principle than practicality. Their
distinction varies from physician to physician but most of all
from patient to patient. I admit that in most cases I must have
concentrated first and foremost on the will to heal, but also had
quite a number of patients — and I preferred those — where I
could not and would not make that distinction, where it did only

7. "Der Fall Suzanne Urban," Schweizer Archiv für Psychiatrie und Neur-
ologie, Band 69, Heft 1/2 (1952).

8. "Schuld and Schuldgefühle" (Guilt and guilt feelings), *Merkur* 11, no. 8
(Aug. 1957).

seem possible at the same time to consider both the healing and the possibility of salvation and that from both sides, the physician's and the patient's.

Your analysis of Stavrogin and the trial[9] was of special interest to me. .

30. Ludwig Binswanger to Martin Buber

Kreuzlingen
8 May 1962

My dear Martin Buber,

Thank you kindly for having the two addresses, *Logos*, sent to me; both spoke to me directly. What you say about the two truths is very true and fruitful. The second speech also is extremely valuable to me, since I have worked on Heracleitus myself; but you dig much deeper.[10]

In a new preface to the third edition of my *Basic Forms and Knowledge of Human Existence*,[11] I again recall your decisive importance for this work. We are still extremely close to each other in our emphasis on the importance of the we-ness, particularly vis-à-vis Heidegger. Only when you speak of the "monologizing hubris" with its strongest threat of disintegration (p. 13) would I like to dissent, having just read the second volume of Heidegger's *Nietzche*[12]–because in action and in truth Heidegger is engaged in a hitherto unsuspected *permanent* dialogue with the great philosophers of all times, particularly since to him philosophy and the history of philosophy are identical. I am glad to see how active you still are and how your language and your thought have in equal measure attained to ever greater heights of purity, maturity, and clarity. . . .

9. In "Guilt and Guilt Feelings," Stavrogin is a figure from Dostoevski's novel *The Possessed* (1870). *The Trial* is Kafka's novel.

10. "What Is Common to All."

11. *Grundformen and Erkenntnis menschlichen Daseins*, 3d ed. (Zurich, 1942).

12. Pfullingen, 1961; English translation by David Farrell Krell (San Francisco: Harper & Row, 1979).

31. Martin Buber to Ludwig Binswanger

Jerusalem
14 May 1962

Dear Ludwig Binswanger,

Many thanks for your two letters.

My state of health is anything but satisfactory (my condition is best characterized as constant lability), but the doctors have now permitted me to spend the major part of July and August at the Sonn-Matt sanatorium overlooking Lucerne. During the first week of July and the last week of August, I shall spend a few days in Zurich. Thus I may hope to see you again on one of these occasions. Then we can discuss, among other things, your reservations about my critique of "monologizing." In essence, it seems to involve the fact that I cannot regard what you call "permanent dialogue" *in concreto* as a dialogue at all. Dialogue in my sense implies of necessity the unforeseen, and its basic element is surprise, the surprising mutuality.

I gratefully accept your very kind offer to have your book on melancholia and mania,[13] with which I am not yet acquainted, sent to me.

13. Ludwig Binswanger, *Melancholie und Manie: Phänomenologische Studien* (Melancholy and mania: phenomenological studies) (Pfullingen, 1960).

Correspondence with Maurice Friedman and Leslie H. Farber

32. Martin Buber to Maurice Friedman[1]

Jerusalem
30 January 1956

Dear Maurice,

. . . Please give me some details on the School of Psychoanalysis, particularly what kind of human beings they are. I do not yet see myself in such an institute. But the fact is that some days before your letter my wife said to me: "We did not see enough of the grand wild nature of America." (We saw only the Great Canyon that impressed us very much, but the course of the Hudson we saw only from the railway window.) And I answered: "Who knows — we may yet see more of it." So these are the essential points: (1) The atmosphere must be one where such an attempt of synthetical[2] life as mine can make itself understood; (2) the conditions must be such as to enable us to see the scenery more intensely and I cannot renew the absorbing and tiring experience of an American lecture tour. Of course, I could lecture

---

1. Maurice Friedman (b. 1921), currently professor of religious studies, philosophy, and comparative literature at San Diego State University. He has translated and edited many of Buber's works as well as written extensively on his thought. He was also instrumental in arranging Buber's lecture tour in the United States.

2. Semijocular concept to distinguish his standpoint from that of psychoanalysis.

191

on anthropology (the three subjects you know and two or three others, especially the anthropological view of the 'soul' and that of language). . . . I am now very busy with the encyclopedia (of education) and some other things, so it is rather doubtful if I shall be technically able to write now on Freud. . . .

33. Martin Buber to Maurice Friedman

Jerusalem
2 March 56

Dear Maurice,
. . . The invitation of the Washington School has given me a stimulus to make my critical attitude to certain terms, as libido, the subconscious, the archetypes, theoretically clearer than I have done till now. I hope I shall be able next summer to deal with the whole matter. Of course, the main problem is that of the psychical life as such . . .

34. Leslie H. Farber[3] to Martin Buber
(Original in English)

Washington
13 March 1956

Dear Professor Buber,
As the chairman of the faculty of the Washington School of Psychiatry, it is my great privilege to invite you to give the fourth William Alanson White Lectures this coming winter, the exact time to be arranged at your own convenience. We would like three or four formal lectures from you, scattered over a three-week period. Also, we would wish the opportunity to

3. Leslie H. Farber (1912–81), psychoanalyst and psychologist at the Washington School of Psychiatry (Washington, D.C.) and the Austen Riggs Center, Stockbridge, Mass. At the time of his correspondence with Buber, he was a chairman of the faculty at the Washington School of Psychiatry. He wrote chapter 25, "Buber and Psychotherapy", in *The Philosophy of Martin Buber*, vol. 12 of the Library of Living Philosophers, 1967.

meet with you more informally in small seminar groups over the same period.

As to subject matter, we would of course be interested in any papers you would wish to present from your developing philosophical anthropology. Recently, I was most stimulated to read "Distance and Relation" in a small English journal.[4] You should know that we are rather an eclectic group with no strong allegiance to any particular psychological system and exist outside the orthodox psychoanalytic organization. I mention this so that you may know we would be receptive to any critique you may have written or wish to write on Freud's theories. In a letter to me, Maurice Friedman suggested you had been working on a criticism of Freud's unconscious, as well as his dream theory, which would interest us very much.

The school began about twenty years ago at the instigation of Harry Stack Sullivan,[5] who was generally regarded — even by his opponents — as the most gifted student of schizophrenia and its treatment in this country. Although he had some Freudian background early in his career he turned to a sociological view of mental disorder — similar in many respects to that of George Herbert Mead,[6] with whom he had some contact during his early years in Chicago. It was Sullivan who insisted that psychiatry be described as the study and treatment of "interpersonal relations." In case you have a chance to look at his writings, I should say that there is an unpleasant discrepancy between his theories and his practice. Unfortunately, writing was difficult for him; he was above all a talker. And when he wrote, he was overcome by a pomposity and pedantry, coming both from awkwardness and his compulsion to give his theories "scientific" respectability. Essentially he was a self-educated man, with some scientific background. But he was naïve in philosophy, theology, and the arts. And when he was driven to systematize his ideas, he turned to

4. This essay was first published in the *Hibbert Journal* 49 (1951).

5. Harry Stack Sullivan, (1892–1949), American psychiatrist.

6. George Herbert Mead (1863–1931), professor of philosophy at the University of Chicago.

the theories of modern physics, which only served to widen the split between his private and public selves. Despite this, he was an inspiring teacher with an almost exquisite capacity for relationship. Moreover, he was a man of remarkable courage, willing to oppose the Freudians on all public occasions. Until his death a few years ago, he worked hard to make the Washington School of Psychiatry into an interdisciplinary organization, to be peopled by all the professions concerned with human relations.

Of my own background, I am a psychoanalyst by profession. I had the usual orthodox psychoanalytic training with a Freudian group, later working with Sullivan. It was during World War II that I first ran across a reference to your own writings and managed to get a copy of *I and Thou* from Scotland. I shall not labor the influence this book had on both my life and work, because this will be apparent in the paper "Martin Buber and Psychiatry," which I am sending to you (in fairly rough draft) along with this invitation.[7] I read the paper the other night as part of a public lecture series, sponsored jointly by the school and a local seminar on religion and psychiatry. The discussants of my paper were Maurice Friedman and Reuel Howe,[8] a professor of pastoral theology at the Episcopalian Seminary in Alexandria, Virgina.

If there is anything more you wish to know of our group or its publications, please let me know. Meanwhile, I eagerly await your reply to our invitation.

35. Martin Buber to Leslie H. Farber
(Original in English)

Jerusalem
1 April 1956

Dear Dr. Farber,

I thank you for your invitation and your very interesting paper. I was rather surprised by the great spiritual freedom under-

7. See "Martin Buber and Psychotherapy" in Schilpp and Friedman, eds. *The Philosophy of Martin Buber,* vol. 12 of the Library of Living Philosphers, (Cambridge: Cambridge University Press, 1967), 577–601, particularly the section "Buber and Sullivan," 585ff.

8. Reuel L. Howe (b. 1905), theologian and educator.

lying it. We need now, in psychology and elsewhere, a phase of real freedom. I was impressed by what you say, in the paper and in the letter, about Sullivan; obviously nothing was lacking but just that freedom.

I should like to give — next winter, in January, I think — as you suggest, three or four lectures for your public and to do some seminar work with small groups. I am thinking of devoting a part of the lectures to anthropological problems (as that in "Distance and Relation") and the rest to a critical revision of some psychological terms. The ultimate question should be: What can anthropology, as I understand it, give psychology?

Of course, I should like to know somewhat more about what your group has done and has published till now. It will help me to see the particular problems that are involved here. . . .

36. Leslie H. Farber to Martin Buber
(Original in English)

Washington
9 April 1956

Dear Professor Buber,

I am delighted that you will give the William Alanson White Lectures in January 1957. . . .

Perhaps I can tell you a bit more about our group. The William Alanson White Foundation is the parent organization of the Washington School of Psychiatry and the journal *Psychiatry*, both of which have been in existence since 1939. . William Alanson White,[9] whose name the foundation took, was for many years the superintendent of St. Elizabeth's Hospital in Washington — one of the oldest and most humane psychiatric institutions in this country. White had been one of Sullivan's teachers and moreover was esteemed by psychiatrists of all theoretical persuasions. So much for the bare structure. What would distinguish our group from other psychiatric or psychoanalytic groups would be our continuing concern with the treatment of schizophrenia.

9. William Alanson White (1870–1937), American psychiatrist.

Though most of us have been trained in psychoanalysis, Freud's theories of the narcissistic nature of schizophrenia were of little use to us. We learned early that it was often possible to have rather intense relations with schizophrenics, but these relations — as I indicated in my paper — were easily fragmented, the consequence being a growing preoccupation with our own failures in sustaining these relations. I shall send you a number of reprints, many of which will have to do with what is usually called 'countertransference' in Freudian circles.

In the middle thirties Frieda Fromm-Reichmann (Erich Fromm's first wife) came to Washington as director of treatment at Chestnut Lodge Sanatorium, a private hospital on the outskirts of Washington, where most of us had some of our training. She too had been interested in the treatment of the psychoses in Europe. Next to Sullivan, I suppose she has had [the] most personal influence on the group. I will try to include some of her papers. You will notice that she had little of Sullivan's chronic exasperation — or his grandiosity, for that matter. On the other hand, she was apt to romanticize the schizophrenic, regarding him as [a] misguided genius. Where Sullivan turned to the theories of physics, Frieda Fromm-Reichmann turned to the romanticism of the nineteenth century, falling back on such terms as "empathy," "spontaneity," etc. As you can see, a portion of my paper alludes to the conflict between Sullivan and Fromm-Reichmann. Sullivan was the first chairman of the faculty of the school, Fromm-Reichmann the second, and I am the third.

I have been in office for only a year. In fact, I have been back in Washington for only the last two years. After World War II, I chose not to return to Washington. Instead, I went to San Francisco, where I spent some seven years in private practice and teaching, leading on the whole a rather isolated professional life. However, I think the solitude allowed me to develop my own notions with greater freedom than I would have had, had I returned to Washington. It was in San Francisco that I heard you speak in 1950 — once at Stanford University and again at a synagogue in San Francisco.[10] I shall never forget the several rabbis

10. Farber can only have heard Buber in San Francisco in 1952.

who attempted to introduce you, evidently having no more to go on than a hasty perusal of the dust jacket of one of your books would allow.

One analyst in our group is a good friend of Paul Tillich's[11] and has been responsible for his giving several talks in Washington. There are also a couple of analysts somewhat interested in Zen Buddhism. One of them, Margaret Rioch,[12] will be in Europe [during] the month of May. If you could give me your address for that month, she will make some effort to get in touch with you. I believe she will be able to answer any other questions you may wish to ask. Margaret, incidently, is a great admirer of your novel *For The Sake of Heaven*. I am grateful for your comment on my paper. I believe that your lectures and seminars here will [have] an enormously liberating effect on the school — and ultimately on psychiatry generally in this country.

37. Martin Buber to Leslie H. Farber
(Original in English)

Jerusalem
1 September 1956

Dear Dr. Farber,

[For] some time I [have owed] you a letter, but the lecturing tour through western Europe [three countries, three languages, three months] has proved too much for me and on coming home I could not think of anything but rest. But certainly Mrs. Rioch and Maurice Friedman have informed you sufficiently or nearly so.

As I have found out, meantime, you were right in asserting that you had suggested three to four lectures. To make it four,

11. Paul Tillich (1886–1965), German Protestant theologian. Before emigrating to the United States in 1933, he was a close collaborator of Buber's, especially in the movement of religious socialism.

12. Margaret Rioch, an analyst herself, was the wife of David McKenzie Rioch (b. 1900), one of the pioneers of neuropsychiatry. At the time, he was on the staff of the Walter Reed Army Medical Center, Washington, D.C. Margeret Ricoh was an active participant in Buber's seminar "The Unconcious."

[since] I cannot think of preparing more than two new ones. I must make use of two earlier lectures that are not yet known in America. One of them, "Distance and Relation," to be sure has been published in English[13] and you have read it. This is the basic one, and it will be methodologically necessary to begin with it. It will certainly need a lot of interpretation, but this might be given in the form of answers to questions, so [that] the rather exact composition should not suffer by enlargements. Tell me please what you think of it.

The second lecture should be "Elements of the Interhuman"[14] in an abridged form. Here too discussion is desirable, but here it is not so essential as in the first case.

The subjects of the two new lectures are 1) Guilt and Modern Psychology,[15] 2) Some Basic Concepts of Psychology.[16] About the first, Friedman has written me after his conversation with you. The second will be the place to deal with the theories of the unconscious and Freud's [theory] of dreams.

The two of them present great difficulties to the lecturer who, himself no psychologist, has to explain this critical attitude to people imbued [with] modern psychological thought. Therefore a thorough discussion will be necessary. But the main part of this could and should be transferred to the seminars, which should be devoted to the reexamination of the leading psychological concepts and to the explanation of some anthropological concepts mentioned by me, [such] as [acceptance], confirmation, etc. The seminar work must be based on a somewhat systematical questioning on the part of the participating psychologists. In order to be more or less systematical, the sequence of the problems

13. See letter 34, note 4.
14. "Elemente des Zwischenmenschlichen," in *Knowledge of Man*, 72–88.
15. "Schuld und Schuldgefühle" (Guilt and guilt feelings), first published in *Merkur* 9, no. 8 (Aug. 1957), 705–29.
16. Buber never completed writing this lecture, which was to deal with the unconscious and Freud's theory of dreams. Its outline has been published in *Nachlese* (Heidelberg: Lambert Schneider, 1965); trans. and with an introduction and explanatory comments by Maurice Friedman, Credo Perspectives series (New York: Simon and Schuster, 1967).

should be premeditated and also communicated to me beforehand. It is of course desirable that psychotherapeutic "cases" be
used (in short) as examples, but [it] must be understood [that I
will] not deal at all with the therapeutic side of the matter insofar
as questions of principle do not arise.

I am grateful to you for sending me some very interesting material, and especially the books of Sullivan. The chapters I read
till now are deeply stimulating and the main practical point of
view seems to me [very] near to mine.

38. Leslie H. Farber to Martin Buber
(Original in English)

Washington
25 October 1956

Dear Professor Buber,

. . . Of the lectures themselves, I approve heartily of beginning
with "Distance and Relation" — a paper which seems crucial to
me in your anthropology. I doubt that more than a handful of
your audience will have seen it. I know that I came upon it only
through having a friend of a friend photostat it for me in a seminary library. I agree it will require some interpretation and elaboration, which can issue from questions put to you by the smaller
seminars. It should not be abridged, for it is already so concise
and economical in its reasoning as to offer considerable difficulty
to the casual reader or listener. I do not know the next paper you
mention — "Elements of Between Man and Man," if my translation is correct. I have noticed though, if this is relevant, that
those friends of mine who were baffled by the poetic syntax of *I
and Thou* did very well with *Between Man and Man*, since the form
of the latter was more familiar to them. I look forward with ex-
citement to the subjects of your two new lectures, even while I
understand the difficulty of contending with an audience satu-
rated with modern psychological theories about dreams and the
unconscious. Yet I think the time is a good one for an anthropological view of the subject, for by now the novelty of these

same psychological theories has worn thin: they are no longer
so startling that people believe them anthropological. Or perhaps what I mean is ontological. I neglected to mention, as I
was talking about "Distance and Relation," that I shall try to
have those people who will take part in the smaller seminars
familiarize themselves beforehand with that essay, as well as
other writings of yours. In this way, perhaps, the seminars can
become somewhat systematic. If it is agreeable to you, we will
record the seminars in such a way that [the] technology of recording will be inconspicuous, and later have typescripts made
for your perusal. . . .

39. Leslie H. Farber to Martin Buber

Washington
29 December 1956

Dear Prof. Buber,
. . . I commiserate with you over your task of "analyzing the
usual analysis of the unconscious." In my own humble efforts in
this direction I have usually ended with the sensation that I was
foundering in a thick pea soup.

Correspondence of Robert C. Smith
with Martin Buber and C. G. Jung

40. Robert C. Smith to Martin Buber

Villanova, Penna.
14 May 1960

Dear Prof. Buber:

I am . . . working toward the doctoral degree in the field of philosophy of religion at the Temple School of Theology in Philadelphia. My major professor is Dr. Richard Kroner, formerly of the Union Theological Seminary in New York City. The subject of my dissertation is "Religious Knowledge and Experience in the Writings of Carl Jung and Martin Buber." You may be interested to know that I was stimulated to pursue this topic upon reading your little book, *Eclipse of God*. I have traced down all your references to Jung's writings and read extensively on the subject. Basically I am in agreement with your critique and with most of your conclusions. I have found your analysis of our present spiritual crisis profound and intensely stimulating. Indeed the pursuit of this topic has been more than an intellectual inquiry, it has been a personal quest and search in which I feel deeply involved. At times I have been tempted toward that kind of psychological interpretation of the world that Jung represents. Time and again I have had my misgivings about it. As you have pointed out, he transgresses the boundaries of his discipline at the crucial points. You may also be interested to know that I have had a couple of lengthy discussions with Maurice Friedman

201

about the topic and have appreciated his courtesy in letting me read the articles and your reply to your critics in the volume for the Library of Living Philosophers that he is editing. As you might expect there are many questions that could be further clarified. I shall list some of these and if you would be so kind as to attempt an answer (either in English or German) I should be greatly in your debt.

1. Is your basic distinction between the attitude of I-Thou and I-It an ontological distinction, an epistemological distinction, or an ethical distinction?

2. Is it legitimate to speak of I-Thou knowledge and I-Thou experience? I do not think so, but many of your critics do this. Do they misunderstand you here?

3. Would you agree with Prof. Agus in "Modern Philosophies of Judaism" that "I-Thou reveals a profound psychic experience"? p. 234)

4. Is the I-Thou relation grounded in psychic experience? (Your dream of the double cry would seem to indicate this. *Between Man and Man*, pp. 1–2.) If so, how does I-Thou transcend psychic experience?

5. Can we say that the I-Thou relation is the "knowledge of faith"?

6. When I wrote to Prof. Jung about the nature of this study he replied "the trouble is, that the critiques of his work are unaware of the limitations imposed by the theory of cognition (epistemology)." I would go further and maintain that no theory of knowledge is possible within the legitimate bounds of psychology. Would you agree?

7. I do not feel that Jung has adequately answered the criticisms you raise but I also feel that you have not completely answered his criticisms of your position. Let me select certain sentences from his reply to you and pose them anew. a. "It is noteworthy that he takes offense at my assertion that God cannot exist apart from man and considers that to be a transcendent statement. And yet I say expressly that everything, without exception, which is asserted about 'God' is a human, i.e. a psychological assertion.

Is this untrue? Is the image which we have or make for ourselves of God ever 'detached from man'?" (Reply to Buber, spring 1957, p. 6, 7 originally in *Merkur*, May 1952.) You speak to this question by saying that "Not only statements about God, but all statements in general are 'human,'" but you do not state whether all statements are in the first instance psychological. If so, as you know they are open to analysis and reduction. The crux of the matter is: Are all religious and metaphysical statements psychological as Jung claims?. b. "My critic does not seem to be aware that when he himself speaks of God his assertion stems first of all from his conscious attitude and then from his unconscious presuppositions." (Reply to Buber, p. 6.) Would you comment?

8. Do you believe that God reveals himself through our unconscious, i.e. unconscious image, as well as through 'meeting' and 'encounter'?

9. What place do you give to the function of the unconscious?

10. Do you believe that God is unconditioned?

11. You say Prof. Jung is a modern gnostic but wherein consists his dualism?

12. Do you feel that Jung, like Spinoza, is holding out essentially a life of monologue?

13. Do you believe Jung is reducing God to an object? Does he forget that God is always the Subject who meets us? You don't say this explicitly but you imply it.

These questions I have posed remain some of the unanswered problems that still bother me. In the shortness of space it is not possible to express these issues as fully as I desire. I realize full well that in answer to these questions much could be said. I should be most happy if you would indicate some clarification directed toward some of the questions. Again may I express my deepest gratitude for your searching analysis of the religious crisis of our age.

If you would be able to reply by July 1, 1960, it would be greatly appreciated.

Sincerely yours,

41. Martin Buber to Robert C. Smith

Jerusalem
2 June 1960

Dear Mr. Smith,

My time is fully taken up by trying to finish some unfinished work. Therefore I cannot answer your questions according to your wish. But I will give you the indispensable minimum of information.

Question 1 : An ontological distinction.

2. No 'knowledge' in the objective sense and no 'experience' in the psychological one; the usual terminology proves unsufficient, when you transcend its premises.

3. I do not like 'psychic' here: there are experiences of the whole person, 'psyche' becoming in comparison with it a necessary abstraction.

4. Dreams are not I-Thou relationships at all, but the hint at it.

5. Such a definition would be an unallowed simplification.

6. Too complicated to go here into it.

7. 'Cannot exist' is not a 'psychological assertion' but an ontological denial — even a simple statement like the following "I have received your letter as the expression of a living human person" is not to be determined as 'psychological', although it obviously has a psychological side and can therefore be reduced to a psychological assertion.

7 b. Just the same.

8. God can reveal himself by anything, but we must be more cautious dealing with such revelations than we generally are inclined to be. Your question is not put with sufficient clearness.

9. I have dealt with it at length in my seminar on the unconscious at the Washington School for Psychiatry and have in mind to elaborate it by writing in the course of this year.

10. I am avoiding making assertions on what God is or is not, the logical law of having to chose between contradictory assertions not being appliable here, as already Nicolaus Cusanus knew ("complexio oppositorum").

11. There is not dualistic gnosis only (cf. the book of H. Jonas); the gnosis based on the idea of original unity is not dualistic. Jung's "reintegration," for instance, develops a gnostical motive.

12. Jung is essentially a monologist. Spinoza was much less so, as I could prove.

13. I do not remember Jung speaking anywhere of God as "the Subject who meets us" or the like of it, I do not think he can do it, his God being in the last instance identical with the Great Self.

Sincerely yours,

42. Robert C. Smith to C. G. Jung

Villanova, Penna.
10 June 1960

Dear Dr. Jung:

Sometime ago I wrote to you[1] seeking to learn if your article "Religion und Psychologie" had been translated into English. At the time Mrs. Jaffe told me that she was not aware of a translation. Since then through much research I have found that Dr. Robert Clark of Philadelphia has made a fine translation of your article in *Spring*, 1957. If it were possible I feel it would be most helpful if the article were included as a part of your collected works.

At present I am completing my doctoral research. The topic of my dissertation is "Religious Knowledge and Experience in the Writings of C. G. Jung and Martin Buber." The problems generating out of that interchange you had with Prof. Buber back in 1952 remains the starting point of my thesis. I have read widely your writings and those of Prof. Buber and feel that there are crucial differences between his point of view and your own but nonetheless I still feel that the misunderstandings are just as in

1. Robert C. Smith had written to C. G. Jung earlier, before he had decided on the topic of his dissertation, discussing Jung's reply to Buber, titled "Religion and Psychology", which had first appeared in the German language journal *Merkur* 6 (5 May 1952), 467–73.

evidence. Just recently I asked Prof. Buber many questions that center around those points that you raise and which still pose difficulties. You may be interested in some of them I have posed to him.

Question: "I do not feel that Jung has adequately answered the criticisms you raise but I also feel that you have not completely answered his criticisms of your position. Let me select certain sentences from his reply to you and pose them anew. 'It is noteworthy that he takes offense at my assertion that God cannot exist apart from man and considers that to be a transcendent statement. And yet, I say expressly that everything, without exception is a human, i.e. a psychological assertion. Is this untrue?'"

Answer: "'Cannot exist' is not a 'psychological assertion' but an ontological denial — even a simple statement like the following 'I have received your letter as the expression of a living person' is not to be determined as 'psychological', although it obviously has a psychological side and therefore can be reduced to a psychological assertion."

Question: "You say that Prof. Jung is a modern gnostic but wherein consists his dualism?"

Answer: "There is not dualistic gnosis only (cf. the book of H. Jonas); the gnosis based on the idea of original unity is not dualistic. Jung's 'reintegration,' for instance, develops a gnostical motive."

Question: "Do you feel that Jung, like Spinoza, is holding out essentially a life of monologue?"

Answer: "Jung is essentially a monologist. Spinoza was much less so, as I could prove."

Question: "Do you believe Jung is reducing God to an object? Does he forget that God is always the Subject who meets us? You don't say this explicitly but you imply it."

Answer: "I do not remember Jung speaking anywhere of God as 'the Subject who meets us' or the like of it, I do not think he can do it, his God being in the last instance identical with the Great Self."

Now these are serious charges if they are true. It would be of great help to me if you would take the time to comment upon these interpretations, particularly the charge that you are a monologist and that you reduce God to an object. Buber would insist that the transcendent cannot be known in the objective sense or experienced in the psychological sense. This is a crucial question and I believe that most religious thinkers would agree that religious knowledge and experience are not 'knowledge' and 'experience' in the sense that can be applied to phenomenal objects. Indeed one of your followers, Dr. Fordham has seen this. He insists that religion rests upon a kind of reality that can't be experienced (Quoted by Dr. Philp in his book, *Jung and the Problem of Evil.*) Would you agree with him or not?

God cannot be made into an object of knowledge and experience and still remain God, then we are speaking of the unconscious image and should clearly say so. I know this is what you mean but I feel that your use of the term God in your writings has brought about much misunderstanding. In spite of the fact that you say that you are speaking of God as a human experience it appears to me that you use the term rather loosely in both a symbolic and further in a participating or active sense. Nor do I feel that matters are helped when you speak of God's relativity. Surely the unconscious image is relative to man but religion speaks of something quite other when it refers to a transcendent absolute.

I would be most happy if you could help to elucidate precisely your own understanding in these matters so that I may not misrepresent your true position in my dissertation. May I express to you my profound thanks for your keen analysis of the crisis of our times and my gratitude for the insights that I have received through your writing. If it would be possible to get an answer off by July 10th it would be greatly appreciated.

Sincerely yours,

P.S. In your other letter you said "the trouble is, that the critics of my work are unaware of the limitations imposed by the theory of cognition (epistemology)." Would you agree that no theory of knowledge is possible within the limits of psychology?

43. C. G. Jung to Robert C. Smith

Zurich
29 June 1960

Dear Mr. Smith,

Buber and I start from an entirely different basis: I make no transcendental statements. I am essentially empirical, as I have stated more than once. I am dealing with psychical phenomena and not with metaphysical assertions. Within the frame of psychical events I find the fact of the belief in God. It *says:* "God is." This is the fact I am concerned with. I am not concerned with the truth or untruth of God's existence. *I am concerned with the statement only,* and I am interested in its structure and behaviors. It is an emotionally 'toned' complex like the father or mother complex or the Oedipus complex. It is obvious that, if Man does not exist, no such statement can exist either, nor can anybody prove that the statement 'God' exists in a nonhuman sphere.

What Buber misunderstands as gnosticism is *psychiatric observation,* of which he obviously knows nothing. It is certainly not my invention. Buber has been led astray by a poem in gnostic style I have made forty-four years ago for a friend's birthday celebration (a private print),[2] a poetic paraphrase of the psychology of the unconscious.

Every pioneer is a monologist, until other people have tried out his method and confirmed his results. Would you call all the great minds which were not popular among their contemporaries, monologists, even that "voice of one crying in the wilderness"?

Buber, having no practical experience in depth psychology, does not know of the *autonomy of complexes,* a most easily observable fact however. Thus God, as an autonomous complex, is a *subject* confronting me. One must be really blind, if one cannot get that from my books. Likewise the *Self* is a redoubtable reality, as everybody learns, who has tried or was compelled to do something about it. Yet I define the Self as a *borderland concept.*

---

2. *Septem Sermones ad Mortuos.* Cf. Maeder, 19 Jan., 17n. 1.

This must be a puzzler for people like Buber, who are unacquainted with the empiricist's epistemology.

Why cannot Buber get into his head that I deal with psychical facts and not with metaphysical assertions? Buber is a theologian and has far more information about God's true existence and other of His qualities than I could ever dream of acquiring. My ambitions are not soaring to theological heights. I am merely concerned with the practical and theoretical problem of how-do-complexes behave? For example, how does a mother-complex behave in a child and in an adult? How does the God-complex behave in different individuals and societies? How does the Self-complex compare with the Lapis philosophorum in Hermetic philosophy and with the Christ-figure in patristic allegories, with Al Chadir in Islamic tradition, with Tifereth in the Kabbala, with Mithras, Attis, Odin, Krishna and so on.

As you see, I am concerned with *images*, human phenomena, of which only ignorants can assume that they are within our control or that they can be reduced to mere 'objects'. Every psychiatrist and psychotherapist can tell you to what an enormous degree man is delivered over to the terrific power of a complex, which has assumed superiority over his mind. (Vide compulsion neurosis, schizophrenia, drugs, political and private nonsense etc.) Mental possessions are just as good as ghosts, demons and gods.

It is the task of the psychologist to investigate these matters. The theologia certainly has not done it yet. I am afraid it is sheer prejudice against science, which hinders theologians to understand my empirical standpoint. Seen from this standpoint the 'experience of God' is *nolens volens* the psychical fact, that I find myself confronted with the psychical event of a factor in myself (more or less represented also by external circumstances) which proves to me to be of insurmountable power. For example, a most rational professor of philosophy, being entirely possessed by the fear of cancer, of which he knows it does not exist. Try to liberate such an unfortunate fellow from his predicament and you will get an idea of 'psychical autonomy'.

I am sorry if X bothers about the question of the basis upon which "religion rests." This is a metaphysical question, the solution of which I do not know. I am concerned with *phenomenal religion*, with its observable facts, to which I try to add a few psychological observations about basic events in the collective unconscious, the existence of which I can prove. Beyond this I know nothing and I have never made any assertions about it.

How does Buber know of something, he cannot "experience psychologically?" How is such a thing possible at all? If not in the psyche, then where else? You see, it is always the same matter: *the complete misunderstanding of the psychological argument:* 'God' within the frame of psychology is an *autonomous complex, a dynamic image, and that is all psychology is ever able to state.* It cannot prove or disprove God's actual existence, but it does know how fallible images in the human mind are.

If Niels Bohr compares the model of atomic structure with a planetary system, he knows it is merely a model of a transcendent and unknown reality, and if I talk of the God-image, I do not deny a transcendental reality, I merely insist on the psychical reality of the God-complex or the God-image, as Niels Bohr proposes the analogy of a planetary system. He would not be so dumb as to believe that his model is an exact and true replica of the atom. No empiricist in his senses would believe his models to be the eternal truth itself. He knows too well how many changes any kind of reality undergoes in becoming a conscious representation.

And my ideas are names, models, and hypotheses for a better understanding of observable facts. I never dreamt that intelligent people could misunderstand them as theological statements, i.e. hypostases. I was obviously too naïve in this regard and that is the reason that I sometimes was not careful enough to repeat time and again: "But what I mean, is only the psychical image of a noumenon" (Kant's thing in itself, which is not a negation as you know.)[3]

---

3. "An object of purely intellectual intuition, devoid of all phenomenal attributes" (*Shorter Oxford Dictionary*). The term was introduced by Kant to distinguish between 'noumenon' and 'phenomenon' as 'an immediate object of perception'.

My empirical standpoint is so disappointingly simple that it needs only an average intelligence and a bit of common sense to understand it, but it needs an uncommon amount of prejudice or even ill will to misunderstand it, as it seems to me. I am sorry if I bore you with my commonplaces. But you asked for it. You can find them in most of my books, beginning with the year 1912,[4] almost half a century ago and not yet noticed by such authorities as Buber. I have spent a lifetime of work in psychological and psychopathological investigations. Buber criticizes me in a field in which he is incompetent and which he does not even understand.

Sincerely yours,

44. Robert C. Smith to Martin Buber

7 July 1960

Dear Prof. Buber,

May I express my deepest appreciation to you for taking the time to answer my many questions even though you were deeply involved in other concerns. From Florence, Italy, Maurice Friedman has written me: "even if he finds the time to answer, which itself is doubtful since he has a whole file of unanswered letters he has not been able to get to and is about to leave for four months in Europe, I cannot imagine that he will be able to answer your dozen questions. To do this he would have to write a whole essay for you and he is hardly in a position to do this. I am afraid you will have to content yourself with what you can get from his books." My profound thanks for your reply!

I am glad to hear that you are planning to elaborate your conception of the unconscious during the course of the year. I have written this to Leslie Farber of the Washington School of Psychiatry and he replies "Am glad to hear he intends to do a particular article on the unconscious because I too would like to make particular reference to it in my own writing. So far, have held back in the hope that he would write such an article."

---

4. Date of publication of *Wandlungen und Symbole der Libido* (orig. version of *Symbols of Transformation*).

You will be interested to know that I wrote quite a strong letter to Prof. Jung listing some of my questions and your replies and asking him particularly to say something about the charge that he is a monologist and reduces God to an object. He was good enough to give me a lengthy reply in his typical "no holds barred" fashion. His misunderstanding of any approach other than his own remains unchanged. He shows that he does not know what the philosophical thinker means by a monologist, and for him subject and object have only a psychological connotation. Nonetheless I feel that perhaps you did not formerly see quite clearly enough the limitations of his specialized vocabulary and the ways that there have been some evidences of growth on Jung's part. Criticism from many quarters has forced him into making more room for faith. It is plainly to be seen though that he has always had the greatest difficulty in recognizing as genuine the contributions of disciplines other than his own.

My deepest thanks and best wishes to you.

Sincerely yours

45. Robert C. Smith to C. G. Jung

Villanova, Pa.
8 July 1960

Dear Prof. Jung,

My thanks to you for taking the time to spell out your own differences with Buber at length. The intensity of your remarks indicates how strongly you feel about the subject. I think though that you go too far when you say that Buber criticizes you in a field in which he is incompetent and does not even understand. As he has said in his reply to you he has no desire whatsoever to criticize your own psychology as such but only to speak of your unacknowledged transgressions into the field of ontology. It goes without saying that there is a sense in which he is incompetent to speak authoritatively of depth psychology just as you are incompetent to speak authoritatively of philosophy of religion. What is important is that we have in the discussion a more genuine dialogue between these two fields. You use the terms subject and self and soul in a very different way from the traditional one. In spite of your protest that others are stupid for not recognizing this you must admit that it is certainly understandable that such is the case.

I do not believe that you are as immune to the charge of being "a modern gnostic" as you would like to make out. Buber does not derive all his impressions from your private print. Throughout your writings you say that you have never been able to believe what you have not been able to understand. But does not faith do precisely this unless it is entirely a 'rational faith' which is but considered reason. Surely you are not a gnostic in the classical sense for you posit no ultimate duality between good and evil but you must admit that there are many gnostic elements in your writings. Malcolm Diamond of Princeton University calls my attention to this when he mentions in a letter to me how you describe the healing of a scientist by your own knowledge of the mandalas (Psyche & Symbol). However I would agree with you that the path of individuation is only open to those who are willing to pursue it. Even Clement of Alexandria found that the pathway to knowledge had to make room for faith. (And by this he no longer meant higher knowledge.) Already he saw that "God being no subject for demonstration, cannot be the object of scientific knowledge" (Strom. IV, ch. XXIV, 156, 1).

If you would read Buber I think you would find that he denies I-Thou knowledge in an objective sense and I-Thou experience in a psychological sense. His distinction between I-Thou and I-It is an ontological one. Of course this is what makes the topic such an intriguing and exciting one. No one can ultimately say whether I-Thou is merely a personal relation or not. If it is, then you are right. If it is more than that as he maintains, then he is correct. And the same thing applies to the problem of selfhood.

Sincerely yours

46. Robert C. Smith to Martin Buber

24 July 1960

Dear Prof. Buber,

Again may I say how much I appreciated receiving your letter of 2 June 1960. I have had the opportunity to discuss your answers with Prof. Kroner when he visited me some time ago. He was interested in your statement that I-Thou is an ontological distinction since he makes a distinction between metaphysics and ontology. I told him that my belief is that you do not. I must confess that we were not quite sure what you meant by 'the Great Self'. Nonetheless we became all the more convinced that Prof. Jung is unable to see these issues in any other than a psychological sense.

I would like to request permission from you to make use of your letter to me in my doctoral dissertation and in a possible future book to be published on my findings on the subject "Religious Issues Between Buber and Jung."

Sincerely yours

47. Robert C. Smith to C. G. Jung

Villanova, Penna.
24 July 1960

Dear Prof. Jung,

I would like to request permission from you to make use of your letter of 29 June 1960 in clarification of your position with Buber for use in my doctoral dissertation and in a possible later book version of the same.

As I noted to you in my last letter, I am quite critical of some of your positions even as further clarified in your letter. Nonetheless I can assure you that I shall do everything possible to give your views a fair and unbiased presentation and to see that they are not quoted out of context and intention. As you know, your views, as those of Buber, are subject to much misinterpretation.

Again may I express my appreciation for the many insights I have gained from your writings. If you agree to my request you may so indicate at the bottom of the present letter if you wish. With every good wish to you.

Cordially yours

Summary of C. G. Jung's Second Letter to Robert C. Smith, 2 August 1960

As this letter has not been published in Jung's collected letters, its text cannot be printed here. In this second letter — which is a reply to Smith's letter of July 8 — Jung claimed that Smith, Buber, and Malcolm Diamond, whom Smith had quoted about Jung's therapeutic work, had misunderstood and misrepresented him. Jung objected to his scientific statements being treated by philosophic criticism, as this inadequate method was leading to appallingly wrong conclusions. He asked Smith not even to mention the fact of Jung ever having written to Smith. He therefore concluded the letter by expressing his wish neither to continue the correspondence nor to have it mentioned at all by Smith in his dissertation. However, he did reply in some detail to Smith's subsequent two letters, and Jung's reply appears here.

48. Robert C. Smith to C. G. Jung

Villanova, Pa.
9 August 1960

Dear Prof. Jung:

I am a bit distressed over the fact that you seem to think I have radically misrepresented your position because I have been bold enough to offer some criticisms that are not exactly to your liking. I assure you that what criticisms I have offered were in no way made to invalidate all that you have had to say. As a fellow searcher for truth I felt compelled to make known my views with regard to your position. You once said that the trouble with Freud was that he was unwilling to drink the bittersweet of philo-

sophic criticism. My impression is that you are also unwilling to
do this if the point of view expressed is at variance with your
own.

You have made it perfectly obvious in all that you have written that you are not a philosopher but an empirical scientist. I
agree with you wholeheartedly and I have no desire to misrepresent you on that account. With regard to the mention of what
Diamond said, I should add that I understand full well that healing only takes place when persons discover things for themselves
and do not rely merely on the therapist's knowledge, however I
was merely citing the way Diamond gave me the reference. Certainly you will have to admit, there are many times when a therapist's theory affects the conceptions of his patients. Regardless of
all that, the question I was really pointing to was whether gnosis
or faith brings about the deeper healing. Obviously, you have
your opinion and I have mine. But the very fact that we do
represents value judgments on both our parts. So you see you
cannot avoid such philosophic assumptions.

I think you will be interested to know that I shall not quote
directly from either of the letters that you have written to me.
But you are asking too much when you ask that I not even mention the fact of our correspondence. This little interchange has
been invaluable to me. Whether you realize it or not, I have
found our correspondence both revealing and enlightening. May
I say that I feel honored to have had the privilege to correspond
with a world-renowned personage like yourself, and again I thank
you for having made your views so plain to me.

Cordially yours

49. Martin Buber to Robert C. Smith

Wengen, Switzerland
11 August 1960

Dear Mr. Smith,

I am not directly interested in metaphysics, only historically.
Instead the concept of ontology is most necessary for my think-

ing, as it makes it possible for me to distinguish categorically between, let us say, any event in being itself and its psychological introjection.

As to your question about what I meant by 'the Great Self' will you please remind me of the context in which I used this term (I have here no copies of my letters at all). I am very glad to give you the permission requested, but would like to read those parts of your dissertation in which you are quoting my answers.

Sincerely yours

50. C. G. Jung to Robert C. Smith

Zürich
16 August 1960

Dear Mr. Smith,

Why can't you understand that the therapeutical performance is a vital process, which I call the 'process of individuation'? It takes place objectively, and it is this experience which helps the patient and not the more or less competent or foolish interpretation of the analyst.

The best the analyst can do is not to disturb the natural evolution of this process. My so-called views about it are only poor means of representing the very mysterious process of transformation in the form of words, which serve no other purpose than to describe its nature.

The process consists in a becoming whole or integrated and that is never produced by words or interpretations but wholly by the nature of the Psyche itself. When I say 'Psyche' I mean something unknown, to which I give the name 'Psyche'.

There is a difference between hypothesis and hypostasis. My hypothesis is that all psychical products referring to religious views are comparable on the basis of a fundamental similarity of the human mind. This is a scientific hypothesis. The Gnostic Buber accuses me to be makes no hypothesis, but a hypostasis in making metaphysical statements.

When I try to establish a fundamental similarity of individual psychical products and alchemistic or otherwise Gnostic noumena, I carefully avoid making a hypostasis, remaining well within the boundaries of the scientific hypothesis.

The fact that I try to make you see my standpoint could show to you that I don't mind the criticism. I only want to defend myself against wrong premises. If I could not stand criticism I would be dead long ago, since I have had nothing but criticism for sixty years. Moreover I cannot understand what my alleged incapacity to stand criticism has to do with the reproach that I am a Gnostic. You simply add to the arbitrary assumption that I am a Gnostic the blame of moral inferiority, and you don't realize that one could make the same subjective reproach to you.

I have accused nobody and if I am attacked I have the right to defend myself in explaining my point of view. There is no need at all to blame me under those circumstances of being intolerant.

Sincerely yours

51. Robert C. Smith to Martin Buber

Box 126 c/o Schuerch
Newbury, New Hampshire
21 August 1960

Prof. Martin Buber
Hotel Waldrand
Wengen, Switzerland
My dear Prof. Buber,

. . . I am delighted that you have offered to look over my efforts. . . . I told you a little about my correspondence with Prof. Jung in my other letters to you. Because of my disagreements with his position he has refused me permission to quote from his letter. Because of your interest in this subject I thought you would appreciate having a copy of our correspondence. Evidently he does not appreciate the criticisms that either you or I have made, and I believe we have both embarked on a thankless task. As you will see he is highly sensitive on this subject. I must request that you keep this correspondence confidential and not make use of it in your further writings. However I would be very much interested in your reaction to it if you would care to venture an interpretation of his highly negative reaction. Frankly I was rather free in the criticisms I offered to him because I felt he could take such criticism in the spirit it was offered. Ah well, one only learns that the psychiatric profession is only too human in this regard.

Are you familiar with Hans Urs von Balthasar's book *Einsame Zwiesprache: Martin Buber?* Scribners & Sons has asked me to review the book for them and give them an evaluation of what its value and interest would be for the American reader. I would be interested to know what you think of the book if you have seen it.

My very warmest and best personal regards to you. I hope that you have a pleasant stay in Switzerland. . . .

Your American friend

P.S. Would you care to venture your own definition of Self or indicate where in your writings you have given such a definition? Would you say that self has for you a transcendent dimension?

52. Martin Buber to Robert C. Smith

Wengen, Switzerland
29 August 1960

Dear Mr. Smith,

I am very busy before leaving here and can answer you only briefly. Your correspondence with Jung is very interesting, and your last two letters to him quite remarkable. As to him, he obviously has not read me at all and so he does not even imagine the existence of another epistemology than the one absorbed in the subject-object relation.

About Jung's concept of the Great Self found at the end of the process of individuation I have written in the course of my discussion with him. With my own understanding of the Self I have dealt in my Washington Seminar on the unconscious that I hope to be able to elaborate next winter.

I know Balthasar's book and appreciate it, but I think it too dogmatical. You cannot be dogmatical and dialogical (*"Zwie-sprache"*) at once.

Cordially yours

53. Robert C. Smith to Martin Buber

Villanova, Penna.
21 September 1960

Dear Prof. Buber,

. . . You will be interested to know that I have received another letter from Prof. Jung since I wrote to you last. He replies to my charge that he is unable to accept philosophical criticism that is not to his liking. This is much more the kind of a letter one would expect to receive from a man of his stature. I am enclosing a copy of this letter for your interest.

In accordance with the permission you granted in your letter of August 11, I have made use of your correspondence with me in my dissertation. I believe that what you have had to say in answer to my questions will be of great interest to the American reader should I ever be able to get this document published in a revised form. What you have had to say in answer to my questions is of much more importance to the basic argument of my study than are the philosophical misconceptions of Prof. Jung. I would like to request your consent for permission to quote from your published writings and our correspondence for the purposes of a possible future book version of this material. Naturally I shall be most grateful to receive your suggestions, comments, and your honest evaluation of my efforts.

Again may I thank you for your interest in my investigation and for your helpful letters which have proved a source of personal encouragement. My very best wishes to you.

Sincerely yours

54. Robert C. Smith to Martin Buber

Villanova, Penna.
11 November 1960

Dear Prof. Buber,

You will be interested to know that Dr. Kroner has read and approved the first draft of my dissertation, subject to certain changes which he has indicated to me. I am now in the process of doing some rewriting so that a final draft may be prepared. I would very much like to know your criticisms so that I could correct any glaring errors before the dissertation is put in final form. Your comments would also be of help to me as I prepare to defend the dissertation before the faculty of Temple University. Would it be possible for you to send me your comments by December 1? If so, it would be greatly appreciated as I would very much like to receive my doctoral degree in February.

Dr. Kroner was in basic sympathy with my critique and conclusions. He felt that I could have been even more severe in criticizing Jung's epistemology. He says that he can not discover any truly Kantian thesis in Jung. Kroner also is not at all happy with the phrase psychic experience. For him experience is never psychic. Do you believe one is justified in using the term experience in a psychological sense?

We discussed your views on Kant. Would you say that Kant's view of God is 'within man'? Kroner claims that if you do that on this point you misunderstand Kant for he believes that Kant's God is the holy author of nature absolutely transcending man.

While acknowledging the enormous contribution of what you have had to say about I and Thou, Kroner thinks you are mistaken when you speak of the I-Thou relation as an ontological distinction. He would think it to be a theological one. He thinks that you never truly define what you mean by ontological. My impression is that you would not make a radical distinction between the ontological and the theological. For myself I think you are somewhat justified in speaking of I and Thou as an ontological dimension but I would have to admit that such usage is not too precise according to traditional usage of the term ontology and appears to originate more from your desire to preserve more than a psychological dimension to human existence. Would you comment?

Kroner also thinks you have not given enough discussion to what he calls the monological dialogue of the self with itself. By this he does not mean simply 'Rückbiegung' or the self bending back upon itself such as the psychological monologue of Jung but the kind of inner dialogue to which Niebuhr[5] refers in *The Self and the Dramas of History.* Do you believe it possible to refer to such inner conversation as dialogue in a genuine sense?

Lastly is it true that while you have no essential dichotomy between spirit and nature that you do tend to set up a kind of dichotomy between nature and spirit by your conception of the movement from I-Thou to I-It?

These are some of the questions that still remain. If you would care to venture to answer some of them I should be most appreciative. Also I would like to receive permission to quote from our correspondence in a future book edition of this material.

I think you said something about expanding your thoughts on the unconscious in book form this winter. If so who will be the publisher and when will this book be available?

With kindest regards.

Sincerely yours

55. Martin Buber to Robert C. Smith

Jerusalem, Israel
13 November 1960

Dear Mr. Smith,

I have been seriously ill since my coming home and therefore I have not been able yet to read your dissertation attentively and I

5. Reinhold Niebuhr (1892–1971), American Protestant theologian and so-cal critic. He taught for many years at the Union Theological Seminary in New York City.

cannot say when I shall be able to do it. But casually I have made the following notes: . . .

. . . To what you say at the end of p. 168 and at the beginning of p. 169, you must compare what is said in my postscript[6] to *I and Thou* about the concept of an absolute person. . . .

What I could read till now of your disseration, I have found interesting and a part of it even important.

Sincerely yours

56. Martin Buber to Robert C. Smith

Jerusalem,
4 January 1961

Dear Mr. Smith,

I have been ill for some time, but am feeling somewhat better now and am taking up my correspondence again. So I want to answer, if only briefly, some of the questions of your letter of 11 November.

I never thought that Kant's view of God is 'within man'. The problem of divine existence has in my opinion haunted Kant all his life. It broke out, if we may say so of a problem, in his amazing *Opus postumum*, about which I have written.

I do not understand what you mean by a theological distinction, as I am basing my conception primarily on the simple experience of a relationship between oneself and other human persons. This is a reality in which I am finding myself and I decline to introject it into the psyche. I say expressly that the duality of the relationships is something that makes man what he is and that only expresses itself in his dual experience. Therefore I call it ontological.

You will find some remarks on the so-called "Monological dialogue of the self with itself" in my address on language of this year, published in *Wort and Wirklichkeit*, herausgegeban von der

6. "Afterword to I and Thou," which appeared for the first time in German in the 1957 edition of *I and Thou*, is included in this volume.

Bayerischen Akademie der Schonen Künste, in Verlag von R. Oldenbourg, Munchen. The passage I mean is to be found on p. 19 ss.[7]

The essay on the unconscious will be the last in a volume of anthropological essays. The English translation of it will be published by Harper. I hope to be able to write it down in March so it can be translated in April.

With kind regards.

Sincerely yours

57. Robert C. Smith to Martin Buber

Villanova, Penna.
16 June 1961

Dear Dr. Buber,

Yesterday was a very exciting day for myself and the members of my family. I was awarded the doctoral degree by Temple University. Again I would like to thank you for your help in answering the many questions that I asked. . . .

. . . I do hope that this note finds you in the best of health. By the way I was sorry to learn of Jung's recent death. His death got very extensive coverage in papers and magazines in this country.

Sincerely yours

7. This essay was published in English as "The Word That Is Spoken" in the volume of collected essays, *The Knowledge of Man* (New York: Harper & Row, 1965), 110–20. It is included in this volume.

Dialogue

The Unconscious

1

There is a story in Confucius's *Analects* about a disciple who spent some time at the court of one of the kings "clearing up concepts." As long as they are unclear, everything in the kingdom is doubtful. Concepts become problematic because they do not show a concrete context that can be controlled. Every abstraction must stand the test of being related to a concrete reality without which it has no meaning. This revision of concepts entails a necessary destruction if the new generation is not to be the lifelong slave of tradition.

The History of the Unconscious: What Leibnitz says about "small imperceptible perceptions" is near the unconscious, but it is not the same thing. He is talking about elements of the soul-process. Plotinus had a clear doctrine of the unconscious: "We do not know all that occurs in any part of the soul just by the fact of its occurring. We know it only when it has penetrated the whole soul" (Fourth *Ennead*, 8, 8). "For it is very possible that even without being conscious of having something one has it in himself and even in a form more effective than if he knew it" (Fourth *Ennead*, 4, 4). "The consciousness seems to obscure the actions that it perceives and only when they occur without it, are they purer, more effective, and more vital" (First *Ennead*, 4, 10). The unconscious is a vital force in me, and if I try to make it conscious, I may spoil it. I cannot in utter seriousness accept the term soul. Consciousness has degrees. The penetration of the whole soul is not necessary for consciousness.

227

Nicholas Cusanus does not use the term, but he speaks about different modes of divine participation in our existence and this corresponds to different degrees of self-knowledge.

Leibnitz's views find their best exposition in his preface to *Nouveaux Essais:* "In every moment in our inner being there is an infinite multitude of perceptions that are not accompanied by apperception and reflection but represent only changes in the soul itself — changes of which we are not conscious because these impressions are either too feeble or too many or too uniform so that they do not show sufficient marks of distinctions. Nevertheless, they can have their effect in unison with other perceptions, and they can be valid in the totality of impressions if only in a somewhat vague and indistinct mode." This is near to the modern psychological concept of the unconscious, but unlike Plotinus it is a description rather than a theory. Nevertheless, the influence of the idea of Leibnitz was very strong. Novalis's remarks on the unconscious depend on Leibnitz and so do those of other German romantics.

In German philosophy Hamann, the antagonist of Kant, has much to say on this subject. In the eighteen forties C. G. Carus, the father of modern psychology, builds his psychology on just this: "The key to the knowledge of the nature of the life of the conscious soul lies in the region of unconsciousness." He means we cannot understand any conscious phenomenon without understanding its unconscious basis. Eduard von Hartmann made of the unconscious the solution to the riddle of the world. Instead of the will of his master Schopenhauer he made the unconscious the movement of creation. He trivialized Schopenhauer.

Freud knew Carus and Von Hartmann. He gave a clear definition — physiological but not biological. Freud was an enraged antivitalist, a real mechanist. One does not find the vitalist current of Bergson in Freud.

The main argument Freud repeatedly mentions as opposed to his doctrine of the unconscious is that the unconscious cannot be psychical because the psychic is conscious. In opposition to this Freud stated that there are occurrences in human beings beyond conscious knowledge but dynamically effective. This is a curious, false alternative — between the unconscious as *only* physiological or *only* psychic. Certain unconscious processes functioned in such a way that they had the property of mind.

REED: It was a tautologous consequence of the popular definition of mind.

DR. EDITH WEIGERT: Freud believed in the division of mind.

BUBER: Just so. Is it one or the other? The unconscious to Freud is not a phenomenon, but it has effects on phenomena. This is not a substantive dualism but a functional one. Despite the revolution in the teachings of Jung, in all his writings too, he puts the unconscious into the *psychic* category and so in all modern psychology. What is the radical difference between physical and psychical phenomena and what is the criterion for subsuming any phenomenon here or there? And why cannot the subconscious be subsumed in one place or the other? Not only the distinguishing of two substances, as in all philosophy, but even the distinguishing of two functional realms is not sufficient.

The *physical* and the *psychical* represent two radically different modes of knowing: either the senses or 'inner sense'. What is the radical difference between phenomena given by the outer senses and those given by the inner sense? Feeling — pure psychic process in time — cannot be found as physical. My memory retains the process but by a new process in time. Physiology deals with things that are to be found, psychology with things that are not to be found. The assumption that the unconscious is either body or soul is unfounded. The unconscious is a state out of which these two phenomena have not yet evolved and in which the two cannot be at all distinguished from each other. The unconscious is our being itself and these two are evolving out of it again and again in every moment. In order to become phenomena, the unconscious must dissociate itself — one of the methods of this dissociation is analytical psychology.

Not everything that is, is a phenomenon. The region of a phenomenon is limited. The psychic is pure process in time. There are meeting points between the physical and the psychic — conscious ones — but we must distinguish between the two realms

Psychic process *cannot* go on in the brain whatever the relation between the two may be. *"Die Seele ist nicht befindlich."* In order to grasp the physical as a whole I need the category of space as well as time. But for the psychic I need time alone.

I mean what modern psychology means by the unconscious — this dynamic fact making itself felt by its effects, effects which the psychologist can explore. For example, if there *are* archetypes we learn something of them by their effects. The archetypes themselves, says Jung, can never be sensed, but they influence life in such and such a way that can only come out of this 'anima'. I don't contest at all that psychology is right in saying there are things that influence our life and that come out in certain conscious states. We cannot say anything about the unconscious in itself. It is never given to us. But we can deduce from certain conscious states that there must be certain things. The radical mistake of Freud was to think that he could have it and not have it. The psychoanalyst cannot understand the unconscious of the other, but he can understand the conscious of the other as a primary thing — there is immediate understanding between man and man. Wilhelm Dilthey tried to analyze *das Verstehen* — the understanding of one another.

2

MAURICE FRIEDMAN (summary and speculation): The basic distinction between the physical and the psychic, though not clear cut, does not follow into the unconscious, which is nonphenomenological and prior to the split between psychic and physical. Freud's logical error, followed by all schools of psychoanalysis, places the unconscious within the person alone. Hence reality is seen as psychic rather than interhuman.

BUBER: Most psychological schools, especially that of Jung, assume that there is a nonphenomenological yet psychical reality. This means the assumption of a rather mystical basis of reality. We know from continuous life experience only about being, comprehending the two directions and two kinds of phenomena. The assumption of a psyche that exists as something exists in space should be either a metaphor or an entirely metaphysical thesis about the nature of being for which we have no basis at all in experience. Freud remained in the last instance a radical physiologist. Jung dealt wrongly with the problem, and Freud did not deal with it at all. Freud takes these questions lightly till the end. Freud does not speak explicitly of the psyche but of what is 'psychoate'. He never defines it. Freud was a simplificator, just as in the social field Marx was before him, that is, one who places a general concept in place of the ever-renewed investigation of reality. A new aspect of reality is treated by the simplificator as the solution of one of the riddles of being. Fifty years of psychotherapeutic thought have been based on this dangerous manner of thinking. Now this period is at an end.

REED: Freud, like the positivists, was not concerned about such questions, but Freud has some explicit metapsychological theorizing.

BUBER: Yes, at the end, but he would not give up what went before and therefore could not accomplish anything thereby. Besides his school clung to his former theories. They had built a whole doctrine and practice on it. But it was a great attempt to grasp the problems in a philosophical manner — a tragic attempt. A thinker who begins anew without daring to begin anew in all earnest must fail. Some thinkers could only avoid it by leaving everything in the state of problems ever renewing themselves. This is the specific responsibility of the thinking man in the face of reality.

DR. TUCKER: Would you equate the psychic with consciousness?

BUBER: There are many degrees of consciousness. Therefore, if in a certain sphere there are so many spheres, I would rather not make it basic. But I cannot define what the psychic is. The main way of thought is again and again to criticize concepts and definitions and face them with a reality that those thinkers did not know about. I decline to define not only because I do not know, but also in the interests of this dynamic of thinking. But the psychic that is going on in this moment cannot be itself sufficiently an object to make a definition possible.

TUCKER: Would you equate the psychic with mind?

BUBER: The psychic we know directly without problem, but 'mind' is an indispensable objectification.

DR. LESLIE FARBER: One of the arguments Freud gives for the unconscious is posthypnotic phenomena. The subject of the unconscious is usually one of suggestion, that is, the person will fall asleep and do so and so. And as we know well by now there is no identity between sleep and hypnosis.

BUBER: What in this hypnotized person is being influenced? Carus would say the psyche. This is just the doubtful point. I would say not the psyche but that nonphenomenal unconscious that dissociates itself into the physiological and psychological. Upon his waking out of hypnosis the first thing that happens is this dissociation. The first thing that happens, therefore, is the contact between the two states rather than the common sphere.

FARBER: I find something here that makes the forgetting of dreams more understandable. One reason they leave so quickly unless they are objectivized in such fashion in psychic awareness is that they do not exist as such.

BUBER: Do we know dreams at all? *Have* we a dream as I have this glass? We have the work of shaping memory. But how can I accept this as the reality he dreamed rather than his attitude in relation to the 'dream' that I can never know in itself. This is the first question. The second is that of the 'content' of dreams and with it Freud's whole theory of repression. What is the main difference between the state of waking and the state of dreaming? We are inclined to think the rhythmical recurrence of dreams is analogous to the conscious state of the soul. Yet we cannot compare a dream to any other phenomenon. In the dream itself it seems we have a certain feeling of consciousness. Its relation to consciousness in psychic life is a real problem. What is the general connection between parts of conscious life? Something very different. Freud has not even tried to deal with these things. Sometimes when I am waking I make a violent effort to detach myself from the world of dreams and enter the common world of man (Heracleitus).

Another question: Some contents that we have in conscious life appear again in dreams. What is the identity and nonidentity of the dream-object with that in waking life? A fourth question: As we all know, there is in conscious life an ordering force. Any morning anew when we awake a power begins to make us act and to live in a common cosmos. There is a hegemony. Nothing of this kind is going on in dreams. They have a certain continuity and connection of their own. What is the nature of this difference? A psychological theory of the dream is made terribly difficult by the fact that the dream is not given us as an experience or an object of investigation or something that can be compared with the conscious. In my old age I have not arrived at a state of equanimity about the dreams I have every night. Freud dealt with it as self-understood. The Taoists never ceased to think about the problem of dreams. The dream is a problem really neighboring that of death. Shakespeare's comparison is not metaphorical, for both are unknown by their very nature. We think we know the dream of our shaping memory, but there is a substrate that eludes us.

MOLLEGEN: Does the shaping memory exist in the dream too?

BUBER: That's a very different kind of shaping memory. In conscious life we can see a legend born in utter innocence. This may go on in dreams, but we cannot know it. There is no objective preservation of a dream whereas other memories have the check of other witnesses.

EDITH WEIGERT: The dream has much similarity with some productions of psychotics; both are disorganized.

BUBER: The human being in the condition of the ordered world does not tolerate something disordered.

WEIGERT: It is very important that we penetrate into his private world in order to break through the disorganization.

BUBER: Here is just the difference. You cannot try to come in touch with the dreamer. As soon as you succeed, there is no more dreaming. It is a dynamic difference.

WEIGERT: You can try to get in touch with the psychotic later when he is less anxious and better organized and this is what we do with the dreamer.

BUBER: No, I can try to come in touch with the schizophrenic. I cannot get in touch with a dreamer. The schizophrenic remains a schizophrenic and something in him becomes common. There is nothing common with the dreamer.

DR. WEININGER: Sometimes he comes out of sleep with something changed in his consciousness.

BUBER: He lies awake in a state of unusual lucidity, but this is passing from sleep into a state of lucidity. I remember and others have confirmed that there are nights of extraordinary lucidity without sleep. The solving of problems in sleep also occurs there. It is an extraordinary awakeness — much more than in the common world. This is not dream or sleep.

MRS. MARJORIE FARBER: Is a dream not like a work of art minus a conscious 'creator'?

BUBER: Imagination is not bound to a certain connection of images. It is not responsible in relation to facts. It has its own laws, but it is not bound to a certain material. But the man remembering dreams would not change anything consciously, willingly. There is a tension of will not to change anything in the dream. In imagination I have a sense of dynamic process of which I am the subject. This distinguishes it from a night of images. This latter is similar to the dream, but in the dream the single appearances are always connected with one another. The dream is epical — a series of events connected with one another — but these flights of images (faces) are entirely dissociated from one another. It has something in common with psychotic *Ideenflucht* (Binswanger).

MARGARET RIOCH: Are you equating the world of sleep and dreams with the unconscious?

BUBER: No, dreams are one of the forms of the unconscious. The so-called soul and the so-called body are not separated from one another, but there is a detached world. I don't differ at all from the analytical schools in this. I accept everything that they call unconscious as such. Some psychotic processes are this — as far as I cannot distinguish a psychic process.

FARBER: The dream is similar to some of the things that go on in psychosis.

KVARNES: In both you can observe it and not be part of it.

BUBER: You can have some dialogue with the schizophrenic.

KVARNES: The patient can drift in and out of psychosis in the course of one interview. In so far as he is psychotic you cannot reach him.

DR. CAMERON: In cases where therapy has progressed successfully there are cases where distance is lost between therapist and patient — dialogue. I have a bearded German patient, very ill, a schizophrenic with whom I had a false relation. Then he was struck by another patient and withdrew entirely into his own world. When I became aware that this kind of sharing was an essential factor in the relationship, then distance reappeared. He told me his dream and he got better.

BUBER: There was a schizophrenic among my friends whose illness I followed for years. He had a wife with astonishing will power who wanted to see him recover once for all; I doubt if such is possible. If this man lives long enough, some of the same or similar events recur. In order to heal him, she visited him in the catatonic moments when he assumed attitudes, positions, and movements some of which are not possible to a normal man. This woman tried and succeeded in imitating him and made the same movements as he. A curious thing then occurred. He let her into his particular world — took her in. Some schizophrenics want to introduce another person from the base common world of man into the particular one — the only one of real value. The influence was positive. Perhaps in the same measure as he let her in, he came out — he appreciated more a world common to the two of them. (EDITH WEIGERT: *Folie à deux*.) About twenty-five years afterward, after this man for a series of years had been normal — a professor in the university respected by all — I saw him and he told me of his wife that she does not venture to go out of her house or even leave her bed by day. The man was seemingly normal. We talked for some hours. But when I left, he told my wife that he had been very useful to the British through his connection with the stars.

Our common world is to the schizophrenic a world of illusions, conventions. Their particular world is the real one. They even have a double stream of memory.

DR. CAMERON: The absence of distance is characteristic of schizophrenia.

BUBER: In the dreams that we remember there is sometimes

an interposition of spaces, meaning that here things are going on and here other things, not intermingling. Here there are, so to speak, two planes, two space dimensions going on, one in the face of the other. Even more curious are appearances in time. I once had a dream in which at one moment I walked forward and a wind was blowing into my face, and I said to myself in the dream, "Ah, this is the other time." I felt not only the one line of time going on from birth to death, but also as if there were another line of time coming toward me, striking me. In reflection I thought, "Oh, this is the same thing with space as with time." In dreams there is a connection of things entirely different from waking, but it exists. There was a time in my life when I knew very much of dreams and then less and less, so now it is only remembering. What Rank wrote on dreams is rather interesting.

WEIGERT: The decrease in interest in dreams is because the interpretation of dreams is an art.

BUBER: In its very reality the dream is inaccessible. The hypnotic dream is very different from the usual one. A certain dream went on until in a moment I felt in the dream, "It is not as it should be — what now?" As if I were writing a story and thought of changing it. From this moment on the same scene occurred again and again with some variants. Finally, I succeeded in changing the last scene and it went on. This recurred many times. When awake I thought there is a certain moment of will in the dream though not felt as such in the dream.

DR. SMITH: What do you consider the implications you see in the unconscious and shaping memory of a dream?

BUBER: Dreams are not the best example because of the difficulty of making dreams a material of research.

SMITH: Dreams in practice are dealt with along lines you suggest more than the theories of dreams do.

BUBER: First I should advise to observe what the waking man does with the dream. In the last ten years or so I have the impression of a certain change in psychotherapeutic practice in which more and more therapists are not so confident that this or that theory is right and have a more 'musical', floating relationship to their patient. The deciding reality is the therapist, not the methods. Without methods one is a dilettante. I am for methods, but just in order to use them, not to believe in them. Although no doctor can do without a typology, he knows that at a certain moment the incomparable person of the patient stands before the incomparable person of the doctor; he throws away as much of his typology as he can and accepts this unforeseeable thing that goes on between therapist and patient. This change goes along with a 'medical realism' which, unlike the ordinary use of the term, is no acceptance of general concepts but accepting this situation as it is in its uniqueness. Although I am not allowed to renounce either typology or method, I must know in what moment I must give them up.

DR. DAVID RIOCH: Could you differentiate giving up hypotheses for data from giving them up for the unique?

BUBER: People cannot communicate about objectified things except in a certain common language.

RIOCH: You have past experience, present experience, and formulation.

BUBER: Yes, but formulation is secondary.

RIOCH: Formulation is primary since you can't have a datum without formulation.

BUBER: Experience is the presupposition of all formulation. I mean the real meeting of therapist and patient which precedes formulae and data.

RIOCH: There is a distinction between hypotheses based on data and hypotheses based on inference, for example, the unconscious, hostility, and love. A lot of these derivations are being given up, and quite usefully.

BUBER: Yes, I don't contest it. But the main thing is what is different from other experiences and inferences and not what is common.

RIOCH: Do you know anyone who has had a night of lucidity without having worked diligently on a problem beforehand?

BUBER: Yes, myself—in general not, but once or twice as a surprise, with a character of continuous surprise, and it determined the course of my other thought afterward.

RIOCH: When you get something, is it necessary to check it?

BUBER: Never in the process itself, sometimes afterward. The sad thing is that I forget it.

3

FARBER: There seem to be three areas of implications of your theory of the unconscious: for Freudian theory, for the dialogic as compared to the psychological approach, and for therapy in general.

BUBER: I don't know about the implications of my ideas in various fields. When I am asked, I begin to think about them. I was about forty when I began to think about these things. I got the impression that different men in different fields became interested and wanted to transpose these ideas. I was willing to be used. In 1923 or so the psychotherapists began to be interested and wanted to talk with me. And I talked and talked. They, not I, made the implications. I will try tonight, but I have no conclusions or consequences. If you ask me a question, I will just begin to think about it.

FARBER: Since you say Freud made a mistake in making the unconscious psychic, what does your theory imply concerning Freud's bringing over the contents of the unconscious to consciousness — for repression, fixation, transference, and free association?

BUBER: Making the conscious unconscious means there are repressed elements which the patient did not want to keep. He put them down into Acheron, and now the therapist induces him to bring them out into the open. If the unconscious is not something psychic that can be preserved in the underground but just a piece of human body and soul existence, it cannot at all again be raised as it was. We do not have a deep freeze which keeps fragments, but this unconscious has its own existence which can again be dissociated into physical and psychic phenomena, but it can mean a radical change of the substance. This radical change can be brought up by the patient under the supervision, help, and even initiative of the therapist. This new dissociation can be brought up in very different ways, but every time a radical change is going on. What is the meaning of this curious co-operation between two persons in the course of which this change and elaboration is being made? Transference is a presupposition of this, but even the concept of transference changes radically if it is not to make the unconscious conscious but the elaboration of dissociated elements. This is a unique cooperation, the material of which is just a lump of the substance of the other. If the aim is to bring up something that is lying in the underground, then the therapist is only a kind of midwife. But if this work means real and sometimes radical change of the substance, then transference implies eminently a certain influence of the therapist on the very act being made. The patient has the impression of discovery going on in relation to something contained in his soul and in unconscious form. This is a mistake of the patient induced by the relation between him and the therapist. He brings up what he senses is wanted of him. I would ask the therapists of the world to examine anew the nature of this unique transference relationship.

MARGARET RIOCH: This puts great responsibility on the therapist.

BUBER: *Yes.* Since something is made and produced, rather than just being brought up. No other relationship produces such strange phenomena. The responsibility in this new concept is shared and is not only up to the therapist.

FARBER: Freud moved from hypnosis to free association. How would you describe free association?

BUBER: It is usually described as putting the patient in such an attitude that he does not direct his thoughts but lets himself say what comes to mind. My question is: is this indeed free association? What makes us think it is free?

FARBER: It is clear — we agree it is rare — the patient would not need our help if he could free associate.

BUBER: There are two kinds of therapists, one who knows more or less consciously the kind of interpretation he will get and the other, the psychologist who does not know. I am entirely on the side of the latter, who does not want something precise. He is ready to receive what he will receive. He cannot know what method he will use beforehand. He is, so to speak, in the hands of his patient. You cannot interpret different material by the same method. Take, for example, literary texts. You cannot interpret poetry by the same methods as a novel. In the world of patients the differences are greater than this. In the interpretation of dreams, if a therapist is not a Freudian, Jungian or Adlerian, but is what the man puts to him, he is a better therapist. There is more in common to literature than to people. The interpretation of dreams becomes more and more difficult without categories. He must be ready to be surprised. From this a new type of therapist may evolve — a person of greater responsibility and even greater gifts, since it is not so easy to master new attitudes without ready-made categories. I see this new willingness to be surprised in the writings of Sullivan. This has an analogy in the physical sciences where terminology is being changed. New terminology is needed to express Niels Bohr's theory of complementarities — the one I think most important of the theories of our day.

EDITH WEIGERT: I understand about liberating ourselves from categories, yet one needs some charted expectations. Is there not a middle way which will avoid preconceived ideas yet have some line of direction of expectation of what is to be found?

BUBER: The usual therapist imposes himself on the patient without being aware of it. What I mean is the conscious liberation of the patient from this unconscious imposition of the therapist — leaving the patient really to himself and seeing what comes out of it. The therapist approaches the patient, but he must try to influence him as little as possible, that is, the patient must not be influenced by the general ideas of the school. The patient must be left to himself, if I may say so, with the humility of the master, and then the therapist awaits the unexpected and does not put what comes into the categories. (Analogous to the interpretation of the poem.) It is much easier to impose than to use the whole force of the soul to leave him to himself and not to touch him, so to speak. When I read of an unknown poet, I cannot use any method when I receive this poem. If you judge Eliot by Keats you fail. The real master responds to uniqueness.

MAURICE FRIEDMAN: Is the unconscious, instead of a psychic sphere within, a sphere which has *more* direct contact with and part in the interhuman than the psychic? If so, would notions such as introjection and projection be partially open to question on this ground?

BUBER: This must be rethought, but it will take time — twenty years. The new therapist may not be called a psychologist or psychotherapist by that time. In certain crises of later childhood I feel that more decisive formation is going on than in infancy. Social and cosmic puberty is what I refer to, and not just to sexual puberty, for they may not occur. We need new terms and a new approach. If it will be done, it must be by new methods, by new insights. If the unconscious is that part of the existence of a person in which the realms of body and soul are not dissociated, then the relationship between two persons would mean the relationship between two nondivided existences. Thus the highest moment of relation would be what we call unconscious. But unconscious should have, may have, will have, more influence in the interhuman than the conscious. For example, in shaking hands, if there is real desire to be in touch, the contact is not bodily or psychic, but a unity of one and the other. The unconscious as such does not enter easily into action. I pronounce a word, you receive it — the unconscious has no such means at its disposition. The unconscious sometimes leads to a half-articulated exclamation which all the prepared words cannot, however. The voice becomes the direct instrument of the unconscious in this case.

DR. RYCOFF: The patient suffers infinitely more from preconceptions than the therapist (his defenses). Does openness on the part of the therapist lead him to drop these defenses?

BUBER: Are you sure this is the normal attitude of the patient? In the time of strongest transfer is there not the need of the patient to give himself up in his unconscious into the hands of the therapist so that contact may arise between them?

RYCOFF: He cannot do this. He suffers from repetition — uses the same devices time after time and does not see the new in the situation.

BUBER: One doctor kept a diary on such things, and a year later laughed at his diagnoses.

RYCOFF: You would put your emphasis on the *receptivity* of the therapist?

BUBER: Yes, but I am not sure receptivity is the right word. But the therapist must be willing — so that the patient trusts existentially.

FARBER: Does your theory imply that healing takes place through meeting rather than through insight and analysis?

BUBER: A certain very important kind of healing — existential healing — takes place thus, healing not just of a certain part of the patient, but of the very roots of the patient's being.

DR. NELKIN: What would you think of saying that healing leads to meeting? Patients use devices to prevent meeting, and this is called disease. But if these devices are abandoned, that meeting may occur?

BUBER: I'm doubtful about this. Do you mean that the *patient* is the cause of the meeting's not taking place? There are certain difficulties on the side of the patient and some, perhaps not less, on the side of the therapist. Not everyone is a therapist who thinks himself one even though he has studied and has the given abilities. Let us look at the kind of relation called trust — existential trust of a whole person to another. What we call in general life trust has a particular representation in the domain of healing, and so long as it is not there, this need to give up into the hands of the therapist what is repressed will not be realized. I know some therapists in Europe rather intimately that were gifted and knew a lot, masters of methods who realized it took a long time to overcome the patient's difficulties (but who did not have trust).

FRIEDMAN: Does your view of the unconscious and of therapy imply confirmation instead of observation and transference? Or do transference and confirmation complement or include each other?

BUBER: Let us divide this question in two. Confirmation in this context is too general a term. A certain kind of confirmation should be specified. Secondly, confirmation does not replace transference, but if meeting is the decisive factor, the other concepts would change also, in both their meaning and their dynamic. Everything is changed in real meeting. Confirmation can be misunderstood as *static*. I meet another — I accept and confirm him as he now is. But confirming a person *as he is* is only the first step, for confirmation does not mean that I take his appearance at this moment as the person I want to confirm. I must take the other person in his dynamic existence, in his specific potentiality. How can I confirm what I want most to confirm in his present being? That is the hidden, for in the present lies hidden what *can become.* His potentiality makes itself felt to me as that which I would most confirm. (In religious terms, his created purpose.)

FRIEDMAN: Is there a special kind of confirmation for therapy?

BUBER: I am inclined to think that in the strongest illness manifesting itself in the life of a person the highest potentiality of this person is manifesting itself in negative form.

UNIDENTIFIED SPEAKER: In healing this illness, is the therapist confirming the negative?

BUBER: The therapist can influence in a direct way the growing up of potentialities. Healing is not the bringing up of the old, but of the new, not bringing up of zero, but counterbalancing with the positive.

WOLFGANG WEIGERT: Don't I dissociate every time I become aware of myself? What is dissociative experience?

BUBER: The unconscious is not a phenomenon, either physiological or psychic, and we never experience it directly but only know it by its effects, by the dissociation of the lump into body and soul phenomenon. Dissociation is the process of its manifesting itself in inner and outer perceptions. The conscious life of the patient is a dualistic life, as he knows it; his objective life is not dualistic, but he doesn't know it.

W. WEIGERT: Is this dualism an illness?

BUBER: No, it is just the biography of body-soul. No man can know his own unity.

DAVID RIOCH: What can you say about God in healing?

BUBER: In that moment when the name of God is mentioned, most human circles break asunder as persons without knowing it. In that moment the commonness of thinking — the fact of thinking together — is disrupted. The difference between the world with God and without is so enormous that discussion of

God must divide except in a group united by a real common faith. People say God without meaning reality, as a sublime convention of a cultured person.

UNIDENTIFIED SPEAKER: If man cannot know his own unity, does this mean that he can't know his self?

BUBER: To say man cannot perceive his unity as an object does not mean that he can have no conception of his self. In rare moments he may feel the uniting of his forces, each force in its own sphere, united without losing its own essence. This uniting is the precondition of real decisions. A decision made with only a part of a man is not true decision. Man can have in a certain measure the consciousness, the feeling of this coming together of his forces, his acting unity, but he cannot perceive his unity as an object. As long as man perceives the self as an object, he is not united.

DR. CAMERON: Can you enlarge on the nature of the shaping memory?

BUBER: The birth and growth of legends is a good example. Something occurs that is so overwhelming that those who experience it cease to be faithful chroniclers and in utter innocence remember it as a miracle. The memory shapes what occurred.

CAMERON: Are you aware in your dream that you are dreaming, shaping?

BUBER: You cannot remember a dream otherwise than by shaping it. Your inner action is a part of the result of what you call the content of the dream. There is an active part in dreams themselves as well that bears some analogy to action in waking life.

CAMERON: Does this relate to distance? This standing back appears in schizophrenia — "This is crazy."

BUBER: The schizophrenic has a "double memory." He dwells in a common world and in his own world. Example "Der Oberdada" with his diary of Weimer (1910).

MARGARET RIOCH: Is there an essential difference between the teacher-pupil relationship, on the one hand, and the therapist-patient relationship on the other?

BUBER: The two have in common the fact that teacher and

therapist experience the relationship from the side of pupil and patient and not vice-versa. The teacher experiences from his side *and* from the pupil's, but there is no reciprocity there; the pupil cannot and should not experience the teacher's side. If he does, there is no teacher-pupil relation, but it breaks or they become friends. The same thing is true for the therapist and the patient. The therapist must feel the other side as a bodily touch to know how the patient feels it. If the patient could do this, there would be no need of therapy and no relationship. But there is an essential difference. There exists a specific, legitimate, rather problematic but nonetheless legitimate, superiority of the therapist. He cannot go on without it. He must, of course, be humble in it if he is to be a therapist. I don't think a teacher has a real superiority. The therapist in the most favorable cases can heal really. No teacher can teach perfectly. The teacher is a rather tragic person because in most cases learning is fragmentary.

RIOCH: The therapist is fragmentary too. There is no complete development of the person.

BUBER: The existential element means bringing the patient to self-healing, which is the same task as teaching.

Martin Buber and Carl Rogers

REV. DEWITT BALDWIN: [The first 11 seconds on the tape are largely unintelligible.] . . . Dr. Maurice Friedman as a, well, an interpreter or moderator . . . and I'm sure that many of you have been looking forward to this opportunity of seeing the exchange and feeling the [unintelligible] that the two men like Dr. Carl Rogers and Dr. Buber. And so my job tonight is a very pleasant one in [quality of recording improves] bidding you welcome and saying sit back and enjoy at least an hour of time when you can think with two men who want to come to little closer grips with their own ideas. I just want to introduce one person and let him speak of the others. The moderator is Professor Maurice S. Friedman, professor of philosophy at Sarah Lawrence College, Bronxville, New York. Professor Friedman, as those who have been in the conference well realize, is one of the best American interpreters of Martin Buber. He had his undergraduate work at Harvard, graduate work at Ohio State and the University of Chicago, where he took his doctor's degree, and perhaps is best known in relation to Martin Buber for his book, *Martin Buber: The Life of Dialogue.* And so, Maurice, I'll turn over to you and know you'll have a good time.

MAURICE FRIEDMAN: Thank you, DeWitt Baldwin. Gives me a great deal of pleasure to moderate this because I could say I perhaps initiated the dialogue between Professor Buber and Professor Rogers some years ago when someone pointed out to me some resemblances in, in their thought, and I wrote to Dr. Rogers and he kindly supplied me with some papers and then we corresponded a while, and then I sent this material to Buber,

246

including some of Professor Rogers's articles, and so I was very happy indeed when the idea of the two of them speaking here in dialogue came up. I think it is a *most* significant meeting, not just in terms of — [brief largely unintelligible interruption having to do with the position of the microphone] not just in terms of psychotherapy, but of the fact that both these men have [unintelligible] our admiration as persons with an approach to personal relations and personal becoming. There are so many remarkable similarities between their thought that it's also intriguing to have the privilege of seeing them talk with one another and seeing what issues may also come out. And my role as moderator is only, if occasion should arise, to sharpen these issues or interpret one way or another. You don't, I think, need introduction to Professor Buber since the conference is centered around him, and I'm sure you don't need introduction to Dr. Rogers either. He, of course, has been famous for a great many years as the founder of the once so-called nondirective therapy, now, I believe, rechristened client-centered therapy, and is the Director of the University of Chicago Counseling Center, where he has had very fruitful relations with the theological group and the personality and religion courses there. And the form of this dialogue will be that Dr. Rogers will himself raise questions with Dr. Buber and Dr. Buber will respond, and perhaps with a question, perhaps with a statement. We'll let them carry it from there. Dr. Rogers.

CARL ROGERS: One thing I think I would say to the audience before starting to talk with Dr. Buber is that this is most certainly an unrehearsed dialogue. The weather made it necessary for me to spend all day arriving here, and so it was only an hour or two ago that I met Dr. Buber, even though I have met him a long time ago in his writings.

I think that the first question I would like to ask you, Dr. Buber, may sound a trifle impertinent, but I would like to explain it and then perhaps it won't seem impertinent. I have wondered: How have you lived so deeply in interpersonal relationships and gained such an understanding of the human individual, without being a psychotherapist? [Buber laughs; audience laughs.] Now the reason I ask that is that it seems to

me that a number of us have come to sense and experience some
of the same kinds of learnings that you have expressed in your
writings, but very frequently we have come to those learnings
through our experience in psychotherapy. I think that there is
something about the therapeutic relationship that gives us permission, almost *formal* permission, to enter into a deep and close
relationship with a person, and so we tend to learn very deeply
in that way. I think of one psychiatrist friend of mine who says
that he never feels as whole, or as much of a person, as he does
in his therapeutic interviews; and I share that feeling. And so, if
it is not too personal, I would be interested in knowing what
were the channels of knowing that enabled you to really learn so
deeply of people and of relationships?

MARTIN BUBER: Hmmm. It's rather a biographical question.
I think I must give instead of one answer, two. [Rogers: Uhm
huh.] One, [unclear: *"aber"* (German for "but") or perhaps
"rather"] this is only just a particular — is that I'm not entirely a
stranger in, let me say, psychiatry, because when I was a student — it's long ago — I studied three terms psychiatry, and what
they call in Germany "Psychiatrische-Klinik." I was most interested in the latter. You see, I have not studied psychiatry in order
to become a psychotherapist. I studied it, three terms. First with
Flechsig in Leipzig, where I was student of Wundt. Afterwards
in Berlin with Mendel, and third term with Bleuler in Zurich,
which was the most interesting of the three. And, I wanted just
then — I also was a very young, inexperienced, and not very understanding young man. But I had the feeling that I wanted to
know about man, and man in the *so-called* pathological state. I
doubted even then if it is the right term. [Rogers: Oh, I see.] I
wanted to see, if possible to meet, such people, and to establish — as far as I can remember — to establish the *relation*, the real
relation between what we call a sane man and what we call a
pathological man. [Rogers: Uh huh.] And this I have learned in
some measure — as far as a boy of twenty or so [Buber chuckles]
can learn such things.

But what *mainly* constituted what you ask — it was something
other. It was just a certain inclination to meet people, and as far

as possible just to change if possible something in the other, *but also* to let me be changed by him. At any event, I had no resistance — I put no resistance — to it. I — already then as a young man — I felt I have not the right to want to change another if I am not open to be changed by him as far as it is legitimate. Something is to be changed, and his touch, his contact, is able to change it more or less. I cannot be, so to say, above him, and say, "No! I'm out of the play. You are mad." And so from my — let me see — there were two phases of it. The first phase went until the year eighteen, eighteen nineteen [nineteen eighteen], meaning until I was about forty.

ROGERS: Till you're about forty?

BUBER: Just so. And then, in eighteen nineteen, I felt something rather strange. I felt that I had been strongly influenced by something that came to an end just then, meaning the Second, the First World War.

ROGERS: In nineteen eighteen.

BUBER: It ended then, and in the course of the war, I did not feel very much about this influence. But at the end I felt, "Oh, I have been terribly influenced," because I could not resist to what went on, and I was just compelled to, may I say so, to live it. You see? Things that went on just in this moment. [Rogers: Uh huh.] You may call it "imagining the real." [Rogers: Uh huh.] Imagining what was going on. This imagining, for four years, influenced me terribly. Just when it was finished [Rogers: Uh hmm], it finished by a certain episode in May nineteen when a friend of mine, a great friend, a great man, was killed by anti-revolutionary soldiers [Rogers: uh huh] in a very barbaric way, and I, now again once more — and this was the last time — I was compelled to imagine just this killing, but not in an optical way alone, but may I say so, just with my body.

ROGERS: With your feelings.

BUBER: And this was the decisive [unintelligible] or rather the decisive moment, after which, after some days and nights in this state, I felt, "Oh, something has been done to me." [Rogers: Uh huh.] And from then on, these meetings with people, particularly with young people, were the — became — in a somewhat different form. I had a decisive experience, experience of four years, very concrete experience, and from now on, I had to give something more than just my inclination to exchange thoughts and feelings, and so on. I had to give the fruit of an experience.

ROGERS: Sounds as though you're saying the knowledge, perhaps, or some of it, came in the twenties, but then some of the wisdom you have about interpersonal relationships came from wanting to meet people openly without wanting to dominate. And then — I see this as kind of a threefold answer — and then, third, from really living the World War, but living it in your own feelings and [Buber: uh huh] imagination.

BUBER: Just so. Because this latter was really, I cannot say it in another language, it was really a living *with* those people. People wounded, killed [Rogers: uhm huh] in the war.

ROGERS: You felt their wounds.

BUBER: Yes. But feeling is not sufficiently strong — [Rogers: Uh huh] — the word 'feeling'.

ROGERS: You'd like something stronger.

I'm going to make one suggestion, even though it interrupts us a little. I can't face the mike and face you at the same time. [Buber: Oh.] Would you mind if I turned the table just a little?

BUBER: Yes, please, please do.

ROGERS: Then I —

BUBER: Shall I sit here?

ROGERS: Yes. It — move it forward just a little then I think it —

BUBER: Is this right?

ROGERS: That seems better to me. Hope it does to the audience.

FRIEDMAN: While he is changing, I'll interject this, that Professor Rogers's question reminded me of a theological student from a Baptist seminary who talked to me about Professor Buber's thought for an hour, and when he left he said, "I must ask you this question. Professor Buber is so good. How is it he's not a Christian?" [Laughter.]

BUBER: Now may I tell you a story, not about me, but a true story, too, not just an anecdote. A Christian officer — I don't —

colonel, or so — had to explain some people in — I think — in Wales, had to explain them something in the war, in the Second War [unintelligible], to explain them something — soldiers — something about the Jews. It began, of course, with the explanation what Hitler means and so on, and he explained to them that the Jews are not just a barbarous race, they had a great culture and so on; and then he addressed a Jewish soldier that was there and knew something and told him, "Now you go on and tell them something." And this young Jew told them something about Israel and even about Jesus. And, to wit, one of the soldiers answered, "Do you mean to tell us that before your Jesus we have not been Christian people?" [Extended laughter.]

BUBER: Now you go on.

ROGERS: Oh no. [unintelligible — not after this?]

BUBER: No? [More laughter.]

ROGERS: Well, I'd like to shift to a question that I have often wondered about. I have wondered whether your concept — or your experience — of what you have termed the I-Thou relationship is similar to what I see as the effective moment in a therapeutic relationship. And I wonder — if you would permit me, I might take a moment or two to say what I see [Buber: yes, yes] as essential in that — and then perhaps you could comment on it from your point of view.

I feel that when I'm being effective as a therapist [Buber: mmmm], I enter the relationship as a subjective person, not as a scrutinizer, not as a scientist, and so on. [Buber: Uh.] I feel, too, that when I am most effective, then somehow I am relatively whole in that relationship, or the word that has meaning to me is is "transparent." That is, there is nothing — to be sure there may be many aspects of my life that aren't brought into the relationship, but what is in the relationship is transparent. There is nothing hidden. [Buber: Mmm.] Then I think, too, that in such a relationship I feel a real willingness for this other person to be what he is. I call that 'acceptance'. I don't know that that's a very good word for it, but my meaning there is that, I'm willing for him to possess the feelings he possesses, to hold the attitudes he holds, to be the person he is. [Buber: Mmm.] And then I sup-

pose another aspect of it that is important to me is that I think in
those moments I really am able to sense with a good deal of
clarity the way his experience seems to him, really viewing it
from within him, and yet without losing my own personhood or
separateness [Buber: uh huh] in that. And, then, if in addition to
those things on my part, my client or the person with whom I'm
working is able to sense something of those attitudes in me, then
it seems to me there is a real, experiential meeting of persons, in
which each of us is changed. I don't know — I think sometimes
the client is changed more than I am, but I think both of us are
changed in that kind of an experience.

Now, I see that as having *some* resemblance to the sort of thing
you have talked about in I-Thou relationship. Yet, I suspect
there are differences. At any rate, I would be interested very
much in your comments on how that description seems to you in
relation to what you have thought of in terms of two persons
moving or an I-Thou kind of relationship.

BUBER: Now I may try — but allow me to ask questions
[Rogers: uh huh] too, about what you mean. First of all, I would
say, this is the action of a therapist. It's a very good example for
a certain mode of dialogic existence. I mean: Two persons have a
certain situation in common. This situation is, from your point of
view — point is not a good word, but let's see it from your point
of view — it is a sick man coming to you and asking a particular
kind of help. Now, look down [unintelligible — Rogers over-
laps] — what would you see?

ROGERS: May I interrupt there?

BUBER: Yeah, please do.

ROGERS: I feel that if, from my point of view, this is a sick
person [someone pours water], then probably I'm not going to
be of as much help as I might be. [Buber: Mmm.] I feel this is a
person. [Buber: Mmm.] Yes, somebody else may call him sick, or
if I look at him sort of from an objective point of view, then I
might agree, too, "Yes, he's sick." But in entering the relationship, it seems to me if I am looking upon it as "I am a relatively
well person [Buber: mmm] and this is a sick person" —

BUBER: No, but this I don't mean.

ROGERS: — no good.

BUBER: I don't mean this. Let me leave out this word "sick." [Rogers: Uhm.] A man coming to you for help. The difference — the essential difference — between your role in this situation and his is obvious. [Rogers: Uh huh.] He comes for help to you. You don't come to help for him. And not only this, but you are *able*, more or less, to help him. He can do different things to you, but not just help you. And not this alone. You *see* him, really. I don't mean that you cannot be mistaken, you see [Rogers: um hmm], but you *see* him, just as you said, *as he is*. He cannot, by far, cannot see *you*. Not only in that degree, but even in that *kind* of seeing. You are, of course, a very important person for him. But not a person whom he wants to see and to know and is able to. You're important for him. He is, from the moment he comes to you, he is, may I say, entangled in your life, in your thoughts, in your being, your communication, and so on. But he is not interested in you as you. It cannot be. You are interested, you say so and you are right, in him as this person. This kind of detached presence he cannot have and give. And now this is the first point, as far as I see it. And the second is — now, please, you —

ROGERS: [Unintelligible.] Yes, I'm not [Buber: yes], I'm not entirely sure —

BUBER: You may interrupt me any moment.

ROGERS: Oh, all right. I really want to understand that. The fact that I am able to see him with less distortion than he sees me, and that I do have the role of helping him and that he's not [Buber: mmm] trying to know me in that same sense — that's what you mean by this "detached presence"?

BUBER: Yes, hmmm hmm.

ROGERS: I just wanted to make sure I —

BUBER: Hhmm. Hmmm.

ROGERS: Okay.

BUBER: Yes [Rogers: okay]; yes, only this.

ROGERS: Uh huh.

BUBER: Now, the second fact, as far as I see as a fact, is in this situation that you have in common with him, only from two sides. You are on one side of the situation — on the, may I say so,

more or less active, and he in a more or less passive, not entirely
active, not entirely passive, of course — but relatively. And, let us
now look on this common situation from your point of view and
from his point of view. The same situation. [Rogers: Uh.] You
can see it, feel it, experience it from the two sides. Let's begin
from your side seeing him, observing him, knowing him, helping
him — but he — from your side and from his side. You can experience, I would venture to say, bodily, experience his side of the
situation. When you *do*, so to speak, something to him, you *feel*
yourself *touched* by what you do to him. He cannot do it at all.
You are at your side and at his side at the same time. Here and
there, or let's rather say, there and here. Where he is and where
you are. He cannot be but where he is. And this, you will, not
only you will, you want. Your inner necessity may be as they are.
I accept that. I have no objection at all. But the situation has an
objection. You have — necessarily — another attitude to the situation than he has. You are able to do something that he's not able.
You are not equals and cannot be. You have a great task — self-
imposed — a great self-imposed task to *supplement* this need of his
and to do rather more than in the normal situation. But, of
course, there are limits, and I may be allowed to tell you — certainly in your experience as a therapist, as a healing person or
helping to healing, you must experience it again and again —
these limits to simple humanity. "To simple humanity" meaning:
Being, I and my partner, so to speak, alike to one another, on the
same plane. I see, you *mean* being on the same plane, but you
cannot be. There is not only you, your mode of thinking, your
mode of doing, there is also a certain situation — things are so
and so — which may sometimes be tragic and even more terrible
than what we call tragic. You cannot change this. Humanity, human will, human understanding, are not everything. There is
some reality we confront — is confronting us. We cannot — we
may not — forget it for a moment.

ROGERS: Well, what you've said certainly stirs up lots of reactions in me. One of them, I think, is this. Let me begin first on
a point that I think we would agree on. I suspect that you would
agree, too, that if this client comes to the point where he can

experience what he is expressing, but also can experience my understanding of it and reaction to it, and so on, then really therapy is just about over.

BUBER: Yes. This is just what I mean.

ROGERS: OK. But one other thing that I feel is this. I've sometimes wondered whether this is simply a personal idiosyncracy of mine, but it seems to me that when another person is really expressing himself and his experience and so on, I don't feel, in the way that you've described, different from him. That is — I don't know quite how to put this — but I feel as though in that moment his way of looking at his experience, distorted though it might be, is something I can look upon as having equal authority, equal validity with the way I see life and experience. And it seems to me that that really is the basis of helping, in a sense.

BUBER: Yes.

ROGERS: And I do feel a real sense of equality between us.

BUBER: No doubt of it. But I am not speaking now about your feeling but about a real situation. I mean, you two look, as you just said, on *his* experience. Neither you nor he look on *your* experience. The subject is *exclusively* he and his experience. He cannot in the course of, let's say, a talk with you, he cannot change his position and ask you, "Oh, Doctor, where have you been yesterday? [Laughter.] Oh, have you been to the movies? What was it and how were you impressed?" He *cannot* do it. So, I see and feel very well your feeling, your attitude, your taking part. But you cannot change the given situation. There is something objectively real that confronts you. Not only he confronts you, the person, but just the situation. You cannot change it.

ROGERS: Well, now I'm wondering who is Martin Buber, you or me, because what I feel —

BUBER: Heh, heh, heh. [Audience joins laughter.]

ROGERS: — because —

BUBER: I'm not, so to say, "Martin Buber" as, how do you say, with the signs, brackets? Yes — no?

ROGERS: In that sense, I'm not "Carl Rogers" [Buber: I'm not —] either. [Laughter.]

BUBER: Yes, you see, I'm not a quoted man that thinks so and so and so on.

ROGERS: I know.

BUBER: We were just speaking about [Rogers: sure] something that interests us, perhaps, in the same [Rogers: right] measure. You're in another kind, you are always in contact with, in practical contact with —

ROGERS: Now, let's forget that facetious remark, what I wanted to say is this: That I think you're quite right, that there is an objective situation there [Buber: uh huh], one that could be measured, one that is real [someone pours water], one that various people could agree upon if they examined the situation closely. But it has been my experience that that is reality when it is viewed from the outside, and that that really has *nothing* to do with the relationship that produces therapy. [Buber: Umm.] That is something immediate, equal, a meeting of two persons on an equal basis — even though in the world of I-It, that could be seen as a very unequal relationship.

BUBER: Now, Dr. Rogers, this is the first point where we must say to one another, "We disagree."

ROGERS: OK. [Laughter.]

BUBER: You see, I cannot only look on you, on your part of things, of your experience. Let me say — let's take the case that I could talk to him, to your patient, too. I would, of course, hear from him a very different tale about this *same* moment. [Rogers: Yes.] Now, you see, I am not a therapist. I'm interested in you *and* in him. I *must* see the situation. I must see you and him in this dialogue hampered by tragedy. Sometime, in many cases, a tragedy that can be overcome. Just in your method. I have no objection at all to your method, you see? There is no need to speak about it. But sometimes method is not enough, and it cannot do what has been — what is necessary to do.

Now, let me ask you a question that seemingly has nothing to do with this, but it's the same point. You have certainly much to do with schizophrenics. Is it true?

ROGERS: Some. Uh huh.

BUBER: You have, have you, also, to do, let me say, with paranoiacs?

ROGERS: Some.

BUBER: Hum?

ROGERS: Some.

BUBER: Now, would you say that the situation is the same in the one case and in the other? Meaning, the situation as far as it has to do with this relationship between you and the other man. Is this relationship that you describe the same kind of relationship in the one case and in the other? Can you talk — this is a case with a question that interests me very much, because I was interested very much by paranoia in my youth. I know much more about schizophrenia, but I often am much impressed and I would want [unintelligible] like to know, have you — this would mean very much — can you meet the paranoiac just in the same kind?

ROGERS: Let me first qualify my answer to some degree. I haven't worked in a psychiatric hospital. My dealings have been with people for the most part who are able to at least make some kind of an adjustment in the community, so that I don't see the really chronically —

BUBER: Oh, I see.

ROGERS: —ill people. [Buber: Uh huh.] On the other hand, we do deal with individuals who are both schizophrenic and others who certainly are paranoid. And one of the things that I say very tentatively, because I realize this is opposed by a great weight of psychiatric and psychological opinion, but I would say that there is *no* difference in the relationship that I form [Buber: Hum] with a normal person, a schizophrenic, a paranoid — I don't really feel any difference. [Buber: Hmm hmm.] That doesn't mean, of course, that when — well, again it's this question of looking at it from the outside. Looking at it from the outside, one can easily discern plenty of —

BUBER: No, no — I don't mean —

ROGERS: —differences. I don't either. And, it seems to me that if therapy is effective, there is this same kind of meeting of persons no matter what the psychiatric label.

And one minor point in relation to something you said that struck me: It seems to me that the moments where persons are most likely to change, or I even think of it as the moments in which people *do* change, are the moments in which perhaps the relationship is experienced the same on *both* sides. When you said you might talk to my patient and you would get a very different picture, I agree — that would be true in regard to a great many of the things that went on in the interviews. But I suspect that in those moments [Buber: uh huh] when real change occurred [Buber: uh huh], that it would be because there *had* been a real meeting of persons in which it was experienced the same from both sides.

BUBER: Uh huh. Yes. This is, this is really important.

FRIEDMAN: Can I interpose a [Buber begins to talk] question here? As —

BUBER: No. Would you, would you wait a moment? [Friedman: All right, thanks but —] I only want to explain to Dr. Rogers why this question is particularly important [Rogers: uh huh] to me and your answer, too.

A very important point in my thinking is the problem of limits, meaning, I do something, I try something, I will something, and I give all my thoughts, all my existence — *into* this doing. And then I come, at a certain moment, to a wall [Rogers: hum], to a boundary, to a limit that I *cannot,* I cannot ignore. This is true, also, for what interests me more than anything: human effect of dialogue. Meaning by dialogue not just talking. Dialogue can be silent. You could, we could, perhaps, without the audience — I would recommend to do it without an audience. We could sit together, or rather walk together in silence and that could be a dialogue. So even in dialogue, full dialogue, there is a limit set. This is why I'm interested in paranoia. There is here a limit set for dialogue. It is sometimes very difficult to talk to a schizophrenic. He, in certain moments — as far as *my* experience with this, of course, how may I say, a dilettante? [Rogers: uh huh] — I can talk to a schizophrenic as far as he is willing to let me in his particular world that is *his* own; and that in general he does not want to have you come in, or other people. But he lets some people in. And so he may let me in, too. But, in the moment when he shuts himself, I cannot go on. And the same, only in a terribly strong manner, is the case with a paranoiac. He does not open himself and does not shut himself. He *is* shut. There is something else being done to him that *shuts him*. And the terribility of this fate, I'm feeling very strongly because in the world of *normal* men, there are just analogous cases, when a sane man behaves, not to everyone, but behaves to some people *just so*, being shut. And the problem is if he can be opened, if he can open himself, and so on. And this is a problem for humans in general.

ROGERS: Yes, I think I see that as —

BUBER: Yes, now, Dr. Friedman may want to come —

FRIEDMAN: This is my role as moderator. I'm not — the only role I play here — not quite satisfied as to whether in this interchange, just before the paranoiac/schizophrenic, to what extent it's an issue, to what extent it *may* be a different use of terms, so let me ask Dr. Rogers one step further. As I understood what Buber said was that the relationship is an I-Thou one, but not a fully reciprocal one, in the sense that while you have the meeting, nonetheless you see from his standpoint and he cannot see from yours. And in your response to that, you pointed again and again to the meeting that takes place and even to the change that may take place on both sides. But I didn't hear you ever point to suggesting that he does see from your standpoint, or that it is fully reciprocal in the sense that he also is helping you. And I wondered if this might not be perhaps just a difference, if not of words, of viewpoint, where you were thinking of how you feel *toward* him, that is, that he is an equal person and you respect him. [Laughter.]

BUBER: There remains a *decisive* difference. It's not a question of objecting helping the other. It's a question of *wanting* to help the other. He is a man wanting to help the other. [Rogers: Yeah.] And his whole attitude is this active, helping attitude.. This is [Rogers: hhm] — I used to say totality of different by the whole heaven, but I would rather prefer to say by the whole *hell* — difference from your attitude. This is a man in hell. A man in hell cannot think, cannot imagine helping another. How *could* he?

ROGERS: But that's where some of the difference arises. Because it seems to me, again, that in the most real moments of therapy I don't believe that this intention to help is any more than a substratum on my part either. In other words, surely I wouldn't be doing this work if that wasn't part of my intention. And when I first see the client, that's what I hope I will be able to do, is to be able to help him. And yet in the interchange of the moment, I don't think my mind is filled with the thought of "Now I want to help you." It is much more of "I want to understand you. What person are you behind this paranoid screen, or behind all these schizophrenic confusions, or behind all these masks that you're wearing in real life?" [Buber: Huh, uh huh.] "Who are you?" And it seems to me that that *is* a desire to meet a person, not "Now I want to help." It seems to me that it is more that I've learned through my experience that when we can meet, then help does occur, but that's a by-product.

FRIEDMAN: Dr. Rogers, would you not agree, though, that this is not fully reciprocal in the sense that that man does not have that attitude toward *you:* "I want to understand you. What sort of a person are you?"

ROGERS: The only modification I made of that was that perhaps in the moments where real change takes place, then I wonder if it isn't reciprocal in the sense that I am able to see this individual as he is in that moment [Buber: uh huh] and he really senses my understanding and acceptance of him. And that I think is what *is* reciprocal and is perhaps what produces change.

BUBER: [Sighs—audience laughter.] Hmmm. You see, I, of course, am entirely with you as far as your experience goes. I *cannot* be with you as far as I have to look on the whole situation, your experience and his. You see, *you* give him something in order to make him equal to you. You *supplement* his need in his relation to you. You *make* him—may I say so personally—out of a certain fullness you give him what he wants in order to be *able* to be, just for this moment, so to speak, on the same plane with you. But even that is a tangent. It is a tangent that may not last but one moment. It is not the situation, as far as I see, not the situation of an hour; it is a situation of minutes. And these *minutes* are made possible by you. Not at all by him.

ROGERS: That last I would thoroughly agree with—but I do

sense some real disagreement there because it seems to me that what I give him is permission to be. [Buber: Hum. Heh heh.] Which is a little different somehow from bestowing something on him, or something like that.

BUBER: I think no human being can give more than this. Making life possible for the other, if only for a moment. Permission.

ROGERS: Well, if we don't look out, we'll agree. [Laughter.]

BUBER: Now let's go [unintelligible: on?].

ROGERS: I really would like to shift this to another topic [Buber: hmm] because, if as I understand what you've written and so on, it seems to me that I discern one other type of meeting which has a lot of significance to me in my work that, as far as I know, you haven't talked about. Now I may be mistaken on that, I don't know. And what I mean by that is that it seems to me one of the most important types of meeting or relationships [Buber: hmm] is the person's relationship to himself. [Buber: H-hmm.] In therapy, again, which I have to draw on because that's my background [Buber: sure] of experience —

BUBER: Of course.

ROGERS: —there are some very vivid moments in which the individual is meeting some aspect of himself, a feeling he has never recognized before, something of a meaning in himself that he has never known before. It could be any kind of thing. It may be his intense feeling of aloneness, or the terrible hurt he has felt [Buber: hmm], or something quite positive [Buber: hmm] like his courage, and so on. But at any rate, in those moments, it seems to me that there is something that partakes of the same quality that I understand in a real meeting relationship. That he is in his feeling and the feeling is in him. It is something that suffuses him. He has never experienced it before. In a very real sense, I think it could be described as a real meeting with an aspect of himself that he has never met before. Now I don't know whether that seems to you like stretching the concept you've used. I suppose I just would like to get your reaction to it. Whether to you *that* seems like a possible type of real relationship or a 'meeting'? I'll push this one step further. I guess I have the feeling that it is when the person has met himself in that sense, probably in a good many different aspects, that then and perhaps only then, is he really capable of meeting another in an I-Thou relationship.

BUBER: Now here we approach a problem of language. You call something dialogue that I cannot call so. But I can explain why I cannot call it so? Why I would want another term between dialogue and monologue for this. Now, for what I call dialogue, there is essentially necessary the moment of surprise. I mean —

ROGERS: You say "surprise"?

BUBER: Yes, being surprised. A dialogue — let's take a rather trivial image. The dialogue is like a game of chess. The whole charm of chess is that I do not know and cannot know what my partner will do. I'm surprised by what he does and on this surprise the whole play is based. Now you hint at this, that a man can surprise himself. But in a very different manner from how a person can surprise another person —

ROGERS: I hope that perhaps sometime I could play some recordings of interviews for you to indicate how the *surprise* element really can be there. That is, a person can be expressing something and then suddenly be hit by the meaning of that which has come from someplace in him that he doesn't recognize. In other words, he really is surprised by himself. That can *definitely* happen.

But the element that I see as being most foreign to your concept of dialogue is that it is quite true that this otherness in himself is not something to be prized. [Buber: Hmm.] In this kind of dialogue I'm talking about, within — that it is that otherness that probably would be broken down. And I do realize this probably is, in part, the whole discussion of this may be based on a difference in our use of words, too. I mean that —

BUBER: And you see, may I add a *technical* matter? [Rogers: Uh huh.] I have learned in the course of my life to appreciate terms. [Rogers: Uh huh.] And I think that modern psychology does it not in sufficient measure. When I find something that is essentially different from another thing, I want a new term. I want a new *concept*. You see, for instance, modern psychology, in general, says about the unconscious that it is a certain mode of the psychic. It has no sense at all for me. If two things are so different from one another as this *scream* of the *soul*, changing in every moment, where I cannot grasp anything, when I try to grasp it it's away, from one side — this being in pure time, and this what we call the unconscious, that is not a phenomenon at all. We cannot — we have no access to it at all, we have only to deal with its effect and so on. We cannot say this is psychic and this is psychic, the unconscious is something in which psychic and physiologic are, how may I say, 'mixed'?; it's not enough. They penetrate one another in such a manner that we see in relation to this the terms 'body' and 'soul' are, so to speak, late terms [Rogers laughs], late concepts — and consciousness a primal reality. Now, how can we comprehend this one concept, right there? But this is only —

ROGERS: I agree with you very much on that — when an experience is definitely of a different sort, then it does deserve a different term. I think we agree on that.

Perhaps, since I see time is going by, I'd like to raise one other question that has a great deal of meaning to me, and I don't know how to put it. I think perhaps it's something like this: As I see people coming together *in* relationship in therapy, I think that one of the things I have come to believe and feel and experience is that what I think of as human nature or basic human nature — that's a poor term, you may have a better way of putting it — is something that is really to be trusted. [Buber: Hmm.] And it seems to me in some of your writings I catch something of that same feeling. But, at any rate, it's been very much my experience in therapy that [Buber: hmmhmm] one does not need to supply motivation toward the positive or toward the constructive. That exists in the individual. [Buber: Hmm.] In other words, that if we can release what is most basic in the individual, that it *will* be constructive. Now, I don't know. Again, I just hope that perhaps [Buber: yes] that would stir some comments from you.

BUBER: I don't yet see the exact question in this.

ROGERS: The only question that I'm raising is: "Do you agree?" I suppose. Or if I'm not clear, please ask me other questions. I'll try to put it, perhaps, in another way. Well, this would be a contrasting way. [Buber: Hmm.] It seems to me that much of the point of view of orthodox psychoanalysis at least, has held the point of view that when the individual is revealed, I mean when you really get down to what is within the person [Buber: uh huh], that consists mostly of instincts and attitudes and so on which must be controlled. [Buber: Uh hmm.] Now that runs *diametrically* contrary to my own experience which is that when you get to what is deepest in the individual, that's the very aspect that can most be trusted to be constructive or to tend toward socialization or toward the development of better interpersonal relationships and so on. Does that [Buber: uh huh, uh huh] have any meaning to you?

BUBER: I see. I would put it in a somewhat different manner. As far as I see, when I have to do with, now let me say a problematic person, or just a sick person, a problematic person, a person that people call, or want to call, a "bad" person. [Rogers: Uh huh, uh huh] You see, in general, the men who have really to do with what we call the spirit are called not to the good people, but just to the bad people, to the problematic, to the inaccessible, and so on. The good people, we can be friends with them, but they don't — obviously — they don't *need* this. [Rogers: Uh.] So, I'm interested just in the so-called bad, problematic, and so on. And my experience is if I succeed to — and this is near to what you say, but somewhat different [Rogers: uh huh] — if I come near to the reality of this person, I experience it as a *polar* reality.

ROGERS: As a what? A polar?

BUBER: Polar reality. [Rogers: Uh huh.] You see, in general, we say this is either A or Non-A. It cannot be A and Non-A at the same time. It can't. It can't. I mean, what you say may be *trusted*. I would say this stands in polar relation to what can be *least* trusted in this man. You cannot say, and perhaps I differ from you on this point, you cannot say, "Oh, I detect in him just what can be trusted." I would say now when I see him, I grasp him, more broadly and more deeply than before, I see his whole polarity; and then I see how the worst in him and the best in him are dependent on one another, attached to one another. And I can help — may be able to help — him just by helping him to change the relation between the poles. Not just by choice, but by a certain strength that he gives to the one pole in the relation to the other, they being qualitatively very alike to one another. I would say there is not as we generally think in the soul of a man good and evil opposed. There is again and again in different manners a polarity, and the poles are not good and evil, but rather yes and no, rather acceptance and refusal. And we can strengthen, we can help *him* strengthen, the one positive pole. And even perhaps we can strengthen the force of direction in him because this polarity is very often directionless. It is a cha-otic state. We could bring in a cosmic note into it. We can help put order, put a shape into this. Because I think the good, or what we may call the good, is always only direction. [Rogers: Uh huh.] Not a substance.

ROGERS: Right. And if I get the last portion of that partic-ularly, you're saying that perhaps we can help the individual to strengthen the "yes," that is to affirm life rather than refuse it. Is that —

BUBER: M-hmmm. And, you see, I differ only in this word, I would not say "life." I would not put an object to it.

ROGERS: Uh huh.

BUBER: I would say simply "yes."

ROGERS: Uh huh. Uh huh. Uh huh. Uh huh.

ROGERS: You're [to Friedman] looking as though you want to say something. Well, I could —

FRIEDMAN: I'm tempted to —

ROGERS: Well, we could go on forever in the —

FRIEDMAN: My function as moderator, one, is to sharpen is-sues and I feel that there are two interrelated things that have been touched on here, but maybe not brought out, and I feel they're especially important, I'd like to see. When Dr. Rogers first asked Professor Buber about his attitude toward psycho-therapy, he mentioned as one of the factors that enters into his approach to therapy, 'acceptance'. [Buber: Unintelligible.] Now,

Professor Buber, as we saw last night, often uses the term 'confirmation', and it is my own feeling, from both what they said tonight and my knowledge of their writings, that it might be of real importance to clarify whether they mean somewhat the same. [Buber: Hmmm.] Dr. Rogers writes about acceptance, in addition to saying that it's a warm regard for the other and a respect for his individuality, for he's a person of unconditional worth, that it means "An acceptance of and regard for his attitudes of the moment, no matter how negative or positive, no matter how much they may contradict other attitudes he has held in the past," and "This acceptance of each fluctuating aspect of this other person makes it for him a relationship of warmth and safety."[1] Now, I wonder whether Professor Buber would look on confirmation as similar to that, or would he see confirmation as including, perhaps not being accepted, including some demand on the other that might mean in a sense a nonacceptance of his feelings at the moment in order to confirm him later.

BUBER: I would say every true, let's say, existential relationship between two persons begins with acceptance. By 'acceptance' *I* mean — perhaps the two concepts are not just alike — but by 'acceptance' I mean being able to tell, or rather not to tell, but only to make it felt to the other person, that I accept him just as he is. [Rogers: Uhm hmm.] I take you just as you are. But it is not yet what I mean by '*confirm* the other'. Because *accepting*, this is just accepting how the other is in this moment, in this actuality of his. Confirming means, first of all, accepting the whole potentiality of the other and making even a decisive difference in his potentiality. Of course, we can be mistaken again and again in this, but it's just a chance between human beings. I can recognize in him, know in him, more or less, the person he has been — I can say it only in this form — *created* to become. In the simple factual language, we find not the terms for it because we don't find in it the term, the concept, 'being meant to become'. This is

1. Friedman was quoting from Rogers's then-unpublished essay, "Some Hypotheses Concerning the Facilitation of Personal Growth," which became chapter 2 of his *On Becoming a Person* (1961). The quote is from page 34.

what we must, as far as we can, grasp, if not in the first moment, then after this. And now, I not only accept the other as he is, but I confirm him, in myself, and then in him, in relation to this potentiality that is *meant* by him and it can now be developed, it can evolve, it can enter a reality of life. He can do more or less to this scope but I can, too, do something. And this is with goals even deeper than acceptance [acceptance? expectation?]. Let's take, for example, man and a woman, man and wife. And he says, not expressly, but just by his whole relation to her, "I accept you as you are." But this does not mean, "I don't want you to change." But it says, "I discover in you, just by my accepting love, I discover in you what you are *meant* to become." This is, of course, not anything to be expressed in missive terms. But it may be that it grows and grows with the years of common life.

ROGERS: Well, I think that—

BUBER: This is what you mean? [Rogers: Uh huh. Yes, yes.] Good.

ROGERS: And I think that sounds very much like the quality that is in the experience that I think of as acceptance, though I have tended to put it differently. I think that we do accept the individual *and* his potentiality. I think it's a real question whether we could *accept* the individual as he is, because often he *is* in pretty sad shape perhaps, if it were not for the fact we also—in some sense—realized and recognized his potentiality. I guess I feel, too, that acceptance of the most complete sort, acceptance of this person as he is, is the strongest factor making for change that I know. In other words, I think that does release change or release potentiality to find that as I *am*, exactly as I *am*, I am fully accepted—then I can't help but change. Because then, I feel, there is no longer any need for defensive barriers, so then what takes over are the forward-moving processes of life itself, I think.

BUBER: I'm afraid I'm not so sure of that as you are. perhaps because I'm *not* a therapist. [Rogers: Hhm.] And I have necessarily to do with the problematic side in problematic man. [Rogers: Uh huh.] I *cannot* do—in my relationship to him—without just this. I cannot put this aside. I have just, as I said, I have to do with both men. I have to do with the problematic in him. And there *are* cases when I must help him *against* himself. He wants my help against himself. You see, the first thing of all is that he trusts me. Yes, life has become baseless for him. He cannot tread on firm soil, on firm earth. He is, so to say, suspended in the air. And, what does he want? What he wants is a being not only whom he can trust as a man trusts another, but a being that gives him now the certitude "There *is* a soil. There *is* an existence. [Buber apparently hits the table on "is" in these two sentences.] The world is *not* [Buber hits table] condemned [Rogers: uh huh] to deprivation, degeneration, eh, destruction. [Rogers: Uh huh.] Eh, the world *can* be redeemed. *I* can be redeemed *because there is this trust*" [Buber hits table as he says "because there is this"]. [Rogers: Uh huh.] And if this is reached, now I can help this man even in his struggle against himself. And this I can only do if I distinguish between "accepting" and "confirming."

ROGERS: I just feel that one difficulty with a dialogue is that there could easily be no end, but I think that both in mercy to Dr. Buber and to the audience, this is— [Buber overlaps]

[Laughter.]

BUBER: This—what do you say?

ROGERS: I say that out of consideration for you and consideration to—

BUBER: Not for me. Heh heh.

ROGERS: Oh, all right— [laughter] —just consideration for the audience—

FRIEDMAN: May I be so unmerciful as to just ask one last question? And that is: My impression is that, on the one hand, there has been more insistence by Dr. Rogers on the full rec—, full*er* reciprocity of the I-Thou relation in therapy and less by Dr. Buber, but on the other, I get the impression that Dr. Rogers is more client-centered as the—

BUBER: What?

FRIEDMAN: More client-centered—more concerned [laughter] —more concerned with the becoming of the person. And he speaks in his second article[2] of being able to trust one's organism,

2. Friedman was referring to the unpublished manuscript of Rogers's "What

that it will find satisfaction, that it will express *me*. And he speaks of the locus of value as being inside one, whereas I get the impression from my encounter with Dr. Buber that he sees value as more in "the between." I wonder, is this a real issue between the two of you?

ROGERS: I might just give one type of expression to my view on that that puts it in quite different terms than what you've used, and yet I think it really relates to the same thing. That as I've tried to think about it in recent months,[3] it seems to me that you could speak of the goal toward which therapy moves, and I guess the goal toward which maturity moves in an individual, as being 'becoming', or being knowingly and acceptingly that which one most deeply *is*. In other words, that too expresses a real trust in the process which we *are* that perhaps may not entirely be shared between us.

BUBER: Now, perhaps it would be of a certain aid if I add a problem that I found when reading just this article of yours, or a problem that approached *me*. You speak about persons, and the concept 'person' is seemingly very near to the concept 'individual'. I would think that it's advisable to distinguish between them. An individual is just a certain uniqueness of a human being. And if it can, it can develop, just by developing with uniqueness. This is what Jung calls "individuation." He may become more and more and more an individual without making him more and more a *human*. I have a lot of examples of man having become very individual, very distinct of others, very developed in their *such-and-suchness*, without being at all what I would like to call a man. Therefore, individual is just this uniqueness, being able to be developed, so and so. But person, I would say, is only an individual living really with the world. And "with the world," I don't mean *in* the world, but just *in real contact*, in *real reciprocity*

<hr />

It Means to Become a Person," which became chapter 6 of *On Becoming a Person.*

3. Anderson and Cissna suspect that Rogers was alluding to his work on two essays, "A Process Conception of Psychotherapy" and "To Be That Self Which One Truly Is: 'A Therapist's View of Personal Goals.'" Both essays were presented at conferences in 1957, and they later became chapters 7 and 8, respectively, of *On Becoming a Person.*

of the world in all the points in which the world can meet man. I don't say only with man, because sometimes we meet the world in other shapes than in that of man. But this is what I would call a person, and if I may say expressly "yes" and "no" to certain phenomena, I'm *against* individuals and *for* persons.

ROGERS: Uh huh. Correct. [Applause.]

FRIEDMAN: We have reason to be deeply indebted to Dr. Rogers and Dr. Buber for a unique dialogue. It is certainly unique in *my* experience: first, because it is a *real* dialogue, taking place in front of an audience, and I think that is in part because of what they were willing to give us and did give us, and in part because you [the audience] took part, kind of a trialogue, or adding me, a quatralogue in which you silently participated. [Applause — Buber says several unintelligible words during the applause.]

Sources

Selected Reading

Indexes

Sources

Essays

"Distance and Relation." Original in German, "Urdistanz und Beziehung," 1950, *Studia Philosophica-Jahrbuch der Schweizerischen Philosophischen Gesellschaft,* Separatum Vol. X, Basel, Verlag für Recht und Gesellschaft, 7–19; 1951, Heidelberg: Lambert Schneider, 1960, 44pp.; 2d ed., 37pp.; 1978, 4th expanded ed. 57pp. English, trans. Ronald Gregor Smith, 1951, *The Hibbert Journal,* 49, [105]–13; 1957, *Psychiatry* 20, no. 2, 95–104; 1965, in *The Knowledge of Man: A Philosophy of the Interhuman,* ed. M. Friedman, New York: Harper and Row; also several subsequent editions.

"Healing Through Meeting." Original in German, "Heilung aus der Begegnung," 1951, *Neue Schweizer Rundschau,* N.F., 19, no. 6, 382–86; 1952, "Geleitwort," in Hans Trüb, *Heilung aus der Begegnung: Eine Auseinandersetzung mit der Psychologie C. G. Jungs,* ed. Ernst Michel and Arië Sborowitz, Stuttgart: E. Klett, Stuttgart, 9–13; 1965, *Nachlese,* Heidelberg: Lambert Schneider. English, trans. M. Friedman, 1957, in *Pointing the Way: Collected Essays,* New York: Harper; 1967, in *A Believing Humanism: My Testament, 1902–1965,* Credo Perspectives, planned and ed. by Ruth Nanda Anshen, New York: Simon and Schuster.

"Images of Good and Evil" (part 3, chaps. 2–5). Original in German, "Bilder von Gut und Böse", 1952, Cologne: Hegner; 1964, Heidelberg: Lambert Schneider. English, trans. Michael Bullock, 1952, London: Routledge & K. Paul; 1953, trans. Ronald Gregor Smith, *Good and Evil, Two Interpretations: I. Right and Wrong. II. Images of Good and Evil,* New York: Scribner's Sons.

"Religion and Modern Thinking." Original in German, "Religion und Modernes Denken," 1952, *Merkur* 6, no. 2, 101–20; 1953, chapter 5 of *Gottesfinsternis: Betrachtungen zur Beziehung zwischen Religion und Phi-*

losophie, Zurich: Manesse; 1962, *Schriften zur Philosophie,* Kösel and Lambert Schneider, vol. 1 of *Werke,* Munich and Heidelberg, 550–74; 1994, new edition of *Gottesfinsternis,* Gerlingen: Lambert Schneider, 66–99. English, chapter 5 of *Eclipse of God: Studies in the Relation Between Religion and Philosophy,* 1952, trans. Maurice Friedman, Eugene Kaminka, Norbert Guterman, I. M. Lask, New York: Harper; 1957, New York: Harper Torchbooks 12; 1977, Westport: Greenwood; 1979, Atlantic Highlands, N.J.: Humanities Press.

Jung's Reply to Buber, "Religion and Psychology." Original in German "Antwort an Martin Buber: Religion und Psychologie" in *Merkur* 6, no. 5, May 1952, 467–73; reprinted as "Antwort an Martin Buber" in *Gesammelte Werke* 11, Anhang. English, first trans. Robert Clark, *Spring,* 1976; trans. R. F. C. Hull, in *The Collected Works of C. G. Jung,* Bollingen Series, 18, Princeton, N.J.: Princeton Univ. Press, 663–70 (this second translation is included in this volume, with the permission of the publishers).

Buber's Rejoinder. Original in German "Erwiderung an C. G. Jung," 1952, *Merkur* 6, no. 5, 474–76; "Replik auf eine Entgegnung C. G. Jungs," in *Schriften zur Philosophie,* Kösel and Lambert Schneider, vol. 1 of *Werke,* Munich and Heidelberg, 600–603; 1994, new edition of *Gottesfinsternis,* Gerlingen: Lambert Schneider, 147–51. English, trans. Maurice Friedman, *Eclipse of God: Studies in the Relation Between Religion and Philosophy,* 1957, New York: Harper Torchbooks 12; 1979, Atlantic Highlands, N.J.: Humanities Press, chap. 9, Supplement: "Reply to C. G. Jung," 133–37.

"Elements of the Interhuman." Original in German, "Elemente des Zwischenmenschlichen," 1954, *Merkur* 8, no. 2, 112–27; 1954, *Neue Schweizer Rundschau,* N.F., 21, no. 10, 593–608; 1962, in "Die Schriften über das dialogische Prinzip," Heidelberg: Lambert Schneider; also *Schriften zur Philosophie,* Kösel and Lambert Schneider, vol. 1 of *Werke,* Munich and Heidelberg, 267–89. English, trans. Ronald Gregor Smith, 1957, *Psychiatry* 20, no. 2, 105–13; 1965, *The Knowledge of Man: A Philosophy of the Interhuman,* ed. M. Friedman, New York: Harper and Row, 72–88.

"What Is Common to All." Original in German, "Dem Gemeinschaftlichen folgen," 1956, *Neue Rundschau* 67, no. 4 (Dec.), 582–600; 1962, *Logos: Zwei Reden,* Heidelberg: Lambert Schneider. also *Schriften zur Philosophie,* Kösel and Lambert Schneider, vol. 1 of *Werke,* Munich and Heidelberg, 454–74. English, 1958, trans. Maurice Friedmann, *Review of Methaphysics,* 11, no. 3, [359]–79; 1965, in *The Knowledge of Man:*

A Philosophy of the Interhuman, ed. M. Friedman, New York: Harper and Row, 79–99.

"Afterword to *I and Thou,*" 1957, original German first printed in 1958 in the new edition of *Ich und Du,* with an epilogue by the author, Heidelberg: Lambert Schneider, 143–60; in all subsequent editions. English, 1958, 2d ed. of *I and Thou,* with a postscript by the author, translated by Ronald Gregor Smith, New York: Scribner, 121–37; also in 1970 in the new translation of *I and Thou* by Walter Kaufmann, New York: Scribner.

"Guilt and Guilt Feelings." Published first in English, 1957, in *Psychiatry* 20, no. 2, 114–29, trans. Maurice Friedman; original German, "Schuld und Schuldgefühle," 1957, *Merkur* 11, no. 8 (Aug.), 705–29; as a separate title in 1958, Heidelberg: Lambert Schneider, 68pp.; 1960, in *Der leidende Mensch,* ed. Arië Sborowitz, Darmstadt: Wissenschaftliche Buchgesellschaft; 1972, in *Die Sinnfrage in der Psychotherapie,* ed. Nikolaus Petrilowitsch, Darmstadt: Wissenschaftliche Buchgesellschaft, [337]–66. English, 1965, *The Knowledge of Man: A Philosophy of the Interhuman,* ed. M. Friedman, New York: Harper and Row, 121–48.

"The Word That Is Spoken." Original in German, "Das Wort, das gesprochen Wird," 1960, in *Wort und Wirklichkeit,* Bayerische Akademie der schönen Künste, München: R. Oldenbourg 15–31; 1962 in *Logos: Zwei Reden,* Heidelberg: Lambert Schneider, 7–29. English, 1961, trans. Maurice Friedman, *Modern Age* 5 no. 4, 353–60; 1965, in *The Knowledge of Man: A Philosophy of the Interhuman,* ed. M. Friedman, New York: Harper and Row, 110–20.

Letters

1. Buber to Trüb, 18 Oct. 1923; original in German, published in *Martin Buber: Briefwechsel aus sieben Jahrzehnten* (Martin Buber: seven decades of correspondence), vol. 2: 1918–38, in 3 volumes, edited by Grete Schaeder, in consultation with Ernst Simon and in cooperation with Rafael Buber, Margot Cohn and Gabriel Stern, Heidelberg: Lambert Schneider, 1973; letter no. 140, p. 172.

2. Buber to Trüb, 14 Aug. 1925; original in German, published in *Martin Buber: Briefwechsel aus sieben Jahrzehnten,* vol. 2: 1918–38, 1973; letter no. 195, p. 235.

3. Trüb to Buber, 3 Feb. 1926; original in German, published in *Martin Buber: Briefwechsel aus sieben Jahrzehnten,* vol. 2: 1918–38, 1973; letter no. 203, pp. 242–44.

4. Buber to Trüb, 2 Oct. 1928; original in German, published in *Martin Buber: Briefwechsel aus sieben Jahrzehnten*, vol. 2: 1918–38, 1973; letter no. 286, pp. 322–23.

5. Trüb to Buber, 5 Oct. 1928; original in German, published in *Martin Buber: Briefwechsel aus sieben Jahrzehnten*, vol. 2: 1918–38, 1973; letter no. 287, pp. 323–24.

6. Buber to Trüb, 30 Sept. 1935; original in German, published in *Martin Buber: Briefwechsel aus sieben Jahrzehnten*, vol. 2: 1918–38, 1973; letter no. 515, pp. 573–74.

7. Buber to Trüb, 7 June 1936; original in German, from the Martin Buber Archive, The National and University Library, Jerusalem, no. 138.

8. Buber to Trüb, 13 June 1936; original in German, published in *Martin Buber: Briefwechsel aus sieben Jahrzehnten*, vol. 2: 1918–38, 1973; letter no. 535, p. 596.

9. Trüb to Buber, 17 June 1936; original in German, published in *Martin Buber: Briefwechsel aus sieben Jahrzehnten*, vol. 2: 1918–38, 1973; letter no. 536, p. 597.

10. Buber to Trüb, 25 June 1936; original in German, published in *Martin Buber: Briefwechsel aus sieben Jahrzehnten*, vol. 2: 1918–38, 1973; letter no. 538, p. 598.

11. Buber to Trüb, 31 Oct. 1936; original in German, published in *Martin Buber: Briefwechsel aus sieben Jahrzehnten*, vol. 2: 1918–38, 1973; letter no. 554, p. 615.

12. Trüb to Buber, 3 Nov. 1936; original in German, published in *Martin Buber: Briefwechsel aus sieben Jahrzehnten*, vol. 2: 1918–38, 1973; letter no. 555, pp. 616–18.

13. Buber to Trüb, 7 Nov. 1936; original in German, published in *Martin Buber: Briefwechsel aus sieben Jahrzehnten*, vol. 2: 1918–38, 1973; letter no. 556, pp. 618–19.

14. Buber to Trüb, 4 Aug. 1946; original in German, published in *Martin Buber: Briefwechsel aus sieben Jahrzehnten*, vol. 3: 1938–65, 1975; letter no. 91, pp. 113–15.

15. Buber to Trüb, 27 Aug. 1946; original in German, published in *Martin Buber: Briefwechsel aus sieben Jahrzehnten*, vol. 3: 1938–65, 1975; letter no. 94, pp. 117–19.

16. Buber to Trüb, 9 Sept. 1946; original in German, published in *Martin Buber: Briefwechsel aus sieben Jahrzehnten*, vol. 3: 1938–65, 1975; letter no. 9S, p. 119–20.

17. Trüb to Buber, 10 Oct. 1948, original in German, published in *Martin Buber: Briefwechsel aus sieben Jahrzehnten*, vol. 3: 1938–65, 1975; letter no. 144, p. 183.

18. Trüb to Buber, 2 Oct. 1949, original in German, published in *Martin Buber: Briefwechsel aus sieben Jahrzehnten,* vol. 3: 1938–65, 1975; letter no. 171, pp. 213–14.

19. Buber to Gerson, 30 Aug. 1928; original in German, published in *Martin Buber: Briefwechsel aus sieben Jahrzehnten,* vol. 2: 1918–38, 1973; letter no. 285, p. 322.

20. Buber to Gerson, 23 Apr. 1937; original in German, published in *Martin Buber: Briefwechsel aus sieben Jahrzehnten,* vol. 2: 1918–38, 1973; letter no. 577, pp. 644–45.

21. Buber to Ronald Gregor Smith, 28 Dec. 1936, original in German, published in *Martin Buber: Briefwechsel aus sieben Jahrzehnten,* vol. 2: 1918–38, 1973; letter no. 564, pp. 628–29; trans. into English for *The Letters of Martin Buber: A Life of Dialogue,* ed. Nahum N. Glatzer and Paul Mendes-Flohr, Syracuse: Syracuse Univ. Press, 1996; letter no. 495, pp. 453–54.

22. Buber to Rudolf Pannwitz, 1 Jan. 1937, original in German, published in *Martin Buber: Briefwechsel aus sieben Jahrzehnten,* vol. 2: 1918–38, 1973; letter no. 565, pp. 629–31; trans. into English for *The Letters of Martin Buber: A Life of Dialogue,* 1996; letter no. 496, pp. 454–55.

23. Buber to Ernst Michel, 23 Sept. 1949, original in German, published in *Martin Buber: Briefwechsel aus sieben Jahrzehnten,* vol. 3: 1938–65, 1975; letter no. 170, pp. 211–13.

24. Binswanger to Buber, 7 Feb. 1933, original in German, published in *Martin Buber: Briefwechsel aus sieben Jahrzehnten,* vol. 2: 1918–38, 1973; letter no. 408, p. 462.

25. Buber to Binswanger, 23 Oct. 1936, original in German, published in *Martin Buber: Briefwechsel aus sieben Jahrzehnten,* vol. 2: 1918–38, 1973; letter no. 552, pp. 613–14.

26. Binswanger to Buber, 17 Nov. 1936, original in German, published in *Martin Buber: Briefwechsel aus sieben Jahrzehnten,* vol. 2: 1918–38, 1973; letter no. 558, pp. 620–21.

27. Buber to Binswanger, 4 June 1946, original in German, published in *Martin Buber: Briefwechsel aus sieben Jahrzehnten,* vol. 3: 1938–65, 1975; letter no. 84, pp. 103–4.

28. Binswanger to Buber, 10 Jan. 1952, original in German, published in *Martin Buber: Briefwechsel aus sieben Jahrzehnten,* vol. 3: 1938–65, 1975; letter no. 246, p. 303.

29. Binswanger to Buber, 08 Oct. 1957, original in German, published in *Martin Buber: Briefwechsel aus sieben Jahrzehnten,* vol. 3: 1938–65, 1975; letter no. 374, pp. 438–39.

30. Binswanger to Buber, 8 May 1962, original in German, pub-

lished in *Martin Buber: Briefwechsel aus sieben Jahrzehnten,* vol. 3: 1938–
65, 1975; letter no. 483, pp. 546–47; trans. into English for *The Letters
of Martin Buber: A Life of Dialogue,* 1996; letter no. 723, pp. 646–47.

31. Buber to Binswanger, 14 May 1962, original in German, published in *Martin Buber: Briefwechsel aus sieben Jahrzehnten,* vol. 3: 1938–
65, 1975; letter no. 484, p. 547; trans. into English for *The Letters of
Martin Buber: A Life of Dialogue,* 1996; letter no. 724, pp. 647.

32. Buber to Friedman, 30 Jan. 1956, published in German in *Martin Buber: Briefwechsel aus sieben Jahrzehnten,* vol. 3: 1938–65, 1975; letter
no. 345, pp. 405–6; original in English in the Martin Buber Archive,
Jerusalem, no. 217a/419.

33. Buber to Friedman, 2 Mar. 1956, published in German in *Martin
Buber: Briefwechsel aus sieben Jahrzehnten,* vol. 3: 1938–65, 1975; letter no.
349, pp. 408–9; original in English in the Martin Buber Archive, Jerusalem, no. 217a/423.

34. Farber to Buber, 13 Mar. 1956, published in German in *Martin
Buber: Briefwechsel aus sieben Jahrzehnten,* vol. 3: 1938–65, 1975; letter no.
351, pp. 410–12; original in English published in *The Letters of Martin
Buber: A Life of Dialogue,* 1996; letter no. 654, pp. 595–97.

35. Buber to Farber, 1 Apr. 1956, published in German in *Martin
Buber: Briefwechsel aus sieben Jahrzehnten,* vol. 3: 1938–65, 1975; letter no.
353, p. 413; original in English published in *The Letters of Martin Buber:
A Life of Dialogue,* 1996; letter no. 655, p. 597.

36. Farber to Buber, 9 Apr. 1956, published in German in *Martin
Buber: Briefwechsel aus sieben Jahrzehnten,* vol. 3: 1938–65, 1975; letter no.
354, pp. 413–15; original in English published in *The Letters of Martin
Buber: A Life of Dialogue,* 1996; letter no. 656, pp. 597–99.

37. Buber to Farber, 1 Sept. 1956, published in German in *Martin
Buber: Briefwechsel aus sieben Jahrzehnten,* vol. 3: 1938–65, 1975; letter no.
357, pp. 417–19; original in English published in *The Letters of Martin
Buber: A Life of Dialogue,* 1996; letter no. 659, pp. 600–601.

38. Farber to Buber, 25 Oct. 1956, published in German in *Martin
Buber: Briefwechsel aus sieben Jahrzehnten,* vol. 3: 1938–65, 1975; letter no.
358, pp. 419–21; original in English published in *The Letters of Martin
Buber: A Life of Dialogue,* 1996; letter no. 660, pp. 601–2.

39. Farber to Buber, 29 Dec. 1956, published in German in *Martin
Buber: Briefwechsel aus sieben Jahrzehnten,* vol. 3: 1938–65, 1975; letter no.
363, p. 425; original in English in the Martin Buber Archive, Jerusalem, no. 227d/6.

The letters from Robert C. Smith to Buber and to C. G. Jung, and the replies by Buber and by Jung, were all written originally in English and are preserved at the Martin Buber Archive in Jerusalem, file no. 741b. Parts of three letters of Smith to Buber and of three replies by Buber to Smith were published in the *Review of Existential Psychology and Psychiatry* 6, no. 3 (fall 1966). Buber had granted permission to Smith to quote and publish his correspondence with him but Jung had not. Two letters of Jung to Robert C. Smith were published in the second volume (1951–61) of *C. G. Jung Letters*, Bollingen Series XCV, Princeton: Princeton Univ. Press, 1975, pp. 570–73 and pp. 583–84, and permission has been granted by the publishers to reprint them in this volume. Of the third letter, a short summary has been included. Nearly the entire correspondence is reproduced here, with the kind permission of Prof. Robert C. Smith.

40. Smith to Buber, 14 May 1960. Archive no. 741b:1
41. Buber to Smith, 2 June 1960. Archive no. 741b:I1
42. Smith to Jung, 10 June 1960. Archive no. 741b:2
43. Jung to Smith, 29 June 1960. Archive no. 741b:5
44. Smith to Buber, 7 July 1960. Archive no. 741b:6
45. Smith to Jung, 8 July 1960. Archive no. 741b:3
46. Smith to Buber, 24 July 1960. Archive no. 741b:7
47. Smith to Jung, 24 July 1960. Archive no. 741b:4

Short summary of Jung's letter to Smith, 2 Aug. 1960. Archive no. 741b:4

48. Smith to Jung, 9 Aug. 1960. Archive no. 741b.
49. Buber to Smith, 11 Aug. 1960. Archive no. 741b:I2
50. Jung to Smith, 16 Aug. 1960. Archive no. 741b.
51. Smith to Buber, 21 Aug. 1960. Archive no. 741b:8
52. Buber to Smith, 29 Aug. 1960. Archive no. 741b:I3
53. Smith to Buber, 21 Sept.1960. Archive no. 741b:9
54. Smith to Buber, 11 Nov. 1960. Archive no. 741b:11
55. Buber to Smith, 13 Nov. 1960. Archive no. 741b:I4
56. Buber to Smith, 4 Jan. 1961. Archive no. 741b:I5
57. Smith to Buber, 16 June 1961. Archive no. 741b:I3

Dialogue

"The Unconscious." Notes taken by Maurice Friedman of a seminar held by Buber in March–April 1957 at the School of Psychiatry, Washington, D.C., first published as "Das Unbewusste" in German in *Nachlese* in 1965, trans. Grete Schaeder, Heidelberg: Lambert Schneider, 144–72; 1993, 3d edition, Gerlingen: Lambert Schneider. English, 1967, in *A Believing Humanism: My Testament 1902–1965,* Credo Perspectives, planned and ed. by Ruth Nanda Anshen, New York: Simon and Schuster, 153–73.

"Martin Buber and Carl Rogers." Dialogue held at the University of Michigan at Ann Arbor on 18 April 1957. A first transcript was published by Maurice Friedman, who had moderated the dialogue, as an appendix to *Knowledge of Man,* 1965; a slightly abbreviated translation into German appeared in *Integrative Therapie* 3, (1992), 245–60. In this volume a new and more accurate transcription from the original tape, prepared by Kenneth N. Cissna, professor of communication, University of South Florida, Tampa, and Rob Anderson, professor and director of graduate studies, Department of Communication, Saint Louis University, St. Louis, Mo., is published with their kind permission. Anderson and Cissna have recently published their work, with extensive commentary, in book form, as *The Martin Buber–Carl Rogers Dialogue: A New Transcript with Commentary.* Albany: State University of New York Press, 1997.

Selected Reading

Buber's Views on, and Significance for, Psychiatry and Psychotherapy

Farber, Leslie. "Martin Buber and Psychotherapy." In *The Philosophy of Martin Buber*, ed. P. A. Schilpp and M. Friedman, 577–601. Cambridge: Cambridge Univ. Press, 1967.

Fried, Yehuda, and Joseph Agassi. "The Buberians." Chap. 8 of *Psychiatry as Medicine*. The Hague: Nijhoff, 1983.

Friedman, Maurice. "Encounter with Psychotherapy." Chap. 18 of *Encounter on the Narrow Ridge: A Life of Martin Buber*. New York: Paragon House, 1991.

———. "Psychotherapy." Chap. 21 of *Martin Buber, The Life of Dialogue*. 3. Rev. Ed. 1973.

Herberg, Will. "Depth Psychology and Religion: Encounter and Dialogue." *Catalogue of the Washington School of Psychiatry*, 1957–58.

Works Comparing and Contrasting Buber's Views to Those of C. G. Jung

Sborowitz, Arië. *Beziehung und Bestimmung. Die Lehren von Martin Buber und C. G. Jung in ihrem Verhaltnis zueinander*. Darmstadt: n.p., 1955. Published as paper in *Psyche. Eine Zeitschrift für Tiefenpsychologie und Menschenkunde und Praxis*, Bd.II, Heidelberg S.9 ff.

Trüb, Hans. *Heilung aus der Begegnung. Eine Auseinandersetzung mit der Psychologie C. G. Jungs*. Ed. Ernst Michel and Arië Sborowitz. Stuttgart: Ernst Klett Verlag, 1952.

———. "Individuation, Schuld und Entscheidung. Über die Grenzen der Psychologie." In *Die kulturelle Bedeutung der komplexen Psychologie, herausgegeben vom psychologischen Club Zürich*, 529–55. Berlin: Springer, 1935.

Buber's Influence on Gestalt
and on Humanist Psychotherapy

Brice, Charles W. "Betwixt and Between: The Making of a Dialogical Psychotherapy". *The Humanistic Psychologist* 21 (spring 1993): 102–11.

Helg, Felix. "Begegnung und Kontakt. Der Einfluss Martin Bubers auf Fritz Perls und die Gestalttherapie". *Integrative Therapie* 18.Jhg. 1992, 211–44.

Hycner, Richard H. *Between Person and Person: Toward a Dialogical Psychotherapy.* Highland, N.Y.: The Gestalt Journal, 1991.

———. Dialogical Gestalt Therapy: An Initial Proposal." *Gestalt Journal* 8 (spring 1985): 23–49.

———. "An Interview with Erving and Miriam Polster: The Dialogical Dimension in Gestalt Therapy." *Gestalt Journal* 10, no. 2 (fall 1987): 27–66.

———. "The I-Thou Relationship and Gestalt Therapy." *Gestalt Journal* 13, no. 1 (spring 1990): 41–54.

———. *Zwischen Menschen — Ansätze zu einer dialogischen Psychologie.* Edition Humanistische Psychologie. Köln, 1989.

Kron, Tamar. "The Dialogical Dimension in Therapists' Dreams about Their Patients." *Israel Journal of Psychiatry and Related Subjects* 28, no. 2 (1991): 1–12.

———. "The 'We' in Martin Buber's Dialogical Philosophy and Its Implication for Group Therapy and the Therapeutic Community." *International Journal of Therapeutic Communities* 11, no. 1 (1990): 13–20.

Kron, Tamar, and Maurice Friedman. "Problems of Confirmation in Psychotherapy." *Journal of Humanistic Psychology* 34, no. 1 (winter 1994): 66–84.

Kron, Tamar, and Rafi Yungman. "Intimacy and Distance in Staff Group Relationships." *International Journal of Therapeutic Communities* 5, no. 2 (1984): 99–109.

Portele, Heik. "Martin Buber für Gestalttherapeuten, Fritz and Laura Perls and Buber." *Gestalttherapie* 8. Jhg. Heft 1, Juni 1994, 5–18.

Schmidt, Christoph J. "Editorial — Das dialogische Prinzip in der Psychotherapie." *Integrative Therapie* 18.Jhg. 1992, 209–10.

Index of Names

Index of Subjects

287